Islands of Sunshine and Shadow

Islands of Sunshine and Shadow

BERNARD BLESTEL

Copyright © 2013 Bernard Blestel

All rights are reserved. The material contained within this book is protected by copyright law, no part may be copied, reproduced, presented, stored, communicated or transmitted in any form by any means without prior written permission.

Cover Design and typeset by BookPOD

Printed and bound in Australia by BookPOD

A Catalogue-in-Publication is available from the National Library of Australia.

ISBN: 978-0-646-59506-1 (pbk)

eISBN: 978-0-9874643-1-6

Contents

Foreword 1

Part 1

Growing Up 3

Chapter 1
The Babe in the Red Shawl 5

Chapter 2
Scenes from Childhood 21

Chapter 3
More Treasured Memories 51

Chapter 4
Menacing Clouds 71

Chapter 5
Exodus 77

Chapter 6
A Lancashire Hot-Pot Mixed Stew 91

Chapter 7
Christmas 1944 151

Chapter 8
Sarnia Cherie 167

Chapter 9
Family Matters 197

Chapter 10
Trials and Tribulations 207

Chapter 11
Time Well Spent 219

Part 2

New Horizons 245

Chapter 12
The Journey 247

Chapter 13
Australian Transformation 259

Chapter 14
Lending a Sympathetic Ear 275

Chapter 15
Hope Abandoned 285

Chapter 16
Magnificent Venice and the Japanese Annihilation 291

Chapter 17
Shadows Tinged with Hope 299

Chapter 18
The Gift of Life and Its Compensations 305

Chapter 19
Caring for Loved Ones 325

Chapter 20
Faith Rewarded 335

Chapter 21
Marysville Then, Marysville 2009 The Return 357

Epilogue 365

Appendix 367

Foreword

Welcome to the story of my life.

As you journey through these pages. I sincerely hope that you will relate to many of the situations and people set down here. Please don't expect a tale of heroic deeds, or the autobiography of some famous person, perhaps a star, inventor or philanthropist. If that is what you are looking for, forget it. This book is not for you. On the other hand – nothing ventured, nothing gained.

Set down here is the simple story of my journey through what I still call an exciting life, filled with sunshine and shadows. As you turn the pages you will stumble across a world of troubles, which, like all of us, you will have to face or even wrestle with, hopefully winning the battle and emerging once again into the sunshine.

I've tried to spice these pages with humour, for, without laughter, the world is a cold place. But in other parts tears will flow, revealing how humans react towards each other with violence, all too often brought about through the use of drugs like alcohol, heroin, cocaine and so on; while these products supposedly induce happiness or escape from the real world. Names unknown to the generation of my youth.

War and terrorism are also the scourge of the modern world. Not one part of this planet has escaped the greed of man. And then there are the dictators, as governments strive to destroy human decency, leading the majority into a self-centred, godless existence.

I hope as you flick through these pages that you will feel the warmth of love.

Each one of us has a mountain to climb, resting when we reach the summit, surveying the horizon, charting a course before we continue on our way, whether it be long or short to reach a state of tranquillity or planning a course so that the journey is beneficial. And we will encounter others, treading the same path, while their journey may be even more precarious so that we stretch out a hand to ease their burdens.

Reaching the summit is not so important. It is how we finish that counts. In some ways this story has an air of mystery about it, but hopefully you will solve the mystery and find out why we are here, moving through sunshine and shadow.

I thank you for your attention.

Part 1

Growing Up

Chapter 1

The Babe in the Red Shawl

Once upon a time ... all worthwhile stories begin this way – though this is no fairy story. It is 1929 and the start of my journey; though the very beginnings have been remembered and recounted to me by relatives and friends since then.

At this time the 1914-18 war is history; economic depression has replaced the horror of war and a different story unfolds as we visit the granite-built home at No. 9 Les Cotils, St Peter Port in Guernsey. Living here are Charles and Katherine Naper and their three children, Kathleen (Kath), William (Willy) and Frederick (Freddie).

And then, on December 30th a fourth child has come into their lives.

Thin grey wispy smoke was rising outside from a terracotta chimney and mixing with dense fog, giving evidence of a small fire burning in a blackened grate, throwing sparse heat into a bedroom filled with sorrow. The alpha and omega in the life of the young woman lying in an ornate iron double bed. She is covered by a white sheet already wet with perspiration.

Much has happened in this working class home during the last few days. Entering that room you would sense that death would soon pay a visit, yet a calm prevailed, ..."Unmistakable complications" the Doctor diagnosed only to be rejected when the true diagnosis came to light. It was dreaded Toxaemia.

Later, after a difficult labour, then the use of forceps, Katherine finally gave birth to a 12 lb boy on that 30th December 1929.

On that day the mournful sound of a fog horn echoed through the dense fog, warning ships of dangerous submerged rocks that besieged the Isle, it's very tone providing intermezzo background music to the drama being enacted in the sorrowful home on the Blue Mountains.

The house has long since been destroyed. The hard granite was used to fortify a part of the Atlantic Wall against Hitler's enemies. Before that, past generations had enjoyed uninterrupted views of the sea; an ideal site because this hilltop overlooked the neighbouring islands of Herm and Sark and, on a clear day in the distance, Jersey, Alderney and even France could be seen. During the German occupation a number of guns were placed there to protect the seaways between the islands.

Meanwhile, inside the granite house at the end of 1929, the family cherished the help of friends who came to support them wishing to be of some assistance.

The Convent Sisters of St. Josephs arrived at odd times, bringing bowls of soup to feed the hungry children, then leaving after offering prayers for all those within those walls. The youngsters did not understand the state of their mother's condition or of their possible plight if they were to be left without her.

St. Josephs Parish priest, Father O'Brien, a man of great understanding, arrived to administer the last rites. Katherine was a devout Roman Catholic whose unwavering faith upheld her when the darkest shadows fought to extinguish everything she held dear.

In Katherine's case the problems had proved numerous, a never-ending struggle brought on by a husband prone to drink, which often left the family short of money to buy the basic needs for everyday living. Yet the three children never went without food or warm clothing while she all too

Chapter 1 - The Babe in the Red Shawl

often went without herself. Oh yes, times were hard, yet her faith in God saw her through many crises.

It came as a shock to discover that another baby was on the way. Sometimes she blamed Charles for his insistence in gratifying his desires, but then she blamed herself, feeling guilt for being unable to resist him, not having enough strength, while she knew all too well that they could not afford another baby.

The Roman Catholic teaching on such matters did not allow its members to practice safe sex. If a child was conceived, then that was the will of God. In her heart Katherine steadfastly accepted whatever might lie before her, truly believing that God would provide, however hard the journey might become.

When Father O'Brien entered the bedroom he felt a peace within its walls causing him to reflect on a verse in Psalm 46 – "Be still and know I am God..." Yes, God's presence dwelt here as the good Father offered his prayers for a soul that would soon leave this earth.

Katherine felt no fear in the face of death, only remorse at the thought that she would no longer be able to provide the constant needs of her family.

Leaning over her, Father O'Brien surmised that the end was near, having seen the face of death so often in the course of his duties, once again bringing comfort and hope, making the sign of the Cross on her hot forehead. Softly, his clear voice, tinged with a delightful Irish brogue spoke sincerely, giving comfort to those who were mourning; as the flickering flame from the oil lamp cast dancing shadows on the cream coloured walls. Softly, his clear voice intoned – "The Lord giveth and the Lord taketh away..."

He took her hand to give reassurance that he acted as mediator between Katherine and the Almighty.

And then he put his arm around the shoulder of Katherine's sister-law Florence nee Naper and whispered in her ear – "Hold on to your faith because there are times when we do not understand the ways of God. He, in his wisdom, knows that those who love Him will bear witness to their faith as He did on Calvary."

Though the tears came to Florence's eyes, she held her emotions back, trying not to upset the children.

She offered Father O'Brien tea and scones, but he gently refused telling her that he had an important appointment with the Bishop.

"I feel very tempted," he told her. "But the Bishop will never forgive me if I am late."

He replaced his black overcoat over his rounded shoulders; by its appearance the coat had seen many winters, and Florence slipped a few scones into a paper bag and gave them to him, saying – "Bless you Father. Enjoy your afternoon tea." They shook hands, even though she did not belong to his Roman Catholic faith, she attending the Anglican church. Then he left them, passing Charles who lurked in the darkened passage, uncertain about what he was supposed to be doing.

After also shaking hands with Charles, Father O'Brien put his scarf around his neck and went out into the cold, foggy morning.

On his way back he wondered why such a young family should be left motherless. Sometimes, he questioned the ways of God. Perhaps, if he knew all the answers, he himself would be God.

As Charles returned to the bedroom he remembered the parting words of the priest – "May God bless you and keep you in his presence..." Why, Charles wondered, should He keep me in His presence? He knew that he had never bothered with Him. Perhaps it was too late, he thought, as tears turned to sobs. Inside the bedroom Katherine motioned her husband to come close. For once she smelt no alcohol on his breath as she whispered, between a bout of coughing, "Please look after our children..."

Florence was applying a cool compress as Katherine's face took on a new look of extreme anguish and she whispered, between greater bouts of coughing – "Oh, what is to become of our poor baby Bernard?" And once again she drew Charles close. "If you cannot care for him, grant my wish that he will be brought up in a Catholic Order which trains boys to become priests, or..." Then, as an afterthought... "Maybe a childless couple will love him as their own, a good, caring couple..." What else was on her mind

Chapter 1 - The Babe in the Red Shawl

at that moment we can only surmise, but she seemed comforted by the thought, and her anguish slowly subsided.

Katherine released her hold on Charles' wrist and wrestled with her pillow to little effect and Florence quickly went to her aid. An appreciative smile appeared on the dying young woman's face and she lifted her hand to touch the side of her sister-in-law's face, stroking it gently, loving Florence as she would have if they had been true sisters. She had always turned to Florence when Charles had been too drunk for his own good, and her last instructions came gradually, labouring over every word.

"Promise me you will help to take care of my dear children and baby Bernard Anthony. These are the virtuous names I have chosen, and look after your brother, even though he has his faults like all of us – if only he had had our faith... maybe with your prayers he will overcome his drinking? Even so, I love him... see that he carries out my wishes..." As she spoke, Florence knew the end was near and placed her hand on the young dying woman's face, assuring her that her last wishes would be taken care of, though at that moment Florence had no idea how this could happen.

It would have been quite impractical for Florence and her husband to care for any child, because they were employed by the Bailiff of Guernsey, Sir Edward Ozanne and his wife Lady Ozanne, and were only allotted two rooms in the course of their duties.

Florence had married Tom McCormick while both were in their early twenties and both in service by the time they were only fourteen years old. Their union had not been blessed with children. Tom had worked as a gardener and handyman for Sir Edward. In those far off days youngsters from working class families often started working around the age of twelve, some staying with their employers for many years.

This was the case of Florence and Tom, both devoted to Sir Edward and Lady Ozanne, whose only son was killed on active service during 1914-18 Great war, while their daughter Ruth formed a sisterly relationship with Florence. When Ruth died she left an annuity and a house which made it possible for Florence to live comfortably, until she died at the age of 96.

On that night in early January, 1929, Florence was numbed by the thought that her sister-in-law would finally breathe her last, feeling sympathy for the mother going through terrible thoughts while knowing that she had to entrust her young children to another's care. The thought that her husband might re-marry while the new wife might not give the children the same love that a natural mother would give them. Or how a father might cope, while still working on his own. A thousand and one thoughts would pass through the mind of this anguished, dying mother.

The District Nurse arrived to assist with the comfort and care of the young woman whose deep faith had motivated her life. It had given Katherine the strength to deal with the intermittent drunkenness of a husband, who, although he earned a decent enough living as a docker, had spent most of it in the local pub, leaving little or nothing for the necessities of everyday life.

To make matters worse, the working classes suffered greatly through the Depression's stranglehold on the worldwide economy of 1929. It was a year of hunger marches and strikes. The poor became poorer. It would take another war to begin to break down the class system, to introduce a semblance of quality into the lives of the working classes.

As Katherine weakened she surveyed the occupants of the room through bloodshot eyes. Apart from Florence, Charles and the nurse, sitting near the bed was Charles' mother, known as Granny Penny. She was trying to compose herself by knitting away, neither knowing or caring if her effort contributed anything to the garment. Also there was June Le Bargy, a good neighbour who had taken it upon herself to look after young Kathleen and her two brothers, Fred and Willie, during this stressful period.

For the moment June's love and understanding compensated for the likely loss of their mother's love without knowing the outcome of the children's welfare. She hardly dared to think about what might happen to the new baby Bernard Anthony, that poor little mite. Perhaps, she thought, if he had died at birth the situation would have been eased – and then, just as quickly June asked for God's forgiveness for such a thought.

Mothers who contracted puerperal fever before the discovery of Sulphanilamides or antibiotics faced the possibility of dying too early. Such

Chapter 1 - The Babe in the Red Shawl

was the diagnosis in Katherine's case, plus the complication of Toxaemia. Uncontrolled, persistent haemorrhage gave way to the finality of the prognosis making sure that her life was drawing to a close. She appealed to God to be near the children, holding them in His love, especially the baby.

At that moment, unknown to Katherine, the welfare of the newborn was being discussed by his potential adoptive parents Lena and Charles Blestel, a childless couple who had been told that pregnancy was an impossibility. Before the fatal illness struck Katherine, she had talked about the possibility of the Blestel's adopting her fourth child, if he were a boy.

And then, the three remaining children will live with Granny Penny and Albert her son in a cottage in Paris Street, so that the idea of the young family ending up in an orphanage was solved. Granny Penny was a kindly soul, the daughter of a seafaring family, whose fortune had somewhat diminished over the years, though they had still managed a comfortable lifestyle. She had resourcefully meet the family's needs. Learning from her loving parents, Captain and Mrs Purdy, she had received a set of principles that carried her through the loss of two husbands. Then, one of her sons went missing for twenty-two years ,then suddenly, out of the blue she heard that he had drowned in the River Thames. Why he left Guernsey and died in one of London's great waterways remained an unsolved mystery.

As she neared the end of her life, Katherine's eyes, filled with tears lingered on the picture of the Virgin Mary, hanging on the wall opposite her bed. How serene the Holy Mother looked, even though she had born the pain of losing a son. Now she herself was facing the loss of her children not by their deaths but her own. On a chest of drawers, under the picture stood a crucifix, the white ebony figure of our Lord bearing the eternal sins of the world.

Then Florence placed the sleeping babe in his mother's arms, perhaps for the last time. Katherine felt the closeness of her son as her tears mingled on the baby's warm head. She turned to look at Charles and a smile came to her face. Her eyes seemed to focus on something that only she could see, and those looking on thought she might have seen a glimpse of Heaven, such seemed to be her wonderment. And then she whispered "Thank you" as she kissed the baby, drew a few short breaths and ended life's struggle.

Florence removed the little one from his mother's arms and wrapped him in a red shawl, left the room and placed him in a cot near the children's room.

Meanwhile, Charles approached the bed again, as the tears welled in his eyes. He gently caressed the still warm face of his wife.

Slowly, the mist of the last few days began to clear for Charles, and then a well of despair overtook him. Too late, too late now to tell her how much he had loved her. His throat tightened in remorse as he realised he had never really spoken words that mattered regarding that he had never wanted the drink to get the better of him. Spending so much time in the pub ,knowing this had been the cause of terrible suffering for the family--- and now he knew that saying sorry came too late.

He knew that Katherine loved him in spite of his faults. He kissed her gently; her face now released from pain and looking so much like the face he had fallen in love with so long ago. And at last he turned to God, as so many of us do when we are in trouble, and he prayed for the first time in many years.

Downstairs, a thousand and one thoughts crowded through Florence's mind. She knew that she had to contact the new baby's prospective adoptive parents if they were still agreeable to take him on. And she well knew that looking after four children would have been an impossible task for Charles – and constantly seeing the boy would have been a painful reminder of his last mistake.

While Florence thought about all that she would have to do, Charles made his way downstairs past the children's room, without looking at the cot. He opened the front door and stepped out into the fog. He pulled up his coat collar and trudged down the street, his destination the local pub.

The three children had seen their father leave the house and now they crept slowly up the stairs, where they were met by Granny Penny. She had already closed the bedroom curtains and so the room was in semi ---darkness,

Chapter 1 - The Babe in the Red Shawl

indicating to the outside world that the family ithin was in mourning. As she led the three children to bed she whispered to them – "Be brave, my darlings..."

Their mother had explained the seriousness of her condition before the final birth and so they were prepared for the worst in their own childlike way. Yet, as they glanced at their mother's face, trying valiantly to hold back their emotions, it was Kathleen who broke first, giving way to uncontrollable tears. As she sobbed her heart out her grandmother cradled the little girl in her arms, comforting her and knowing that these children were now seeing death for the first time. Fred and Willie joined their sister in the welcoming arms of their grandmother.

As Granny held on to the children she silently prayed to God to uphold them for the sake of their loving mother, who, though utter weariness overtaking her, she still managed prayers trusting someone be found to take on the responsibility of looking after them after she had left this world.

At last they were silent, till Kathleen asked if the baby would be able to stay with her and the boys. The old lady was still for a moment and then she replied very gently – "No, my darlings. I am getting older and the baby needs a young mother. That is why Mr. and Mrs. Blestel have promised that they would love Bernard as if he were their natural son. I pray they will take him and I want you to understand that it would be for the best."

This news was altogether too much for Kathleen to bear and she cried out – "Why did Jesus take Mum and leave the baby? She will be so sad without him in heaven... oh Granny, why?"

"My darling," Granny Penny replied. "There are many things we do not understand. Searching for answers sometimes confuses us, but God will reveal to us when finaly when we meet Him face to face. You must be brave. Mummy always told you to trust Jesus when trouble comes your way. She always knew what to do."

Darkness descended rapidly as the fog thickened, and the wailing sound of the foghorn did nothing to lift the spirits of those within the house at Les Cotils.

There were a few family members together with friends, offering assistance to the family at various times. Rita Fairbrother, as the sister-in-law of Katherine hurried through the smog laden fog to prepare a meal for her grief-stricken relatives. Only ten minutes away she passed Cambridge Park and Castle Carey as quickly as she could.

As Rita made her way into the bedroom Florence embraced her half sister and thanked her for coming. "We can do with your help," she said. "Charles has gone to his usual haunt."

Rita sighed. She loved her half brother but had always longed for his drinking to stop.

Florence, having no phone in the house, made her way to a shop in Candie road to contact the undertaker and Lena Blestel. Mr Beckford, the undertaker, agreed to come at once to make the funeral arrangements, but the Blestels did have a telephone.Florence managed to reach one of their neighbours and asked them to find out if they were still interested in adopting the baby, would they get in touch with her.

That evening, the tasty meal prepared by Rita was left almost untouched by anyone in the family. As Florence wearily cleared the half empty plates into the waste bin, thinking that it was a shame to waste food, she realised that it would take some time for life to get back to normal.

An old-fashioned clock struck six as there was a knock on the door and she opened it for James Beckford. He was a man in his sixties, dressed in formal pin-striped suit. His funeral parlour was in Victoria Road. Though he was small in stature he was a kindly man who was always ready to assist those less fortunate than himself, charging a lesser fee whenever he could if he saw those in need ..

After offering him a cup of tea, Florence led Mr Beckford up to the bedroom where Katherine lay under a white sheet, with a crucifix placed on top of the covering . As he gazed once more at the death, which provided him with his livelihood, he questioned again what road had carried him to this sad moment; yes, he had to do his best for the family. And so that was what he did. As a practical man, he had in fact prepared his own coffin, which,

Chapter 1 - The Babe in the Red Shawl

in the meantime, he used as a wardrobe.so very practical, he often remarked in life we must prepare for death

Once Mr Beckford and Florence had agreed on all the arrangements he left, making his way through the bleak evening to his black Daimler and on to his home in Belmont Road.

A short time later, Lena and her husband Charles, called Charlie, arrived, and Florence, fighting back her tears got down to the reason for their visit.

"This is a very sad time," Florence said slowly , "Doubly so, with the loss of dear Katherine and the uncertainty of what the future will hold for the newborn baby. My brother is incapable of making any decisions right now and so he has left it to me to make the right decision on his behalf. I am acting as the spokesman for the family. We can do no more for Katherine except to make sure that her children are cared for in loving homes. My question to you is – do you still wish to go ahead and loving Bernard as if he were your own – while still accepting that some people will always disregard that he is not your natural son?"

Lena responded with some difficulty... "We have suffered the sneers of some people because we have been childless... we would dearly have loved having a child but it was not to be..."

Lena's life had its share of shadows. She was the youngest child of twenty-three siblings, some living and some who died. Her mother passed away while she was only in her late forties and Lena was raised by her eldest sister Alice, whom she looked on as a mother figure.

And then Lena married Charlie Blestel. Charlie was born in Alderney to August and Mary (Ingrouille) Bletel. The 's' was included at some point during a strained relationship between England and France during the 19th century. Charlie came from seafaring stock. His father sired five girls and one boy but died in his fifties, leaving his wife Mary to buy a donkey cart used to hawk fish around Alderney which is the most northerly island of the Channel Isles. In the early part of the century numerous ships were wrecked along the treacherous coasts and many islanders benefited from those disasters. They would row through turbulent seas to the sunken vessels and retrieve the cargo, making a handsome profit where they could – until the offenders were caught. Bric a brac from those far off days can still be seen in island homes today.

During the early part of the 1914-18 war Charlie had a mishap with an axe. He severed two fingers on his left hand. The wicked said that he did this on purpose to save going to the war, but this was fact ,untrue. In fact he served three years with the Guernsey Light Infantry in the trenches, and encountered some of the most ferocious fighting of that war.

His fondness for condensed milk arose from that time. He often said that it was the only sustenance they sustained before doing battle during that bloody war. This says a lot for Nestles Condensed Milk and may have helped to win the war. What a selling point!

When he was demobbed, Charlie returned to work in the quarries and became a foreman at Manuals, which was considered to be one of the finest Guernsey granite, sources the stone quarried at Bulwer avenue in St.Sampsons.

Charlie married Lena at Holy Trinity Church which was Georgian in style and situated in St. Peter Port. They set up home in Vale Road and later moved to rooms in Cliff Street. This was an early Victorian house built almost at the edge of the cliff, with a view overlooking Castle Cornet. Beyond this, arising out of the sea were the magical islands of Sark, Herm and Jethou. Ferries ply daily, taking visitors and supplies between the islands. On a clear day, looking to the left, one can see the Casquet lighthouse. It was built to warn sailors of the many submerged rocks lying beneath its feet, though many a ship has been lured to those dangerous depths. Passing the devil's graveyard one sees wind-swept Alderney, Charlie's birthplace.

Unlike Lena's, God was not a part of Charlie's life. He did attend Armistice Day parades and other church parades occasionally however, usually in company with his brother in--law   Bill Salmon; they were both ex-servicemen. Charlie was also an ex Grand Master of the Order of Buffalos.

Charlie was known as a hard worker nicknamed Iron Man, such was his strength with a fetish for paying bills the moment they were received. He

Chapter 1 - The Babe in the Red Shawl

was not an easy man to live with, given to sudden, usually unprovoked fits of temper, though these moods subsided as quickly as they erupted. Lena learnt to live with those moods for most of her life. His experiences on the battlefield may have left their mark on his mind, though, like so many others who had been through the war, they rarely spoke of it.

Florence interrupted any thoughts that may have been on the Blestels' minds by bringing the baby into the room. She carefully handed him to Lena who motioned Charlie to come to her side as if to say – "This will be your child too." As her arms enfolded the child, there was the ineffable glow of motherhood on her face and Florence knew at that moment this woman would adore the child always, as if he had been her own in every way. Tears welled in Florence's eyes as she realised that what she had just witnessed would never be hers.

No one in the room could foresee what an extraordinary life lay before that young babe. Up to then, no word had passed Charlie's lips, he was not often emotional, but now his voice quivered as he spoke – "He is a fine child," he said, looking at his wife for approval.

Lena was filled with joy – and misgiving. "Are you sure his father will part with him and not change his mind?" she asked Florence.

Florence understood her anguish and placed a loving arm around her shoulders. "No dear" she said. "His father will not change his mind and the lawyers will see to it that you are the legal parents. No one else will ever have any legal claim on him. Bernard Anthony Blestel will be his legal name. Now, take your son and love him as if you were his natural parents."

After so many years of waiting, those words touched Lena's heart as never before. God, in His heart had answered her prayers.

No sooner had Florence spoken than Charles Naper came into the room, a little worse for wear, perhaps drowning his sorrows. His bleary eyes and slurred speech showed once again that the publican had added more to his purse than his client's pocket could ill afford.

He looked at his sister, asking for a sort of forgiveness ,and, though she loved her brother, she could barely control her anger. She spoke quietly to

Lena – "He has already agreed that you should have the baby. Advocate Langlois will make the baby over to you."

Charles Naper nodded his approval saying – "What else can I do? That baby should never have been born; it's all my fault that my wife is dead!"

As he spoke he burst into uncontrollable sobbing and Lena, while feeling thrilled that the baby would really be hers, went over to Charles and touched him gently on the arm. "No," she said. "You are not to blame. Do not punish yourself. In time you will see things in a different light and you are most welcome to see Bernard whenever you wish. He is still part of you."

Charles muttered a slurred thanks, turned and kissed the baby, an action he never repeated in his lifetime, and with a few unsteady steps he left the room.

Florence embarrassed by her brother's behaviour, took the child from Lena and wrapped him in the red shawl which had been crocheted by Granny Penny, who, though she witnessed all that had transpired in that room, had remained silent. "I've put a few things in a basket for you, things you might need for the baby," Florence said, handing him back to Lena. Then, in a voice that betrayed her innermost feelings she said to Lena and Charlie – "Go now, and find happiness in your son." Then she called in the three children who had busied themselves elsewhere. Fred and Willie entered with Kath following some way behind, not wanting to face the exit of her newborn brother.

Granny Penny went to Kath and took her in her arms. Both knew that the baby would no longer be part of their lives. Each of the children and Granny Penny quickly kissed him and as quickly they left the room, without a word to the Blestels.

But Kath came back, and, still crying, stood in the doorway. "Be kind," she said in fits and starts. "Be kind to him," she said again, looking at Lena and Charlie. Then she left to rejoin her brothers.

The new parents bid a tearful goodbye in that sad house, where one life had ended and another wrapped snugly in a red shawl left that cottage on the

Chapter 1 - The Babe in the Red Shawl

hill. From then on this babe was on the threshold of sunshine and shadows, on a journey that would take him to far distant lands. Lena and Charlie stepped out and into a waiting taxi on that gloomy January day, when the moon suddenly appeared from behind the clouds. This became an omen for Lena that their lives would, from then on, be filled with love.

Florence waved her farewells, standing beside her brother. She knew that Charles did not fully comprehend what had transpired. After a moment, when Charles also did his best to wave, Florence brought them both back into the house.

And so another chapter in life's book had ended, and wiping away her tears, she knew that she must return to her duties. To await another curtain call.

Chapter 2

Scenes from Childhood

It is December 30th 1999. Seventy years have elapsed since the baby in the red shawl was born, and taken to live with a childless couple. That child was yours truly. Today I celebrate my seventieth birthday in warm sunshine in faraway Australia. Seventy years ago the weather was cold and foggy with a melancholy foghorn welcoming me to Guernsey.

It was Mildred, my wife of many years, who encouraged me to set down the incredible journey of ups and downs that we have both experienced over the years. Her childhood days were spent under German occupation and mine as a refugee in England, only returning to Guernsey after the war in 1945.

In a couple of days the world will herald the arrival of the 21st century without knowing what the future may bring with it. For now, as I sit at my desk I recall the past, through those ever present mists of time.

I remained the only child of Lena and Charlie Blestel, though I often wished for a brother or sister. Other children had them so why not me? No one ever explained the complicated procedure that was undergone when I became their offspring. Neither of my parents explained this to me – perhaps they did not understand all of it themselves.

Such was the unenlightened thinking of a very young child in those days. A blank page. During my early years on Guernsey a new word came into my vocabulary – adoption. This was a word that caused me great concern for many years; a word that I wished had never entered my ears. The adult world forgets that a child's mind is ever seeking. Its natural instinct is to store all possible information gleaned from the conversations of adults.

Adoption, adoption? What did it mean?

"He looks like Lena, even though he was adopted."

"They say you begin to look like a person when you live with them."

"Of course, he is not their real child; they are not his real mother and father. His real mother died. Charlie and Lena never had children."

As a child not yet of school age, I was very confused indeed. No, both of my parents are still alive. My Mummy loves me, she is not dead. As she cuddled me close, she expelled those thoughts from my mind. Those others were silly people. Of course, this is my mother. She nurses me when I am sick, bathes my knees when I fall, hugs me when I am afraid, cooks nice food, and gives me birthday parties. She holds my hand when we cross a road, wipes tears and sings me lullabies when I cannot sleep. These thoughts brought me respite, only shattered by remarks by those who should have known better.

My pre-school days were unsettled, darkened by Father's unprovoked bursts of temper. One such occasion comes to mind. He returned home from work in a rage, picked up the wireless set and flung it against the coal cupboard wall. We had no idea why.

In those early years I grew to fear him, not because of a lack of kindness towards me. It was more a case of his not allowing anyone to get close to him. He provided for my welfare, even buying a chicken for us when I fell ill which was a real luxury in those days. When money was scarce in the 1930's the working class, such as we were, had very little cash in our pockets to spend on luxuries.

Chapter 2 - Scenes from Childhood

While Charlie was unable to form a father--- son relationship with me, I cannot remember his, taking part in games, like building sand castles.

I feel sad today when I see young fathers having fun times with their children, though I cannot truly say that I had an unhappy childhood, during my time in Guernsey. But my father's temper did make me sad.

Five years of separation due to the war did not help the relationship. He did care for my welfare and years later I was able to repay his kindness in a minor way after his second marriage failed.

Strangely, he never understood how to control his temper or recognise that his verbal abuse was a form of unkindness to both Mother and me. His behaviour upset us, but he would only laugh, as if it had been a joke.

My first recollection of our living accommodation at Cliff Street consisted of three rooms, a shared outside toilet, no bathroom and a communal clothesline. This was a matter of 'post haste' with the washing; in order to guarantee a space before the rest of the household got there This race also applied to the toilet.

Friday night was bath time, when a large galvanised tin tub was placed in front of the fireplace, after taking it down from a wall on which it was hung, outside the wash house.

The weekly wash was done in a brick construction which housed a round copper bowl which was filled with water. A fire was lit in an aperture beneath it, fuelled by wood, cardboard or paper rubbish, or whatever else one could find. Once the water began to bubble, near boiling point, I would watch as if this was a true witch's cauldron, loving to fantasize. Mother would sprinkle Persil into the water as if producing a magic potion and turning the clothes whiter than snow. A large black kettle, found its home on the hub of the fire place, was in constant use, not just for bathing in the tin bath that that had been placed in front of the fireplace

Also It provided my mother with hot water for cooking nourishing meals' and the fireplace created warmth into the triple-purpose room – dining, sitting and kitchen. Years passed before I enjoyed the use of hot running water in a room set aside for bathing. We had no fancy bottles of shampoo or gel. If you were lucky you would use Lux or Puritan soap or strong, red carbolic soap. The smell still lingers to this day.

A special treat for me was to visit Aunt Alice and Uncle Bill at Burnt Lane. There I was able to ample a real bath complete with sweet smelling shampoos, plus the luxury of a gas geyser supplying hot and cold running water. No more filling of buckets – pure joy.

The house at Burnt Lane held many comforts which we could not afford to enjoy at Cliff Street. There was a separate dining room, a sitting room and three bedrooms which allowed me to stay the night on various visits. The house situated next to a convent which housed the nuns, whom I used to think was penguins

Perhaps I loved Aunt Alice because of her modern conveniences? In her kitchen she had a grey, enamel stove which was fuelled by coal and coke, heating the room wonderfully, much better than our drab blackened stove at Cliff Street, which gave smoke on windy days.

Aunt's house was full of surprises. Walking past a conservatory past and an indoor toilet, one came to a glass door which led to a flight of well-worn stone steps,m halfway up one came to Uncle Bill's workshop. Inside were tools, neatly arranged on the bench and wall, ready for numerous maintenance jobs, that were required around the house. Bill was a handyman who rolled his own cigarettes. Aunt kept him busy with major and minor repairs and he took this in his stride.

After a dozen or more steps one came upon a delightfully well-kept garden, with numerous bushes, trees and a vegetable patch, which supplied my Aunt during the season with fresh produce. Springtime brought the fragrance of flowers, including lily of the valley which greeted you as you entered the garden. The perfume of those Lilies was everywhere, including those beside the wash house window. Inside, the washhouse was very much like ours, without a washing machine or dryer. Aunt relied, as we did, on a copper. Washing clothes in those days was hard work. The steam which arose caused one to perspire, and, if the clothes were particularly grimy, a washboard had to be used. This consisted of a wooden frame in which

Chapter 2 - Scenes from Childhood

was inserted a ripple board of galvanized metal on which the clothes were rubbed. This was certainly harsh on the garments.

A gravel path brought one to a lean-to greenhouse in which she grew delectable black grapes, their sweetness still lingering to this day.

During the thinning season Aunt with scissors in hand would mount a stept ladder and snip away the unwanted leaders, making sure that only the best grapes were produced up to her high standards. Fond memories of my times at Burnt Lane.

Aunt Alice was left to bring up my mother, when at the age of six, her mother died. Lena was the youngest of 23 children! No wonder she only adopted one. Some of those children died in infancy; poor Grandma had few luxuries. Grandfather was a seaman who was away much of the time. It is said that, when the neighbours saw that the blinds were down in their house – Mr. Druce was home from the briny. "The poor soul will have another mouth to feed," they gossiped. Nevertheless, she managed to live for 52 years, dying at her rented house in Cornet St, a very poor district in those days. .

Aunt Alice was rather plump and her legs were bowed. What caused the condition was never ascertained. Some said she had Ricketts Complaint. Bowed leg or not I loved her, though she was raised in poor conditions, she managed to maintain a spotless home, was an excellent cook and was a great one for auctions. She knew a bargain when she saw one, and attending sales she would often snip a cutting off a tree or shrub to flourish in her garden. The auctioneers who saw this would smile and say – "The Salmon garden must surely be the best in Guernsey."

Uncle Bill would never know what he would find when he got home from work as a plasterer. A piece of furniture would be removed and replaced with one of Aunt's latest purchases. The couple had been married for four years when they took my mother under their wing. Uncle was of a quiet disposition and never lost his temper, simply going along with his wife's ideas. They were ideally suited, in contrast to my parents. During the First World War Bill also saw service, like my father. Bill and Aunt were both Christians attending the Vauvert Chapel, opposite their house.

They became caretakers, and, in my mind's eye, I still see her polishing the dark wooden pews, a mob cap on her head and the whole place smelling of Mansion Polish. Also, seeing Uncle Bill mounting a tall step ladder with Aunt issuing warnings for him not to fall. He cleaned the shaded lights assuring her that there were no cobwebs in God's house. With the chores completed there would be slices of Aunt's tasty bread pudding or caraway cake, as only she could make, washed down with a hot cup of tea, or on hot days there was cool homemade lemonade. Oh, those wonderful childhood memories!

I did not only love them for their home comforts, but much more because they were good people and they loved me. They treated me as their blood relative and there was never a word about adoption. Their two children, Jack and Elsie, who were teenagers when I first knew them, accepted me as a true cousin. A shadow had been cast over Auntie and Uncle when their young son Willy died of typhoid fever.

Christmas festivities at Burnt Lane were special. Tinsel and small ornaments drooped from a fresh tree which was illuminated by coloured wax candles. Electricity was yet to arrive in the house; in fact it was I who installed it, working as an Apprentice Electrician from the age 14.

I loved to escape to Burnt Lane whenever Father took a turn. Aunt, like my mother, through their service in home employment, knew how to set a table at Christmas time. Food, which was unseen at Cliff Street appeared on the table in Burn Lane, though my mother always managed to serve nourishing meals.

Aunt Alice held the purse strings, leaving Uncle Bill with enough money for his tobacco, which suited him. She paid all the bills, while this was very different in our household. My Father only gave Lena what he considered to be just enough for food which caused her a great deal of worry, as she tried to make ends meet. Sometimes, margarine would be combined with butter. Father disliked margarine and would have flown into another rage if he had found this out. On these occasions I would do my best to distract him, saying that I felt sick or producing apparent fits of coughing, thus turning the attention to me. When Father's raging storm subsided, he

Chapter 2 - Scenes from Childhood

would leave the house, muttering to himself and returning some time later, changed, as if nothing happened. A strange man.

My mother did not deserve such conduct from a husband she apparently loved. If this was not the case, why did she continue in the relationship? Understandably, prior to the second world war, women tended to remain with husbands who mistreated, them in order to provide a meal ticket for herself and her family. Thankfully, post-war welfare gave such women a number of options. Divorce was no longer the privilege of the rich. Public morality went even further during the 1960's, as the Hippies came into their own, and standards, unheard of before, became the Sexual Revolution.

Having jumped the gun, I will now return to the thirties. I spent my preschool days at Cliff Street, where the sun seemed to shine most of the time. I learnt to accept my father's changes of mood, believing that this was probably the way most people lived. Naturally enough, I realised that this was not actually so, but that came later.

In those days children played in the streets or gardens in comparative safety. Billy Tabel became a playmate of mine, living in Coupee Lane, which was adjacent to Cliff Street. Uneven cobblestones paved the lane that led to Cornet Street, where my mother saw the first ray of light. The houses in that street area were classed as poor, some occupied by families of low morals in those days, it went up---market after the war, housing the head of the Church in Guernsey. --- such is progress. There was a shop on the corner of Coupee Lane and Cornet Street, where Miss le Poidvin sold sweets and other things. The shop had a bay window and appeared straight out of the Victorian era. In those days, I would spend a penny on a bag of sweets like aniseed balls or Collins traditional Guernsey sweets. The taste still tickles my palate today. A few years after the war, the Collins family retired and the factory closed. It was a sad day because the true Guernsey mixture was lost forever. Thankfully, the shop fronts in this quaint area have retained the air of mystery they always had, even though the streets and shops underwent a facelift with bright colours, electricity and clear panes of glass. The shop in Cornet Street is now managed by the National Trust. Charles Dickens would surely have found a place in one of his classic tales for that treasure.

I clearly remember the dark polished linoleum floors with a gas bracket with its flickering mantle illuminating its recesses, where the ghosts of yesteryear lurked; in bygone days they would have been proud to serve Victor Hugo whose purchases were distributed among the poor children of St. Peter Port, and who were entertained by him at Hautville House.

Harsh, fluorescent lighting was yet to arrive, to destroy the magic of this sugar wonderland. If you had unlimited pennies to indulge in all those tempting wares, plain and simple scales governed by brass weights of the correct enumeration, made sure that the customer was given the right amount. Miss le Poidvin would place my favourites on those scales to give me an idea of just how long the sweets would last, until I could afford to come again. Revisiting the shop many years later, I saw that no electronic device had replaced the scales. Memories of those ancient hostelries come flooding back. There were homemade lemonade crystals to quench your thirst on a hot summer's day, sherbet fountains which one drew through a liquorice straw to tingle the tongue and Miss le Poidvin's famous liquorice and aniseed cough mixture, spiced with garlic, which was guaranteed to cure the cough and ease the breathing when winter colds invaded the body.

In those days, with childlike innocence, we explored our bodies, never quite understanding why girls were different. Our parents never explained the birds and the bees to us and sex definitely remained a no, no. TV was yet to show that men and women went to bed together not only to sleep. Puberty came as a great shock to many children. We thought a Stork delivered a baby!

Mr. Sims owned our house at Castle Vaudin which was in a cul de sac off Cliff Street in St. Peter Port. He let various rooms to a Mr. and Mrs. Audoire as well as my parents. This was a part of very old Guernsey and remained the same during our time there. Mr. Sims retained the rest of the house for himself and his wife.

The panoramic view from the upstairs front windows of Audoire's apartment looked out to Castle Cornet, an imposing fortress set in the sea which is now joined to the island by a causeway. The castle was built to guard the island against invading foes long ago.

Chapter 2 - Scenes from Childhood

The White Rock is a harbour adjacent to the castle where ships would anchor, bringing in supplies and returning with produce grown by the islanders. Tomatoes and grapes or the famous Guernsey cows were exported all over the world. Outside the harbour large naval vessels anchored; HMS Nelson and the ill-fated Hood paid regular visits while smaller ships lay at anchor inside the harbour.

Sitting on a window seat in the Audoire's front room I would watch the movements of boats, my mind full of boyish fantasies about the adventures they would encounter. I would think of galleons manned by pirates in combat with the King's Navy. Oh, what joy when we as children travel to Never Never Land!

Mother cleaned rooms for Mr. and Mrs. Audoire and also those of Mrs. du Putron. Mrs. du Putron was the daughter of the Audoires and lived at Pierre Piercee. Mr. Audoire worked at the White Rock and was therefore able to inform me of what vessel would arrive in the harbour. I spent hours on that window seat interested in the sailings. Although I liked Mrs. Audoire, she sometimes frightened me. Due to her age, her right leg became lame and a black stick with a silver knob handle assisted her walking. Sometimes, when Mother and I were with her she would bang the stick on the floor, and, addressing my mother would say – "Mummy, has he been a good boy?" She would then gaze at me through half-closed eyes and continue with words that sent a chill through my heart – "If not, Old Nick lives here," indicating her stick. "I let him out to naughty boys!" What Old Nick would do I was never game enough to find out, but at three years of age one is inclined to believe anything. For me, after those fateful proclamations she conjured up the image of a witch.

Mrs du Putron's family consisted of three girls, Olwyn, Sheila, Jocelyn and John who was two years older than me; Also, another son died before I was born. To be invited to their house was very special to me. I remember birthdays and Christmases when I sampled such delicious delicacies as glace' fruits, lemon and orange slices, homemade sorbet, chocolate mousse or a variety of cold meats served on silver salad platters, mixed with ingredients I had never sampled before. Lemonade and cider punch were made in an adjacent room where Mrs. du Putron bottled preservatives like pickled onions and fruit whose smell permeated the kitchen on bottling days. And, how could I forget them – those huge crackers placed on every plate. The biggest I had ever pulled!

After tea we would play games. Among the assortment was our favourite which was Sardines where we hid in secluded places like cupboards, waiting to be found; after which there was much screeching and laughter by all of us.

Ghost stories sent shivers down spines, sometimes becoming quite frightening. The house lent itself to ghostly games. It was easy to imagine that, on the stroke of midnight a poltergeist or things that go bump in the night might invade us. Strolling along the corridors of this granite house one saw many antiques and family treasures collected over many years, though how some acquired remained a little suspect. One wondered sometimes how they found their way into this interesting house. Was it it through pirates or smugglers. No disrespect to the Du. Putrons.

The du Putron's illustrious family tree spanned hundreds of years. Paintings of their ancestors hung on the walls of the drawing room, many giving allegiance to King and Country. Heavy red and gold curtains adorned the three large windows whose panes were flooded in summer sunlight during Guernsey's warm season. In front of the windows was a Regency-scrolled chaise lounge, covered in rich red velvet giving everyone a warm invitation to sit or lie in sweet repose.

I recollect that there was a white, Adam marble fireplace. On the west wall, upon a marble hearth rested. an ornate highly polished brass fender on which stood also copper coal scuttle together with a hooked brass stand on which hung a poker, tongs, a long-handled shovel: and resting on a lacquered box were fire bellows. When they were pumped, they would encourage the lazy flames to spring to life, spreading warmth on cold winter days. The fire in this room was lit daily, a chore allocated to my mother. Depending on which direction the wind was blowing, soot and dust would come in. When Mother was on her knees polishing away, she received much of that detritus, so, needless to say, this was not her favourite pastime.

Chapter 2 - Scenes from Childhood

When the inclement winter weather passed, it was time for the ritual Guernsey spring clean. Every house was in turmoil; this was the time to banish cobwebs, spiders, grime and dust, which would be replaced by the refreshing smell of Mansion Polish, intermingled with the odour of carbolic soap which was used on the floors, after scrubbing on your knees with a hard wearing brush.

The day of purification began at 6.30am. Toddy Bishop would arrive on his cycle. Strapped across the centre bar were tools of his trade. There was a hard, stiff brush whose bristles would dislodge the transformed coal from smoke into a black residue. The brush could be attached to an extended handle, plus a large sheet, whose whiteness had long since departed, in the middle of which a hole had been cut, covered by a leather flap. This would, at some stage, receive the brush which was now on its extended handle to begin its journey upward in the black environment of the chimney, ultimately to find its way to the top to be greeted by a blue sky.

On this cleansing day Mr. Bishop would make sure that the brush had, indeed ,made its way to the very top. His clothes and cap were by this time black with soot,while he proceeded to bag the residue. He would inform his customer with words I still remember. "It's very good for the garden, Missus, kills those bloody snails so I'll leave a bag. If not for the snails, get your husband to dip his cracker. You know what women say about a black fellow – once a black man, never again a white one." The professional chimney sweep who was so delightfully portrayed in the film Mary Poppins has long since departed, to be replaced by a chemical cube, thus eliminating the sweep's bread and butter. Of course, there were times when fire would roar upif the chimney were cleaned properly. and give the occupants a fright. Sometimes the house would even catch fire.

Sitting on the white mantelpiece was an ornate, Victorian black clock with Roman numerals, measuring time over the decades. There were also Victorian and Edwardian collectables; two French Louis Quinze chairs covered in maroon and gold fabric, and a double settee in matching colours was placed opposite the fireplace. A delicately painted water colour hung on the wall, the flowers presumably grown in the garden. On the far wall there rested a harpsichord with a stool in front of it on which needlework had been stitched long ago, probably by a relative of the family. The harpsichord invited a present –day kinsman to sit and to play 17th century music, befitting the instrument. Legend tells us that, if you remained still at certain times in the quietness of the room, certain melodies of the Masters would drift to your ears. Imagination or fact?

Some people intimated that the ghost of tragic Emilie du Putron was still in the house. She was an exceptionally attractive and intellectual young lady who was about to become engaged to Victor Hugo's son, Francois Victor, when she succumbed to a sudden illness and died in the mid 1860's. Francois had visited the house frequently and listened to her playing till their romanced ended in tragedy. The Hugo family endured much sadness.

Do you believe in ghosts? I do. Wait till the next book – it will send shivers down your spine!

As a child I gazed in awe at the contents of that room. There was a highly polished silver salver in which you could inspect your reflection as you examined its engraving: silver tankards gleamed brightly, together with cut glass decanters, filled with sweet sherry, plus crystal wine glasses set on a gold-edged tray accompanied by a flagon half-filled with the finest port. So many beautiful objects! Fine Chinese ornamental vases filled with flowers of the season, an attractive walnut occasional table upon which lay a Japanese fan, said to have been presented by one of the Royals. Near the fan sat a Rene Lalique bowl and so many paintings, lit at night by two candelabras whose crystals sparkled from the light of many candles. This was surely fairyland and needed very little imagination to feel the presence of the du Putrons as their portraits also dwelt in that room.

Mr. du Putron appeared to be somewhat eccentric. His conversation included philosophical teaching which was not understood by many. He often spoke on the Book of Revelations, also explaining to me that, as a student of astrology, he knew that the stars influenced human behaviours and affairs. I might say that, as a child, all this was far beyond any comprehension, though I listened with an intent ear.

I liked him and enjoyed his company, I suspect because his conversation had a touch of magic about it, even though I did not really understand

Chapter 2 - Scenes from Childhood

everything he said. I often accompanied him to feed the geese and turkeys which were kept on the property. He sold a few of them to the local shops, others ended up on friends Christmas tables, ours included. This was a thank you for my mother. As he talked, I would keep an eye on the poultry which could be quite ferocious, often pecking at our legs.

Young John de Putron often stayed with us when his parents had to attend social functions. He visited us for a few days before Christmas 1937 and seemed healthy and in good spirits, but only a month later he died from a septic appendix. An older son had been killed on a pathway near the house after being hit by his father's car. Then, a few years later another tragic drama became a shadow in the du Putron's, lives. Their daughter Olwyn was electrocuted in Jersey, when she switched on a faulty bedside lamp. No wonder the poor man appeared to be slightly odd. He never recovered from those terrible shadows.

One day I returned from Billy Tabel's home to find my mother in tears. Father had had one of his bouts of temper again. What this was about was never clear, but, between sobs my mother said – "I cannot stand your father's temper any more. What shall I do?" As a four year old I could find no solution to the problem, then, after a while ,Mother took me in her arms and kissed me gently on my forehead. "We will go far away," she said.

"Where is far away?" I asked.

Wiping away my tears she replied – "England." I had no idea where England was, but it sounded exciting. "You must say nothing to your father or he will fly into one of his moods again," she instructed me. The very idea of him flying into one of his bad moods was enough to keep me silent.

My mother spent the rest of the afternoon gathering up clothes and other things that we might need for the journey. I cannot recall what time of the year this took place, but I recall that darkness had fallen when I heard the familiar clomping of hob nailed boots on the cobblestones of our street. It was the sound I sometimes feared, because I never knew what state of mind he would bring with him.

Entering the house he proceeded straight to the wash house without uttering a word ,which set the scene for yet another unpleasant evening. When he returned to the living room a tasty meal of stew was already waiting for him. Sitting at the table held no joy for me, fearing that another wireless set might hit the dust. No words passed between my parents, so,I endeavoured after the meal, to amuse myself playing one-handed Snakes and Ladders. As I waited for another explosion to occur between my parents, a fortunate silence continued, while my stomach, akin to a ship in rolling waters, churned with anxiety. When bedtime arrived there had been no turning of the tide, no sense of security .As I lay in my bed thoughts turned to England, hoping that the situation might right its self preventing us leaving. That I would no longer be subject to fits of temper by a father who seemingly disregarded those who were sympathetically closest to him.

Sadly, due to his temperament I could never feel close to him. I could never feel affection or warmth, though, in retrospect, I realise that he had taken me in as his son and given me a home. Perhaps, subconsciously I chose to reject him as my real father who did not behave appropriately as a real father should? Maybe, if the seeds of adoption had not been sown, the chain of my thoughts might have taken a different path. My mother always showed me love on a different scale and by giving me this love he may have felt deprived of it? Mother rarely administered corporal punishment; a certain look in her eyes would be enough for me.

On the following day, Mother made enquiries regarding ship's sailing times. She had not changed her mind, had no second thoughts. I remember being woken up soon after Father left for work in the quarry. His mood had not changed and he left with his usual grunt, and that was all.

The morning, we left, to go to the boat, fitted our frame of mind. It was cold, dark and dampness filled the air. Father knew nothing of our intended migration, but Mother had left him a note which told him that she could no longer put up with his fits of temper and that it was best for all concerned that we should leave. She also told him that if he acquired a better disposition towards her, she might return. I learnt of this as we walked towards the harbour and a great fear overcame me. What if he had

Chapter 2 - Scenes from Childhood

already discovered our plan? I knew that there would be a terrible response from him against my mother.

Thankfully, such thoughts left me as we approached the old harbour with the boat moored and waiting. Tickets were purchased, and a Docker who knew my mother offered to carry our luggage aboard. Mother accepted his offer, her head hung low, hoping that she would not be recognised by others, while the chaos of the comings and goings of passengers, cranes loading and unloading imports and exports to and from the hold occupied my eyes and ears. A loud blast from the steamer's funnel denoting our imminent departure caused me to clasp mother's hand tightly. The thrill of going to England filled my childlike mind with excitement. Furtively my mother boarded the boat, me in tow, carrying a brown paper bag which contained the clothes that had not fitted inside the suitcase, made her way to the cabin. Once inside, after lifting the suitcase onto a rack and placing the paper bag beside her on the lower bunk, she began to cry. The enormity of what she had undertaken overwhelmed her. As tears also came to my eyes in sympathy, I wondered if her tears were those of dread or thankfulness?

After a while I began to enjoy the adventure, taking in everything that I saw around me. The smell of the sea filled my nostrils as the boat began to move away from the dock. I had the strange feeling that this affinity with the sea happened to me before. Did I have seafaring ancestors? Was the call of the sea instilled in my very body? This question remained unanswered due to the doubts I had about my parentage, a doubt that was with me for many years.

Dawn broke slowly with the promise of a fine day to come. My eyes focused on the islands of Herm and Sark in the distance, as the sun appeared behind those little jewels of the English Channel. Will I ever return, or has Mother relinquished our birthright for a land that might offer her peace? The shadows were now beginning to lift as we looked forward to a stable future. Leaving the Pier Heads the vessel pushed past the Castle Cornet and out to the open sea. A clear blue sky was a good omen as screeching gulls followed in our wake. Then, as we sailed further out to sea, the throb of the engines, the heavy smell of oil, plus the motion, of the boat, thrashing its way through the water caused me to suffer nausea. My churning tummy reminded me of my mother whisking an egg. She suggested that I should go below, but this did no t help. A stewardess had to come with a basin to retrieve whatever was left by a small person who had surely lost his sea legs. Finally ,the sickness left me, and, though I dearly wished to watch the white spray bounding off the sides of the hull, sleep overtook me as Mother gently placed me in my bunk.

I slept until we approached the Solent, the strip of water which led us to Southampton. Climbing up stairs, rubbing my eyes I was eager to catch the first glimpse of the land to which we had escaped. I ran to the ship's rails with the enthusiasm only children experience and feasted my eyes on the scene that lay before me. I saw tall buildings, cranes whose giraffe-like necks were lifting impossible weights and I could smell the oil and saw steam which belched from the funnels of trains as they ran to and fro from the docks.

Was this a dream? So much had happened in twenty-four hours. As I closed and opened my eyes the picture remained. This was real.

Slowly the boat neared the dock; ropes from ship to shore steered the boat to its moorings: the gangplank was lowered and passengers pushed forward to exit the ship. A few of the Guernsey folk spoke in their local patois as they disembarked. They say that the Guernsey patois is understood by those who speak Welsh.

I clutched my mother's hand, feeling secure, yet not apprehending what the future held. Would Father follow us, bringing one of his rages with him? At this thought I squeezed Mother's hand tightly and she returned my squeeze reassuringly. No way was this bond going to be severed.

There were no customs or passport to endure. Just a show of your ticket; so different from today when nearly everyone is under surveillance as if he or she was a potential criminal. Reliving those moments, truly brings back all those memories of yesteryear. In the midst of it all, I wondered whether my mother felt an air of relief, away from Father's moods. Was her relief mingled with a fear of the future? The future is beyond tomorrow to an adult, but to a child it is the approaching hours. The ticking of the clock holds the key to the cross-roads and what destiny has in store for us

Chapter 2 - Scenes from Childhood

widens with age and is reduced to seconds in the final years of sojourn on this planet.

How or where Mother found us a boarding house I never knew. After a short walk from the docks we found the place of her choice. A sign swung in the cool breeze in front of the door, displaying a sailing ship in full sail. It seemed to be sailing with the wind, cutting through the foaming waves. The artist had captured its movement, as it ploughed its way to its destination. Looking at it I felt that I was aboard, bound for a land of FREEDOM. A glass panel door at the entrance to the bar informed would-- be customers that this was THE FREEDOM HOTEL. Each letter shone in red, white or blue. Mother glanced at the sign, nodded to me, and, holding my hand, we entered the smoke-filled lounge. Inside, men and women sat smoking and drinking and chatting, unperturbed by the cigarettes dangling from their lips. In those days there were no warnings on the packets about danger lurking in the lungs which could lead to cancer. The smoke-filled pub is a thing of the past, but the fellowship still exists.

We seemed to be expected. A young girl who later turned out to be the barmaid, named Gloria, with a friendly, cheeky countenance patted my head as she hurried us through the lounge. She asked us if we had a good trip and took us up a flight of stairs onto a landing. Before us were four doors, each one a bedsitter. "Number 3 is yours, Madam. I hope you'll be comfortable. Give a shout if you need anything, ta, ta!" With these words Gloria departed.

Number 3 was a small, comfortable chamber containing a double bed, a single bunk against a yellow distempered wall with a picture hung above it, which depicted a mother, sitting in a rocking chair, nursing a baby. There was an apprehensive look on her face. There was also a modest dressing table on which sat a floral wash basin complete with jug, soap dish and two tumblers. Two white towels hung nearby on a rail and there was a plywood wardrobe painted cream, plus one high-backed wicker chair which completed the furnishings. On the floor lay a rug whose main feature was a tiger's head. The tiger's mouth was open, and, for obvious reasons, I avoided treading on it. This secluded chamber became our home.

It was not the Ritz, but it was clean and comfortable, affordable to Mother's meagre purse.

Stan, our landlord, was a little older than Mother. He had eyes that twinkled and dark, wavy hair and as he spoke he seemed to be very different from my father. Shortly after we arrived there was a knock on the door and Stan came in, carrying a tray with sandwiches and tea.

"A glass of orange juice for the lad," he said, patting me on the head. He spoke with an accent that was unfamiliar to me. Mother searched her purse to pay him, but he stopped her. "It's on the house, missus," he said, waving her away. As she thanked him for his kindness he winked at her saying "See you later, missus." Then he left, looking seriously back for a moment. "Don't open the door to anyone unless I am here," he cautioned.

The ham sandwich soon found its way to my belly, washed down by the delicious fresh orange juice. Mother gave me another sandwich saying – "You must be hungry, eat up." The day held so much excitement for me, though I still had some fears about our situation. Finally, I snuggled down in the warm, comfortable bed and slept the sleep of the gods.

The next morning I awoke refreshed, but, though this might sound strange, I was still concerned about Father's reaction to the note my mother had left behind. Stan brought up our breakfast saying, "Enjoy your breakfast of bacon and eggs." And he also brought a book of coloured photos of the Flying Scotsman roaring towards you in full steam. This became one of my most treasured possessions for many years, only to be lost during the German occupation. "That will keep him out of mischief, " he said, winking at Mother again.

Stan never missed an opportunity to establish a relationship, preferring relationships with women who were alone. This fact was unknown to my mother, who, though, she was vulnerable, did not allow herself to pursue an alliance that might lead to another web of deceit. Stan may well have been an opportunist.

Accepting cleaning employment at the boarding house gave mother a sense of security. She sent a letter to her sister Alice, informing her of our

Chapter 2 - Scenes from Childhood

whereabouts, but not including a precise address and asking Alice not to let Father know where we were. Stan continued to be friendly. I liked his friendly greeting, which was accompanied by a smile and a wink.

One evening, about a week after our arrival, Stan invited us to the theatre. Having never seen a live show, this promised to be very exciting. We arrived early and Stan, taking me by the hand, showed me the picture of the show with the girls looking very glamorous in beautiful pink feathers. "A bit of alright," he said smiling. What he actually meant was a mystery to me at that age. Today, I certainly do know.

The people surged forward as they paid for their tickets and a strange mixture of perfumes invaded my nose. I still recall the thrill of being there. The night will remain in my memory forever – and so will Stan.

As a child I would have accepted him as a father. He was so different from Charlie. If Mother's loyalty to her husband had wavered then; and if she had accepted Stan's advances, our lives would have turned out very differently.

The highlight of the show was a song, sung by a lady with blonde hair and adorned with pink and white feathers. She glided across the stage singing "Daddy wouldn't buy me a bow wow," as she peeped through a volume of feathers with a tiny poodle nestled in her arms, complete with bow and clipped in the latest style. Oh, what a night to remember! After an ice cream cone and a fizzy drink provided by Stan, we returned to the boarding house in jolly spirits. He invited us into his room for more refreshment and I sat down happily on his couch, next to Mother. I learnt later that his wife had left him for a sailor who was very good at dancing the hornpipe – or so the story goes. Then, placing sixpence in my hand and putting his arm around Mother's shoulders he said cheerfully – "Bed time, young fellow. Up those apples and pears and into bed, sleepy head. Mum will be up soon." As a four year old I was not certain why bed was necessary when sleep seemed so far away, but I dutifully accepted the sixpence and bid them goodnight.

At that point Mother removed herself from Stan's embrace and thanked him for a lovely evening. "Goodnight Stan," she said and took my hand to leave the room. Stan followed us to the door and gently kissed her on the cheek. He surprised her by this action which was so unlike that of her husband d who had never shown her affection in this way.

A sense of happiness came over me and, as we mounted the stairs I remarked – "Stan is nice."

Her thoughts seemed to be elsewhere as she replied – "Yes, quite nice."

I am not sure how long we stayed in Southampton. It seemed to me as if we were on holiday and I never wanted it to end. I never knew if Mother regretted having sent that letter to Aunt Alice, but as a result of this Aunt Alice informed Father of our whereabouts. Cousin Elsie and her boyfriend Ted were planning their engagement, and in honour of the occasion they decided to spend a week in Southampton. Aunt Alice had elicited a promise from my Father that he would change his ways – a promise which was soon to be broken, but Elsie and Ted were given the task of finding us. That was no mean task in that busy seafaring town.

To Southampton they came, hoping to find a needle in a haystack. Unsure where to start their search they initially visited various cafes in the main shopping area, to no avail. As the days passed, they almost gave up hope of ever finding us, believing that we may have moved on. Then, out of the blue they discovered us walking down the main street, shopping.

There were tears on both sides as were reunited. Mother was still reluctant to return, fearing the reception she might get from Father, whose temper could rise and fall at the drop of a hat. But Elsie reassured her that he would change. So, against her better judgment she agreed to give him a try and we packed up our belongings. She put a brave face on it, perhaps in the belief that she was doing the right thing by me. A child needs his father?

On my part, I had grown fond of Stan and would have welcomed him into my life, because he was my idea of what a father should be. He showed us many kindnesses and never displayed anger. As we said our farewells we felt sad. Would we ever meet again? We never did; we never spoke of Stan again.

The journey back to Guernsey held reservations about how we would deal with our homecoming, but I was still able to look around with interest. We

Chapter 2 - Scenes from Childhood

sailed down the Solent into the open Channel, passing ships of all shapes and sizes. The throbbing engines brought vibrations throughout the boat--- the swishing of the waves and the circling of gulls hoping to scavenge bits of food offered to the waves by passengers or crew all entranced me. Passengers sat on deckchairs or upturned rafts, wrapped in blankets, as the tossing and rolling vessel ploughed its way to our destination. This time I had no feeling of sickness and considered that a sailor's life might be for me after all. Unfortunately, this ambition never came to pass.

Elsie and Ted accompanied us, perhaps fearing that Mother might change her mind. The berthing of the boat signalled the end of our escape. Several people greeted relatives when we stepped ashore, but Father did not put in an appearance on that murky, rainy day. We had to wait till later to see how he would react. Ted found a taxi and we drove to Burnt Lane to face the music.

Aunt Alice had prepared a meal which she hoped we would share with father, thus pouring oil onto troubled waters, and finally it did the trick because Father did join us and he behaved. I was prepared to resume my coughing, but this was not required. In fact, he promised Mother that he would never display his temper again, (did I detect a small tear on his cheek?) and he apologised for his past behaviour. But he never kept his promise. Aunt Alice made sure that he remained calm before we returned to Cliff Street, and so things went well, considering the circumstances. I often wondered if Mother's thoughts returned to our time in England, and to Stan.

Every so often we met a man who was introduced to me as Uncle Charles. He seemed nice enough and always put a sixpence piece into my hand, which was a lot of money for a boy in those days. But, most of the time he was unsteady on his feet and his breath smelt odious. I only learnt later that beer was the cause of this. How did this man become my uncle? And why was Granny Penny my grandmother, and why did we visit her at Paris Street? What relationship was there to Kath, Fred and Willie? Another mystery was my Aunt Florence. They all showed an interest in my welfare. All this puzzled me for some time – did it have something to do with that word adoption? As nice as they were I did not really want any more intrusions into my life. No, I thought, they did not belong to me, but then – to whom did I actually belong? Even at such an early age, this sense of belonging caused me a great deal of concern.

Mr. Sim's wife died. This was the first time that I came into contact with death. I knew that people and animals died, but I did not expect it to occur in our house. In due course, Mr. Sims invited the household to view his dear wife in sweet repose. So, upstairs we went to observe the lady dressed in a lace nightgown and with a white lace cap on her head. Placed on the lifeless body were three Arum Lilies – which forever remind me of death. It was as if Mrs. Sims were asleep. Everyone present lent over and kissed her. Some person I did not know lifted me up so that I could place my lips on this lifeless image. I will never forget the coldness; it was like touching marble. As a sickly smell entered my nostrils, I hurried to the arms of my mother, who with the other mourners was crying. So this is death, I thought. As we departed, another lady whose name I cannot remember took my hand and said, "You are a brave boy. Don't be afraid. The dear soul has gone to live with Jesus."

Looking up at her I mumbled – "I hope He makes her warm, she is so cold."

Gazing fondly now at childhood photos of my grandchildren enjoying Christmas I remember my own. Oh the joy of those Christmas which are so different in Australia. In those far-off days there were no high-pressure salesmen urging people to buy material happiness, thereby forgetting the real purpose of Christmas.

It was usually cold, frosty and damp in Guernsey, while the smell of roasting chestnuts conjures up the scene under the arches in front of the French Halls. The neighbouring market was surely a sight to behold, where, hanging on display, were turkeys, geese, half a pig, chickens and ducks, and, of course, sides of beef and lamb; all ready to enhance the Christmas tables. Scattered near the entrances were braziers containing hot, roasted chestnuts, attracting purchases by the young and old. This was the time of year when country folk from various parishes arrived at St. Peter Port. It was the time when people met with friends, or stopped to admire the shop windows, dressed in tinsel, holly or mistletoe. Or a manger occupied

Chapter 2 - Scenes from Childhood

the corner of a display, adding warmth and colour and a special charm to passersby. The visitors greeted each other in the Guernsey patois. Many came to stock up for months ahead; to buy farm tools at Leales or some other hardware store. They relied on local stores such as Le Riche or Murdocks or Etors. Representatives from these stores telephoned weekly for orders and delivered them to the relevant doors.

Supermarkets were not yet known. I sometimes wonder if they save time. Firstly, you find your trolley, select the goods off their shelves, then on to the checkout counter and back again into the trolley after which you find your way to your car, stack your purchases into the boot, return the trolley and finally leave the supermarket! Is this progress?

I remember the excitement and wonder of Christmas Eve when a frosty cold bites the air, and snow may fall; thus completing the Christmas card scene with snowballs, reindeer and sleighs. Oh, the expectation and anticipation of it all, as you pressed your face against the window pane in the hope of watching those snowflakes gently falling to the earth. When they did not appear the disappointment was quickly overcome by the thought that a certain red-clothed figure would soon appear; the one, it is said, who lives in Snowland at the tip of the North Pole.

Church bells would ring out the age-old message that a babe was born in Bethlehem on this night, to become the Saviour of the world. Is the world now blind to this message?

Worshippers, warmly clad in scarves and gloves dared to venture out to make their way to various churches for the midnight service, which would announce the arrival of the Messiah.

Much later, during the course of my life, Trinity Church held a midnight service, which I attended with my wife Mildred and her sister Delma and the rest of the family. Mildred and Delma, who had lovely voices, were frequently asked to sing solos or duets.

In the past, carols were sung in the market square by carol singers, or outside one's front door. Sometimes they were lucky enough to be invited in to enjoy mince pies or punch before they were sent on their merry way.

Traditional festive music came to us via the wireless sets, interspersed by our favourite carols. Silent Night usually ended the selection. Young and old would mingle together at the communion table to partake of the bread and wine in thanks to God for sending us His Son.

The expectation that Father Christmas would come down the chimney to bring toys, etc with presents for all the boys and girls, who had been good during the year, was almost too much to bear. And yes, he did arrive on Christmas morn! How the benevolent old man managed to make his way down the narrow chimney never entered our minds. It was magic, and would only be destroyed later by some ill-informed person or other.

Our stockings would contain many precious things. For example, there would be nuts, apples, oranges, bananas, sweets, a ball or a whistle, chocolate, a pencil and a toy or game plus a piece of coal to bring good luck throughout the year. A glass of water and a biscuit would be left for Santa, to refresh him as he went on his way.

The contents of the stockings, compared with what is expected by today's children, were very meagre. Nevertheless, they gave us great joy, then sitting on the floor and unwrapping our parcels in the early hours of Christmas morn we would ignore the cold and revel in the excitement of it all.

This wonderful time was started long ago by St Nicholas, patron saint of Russia ,who gave presents to the needy. The popular name Santa Clause is a corruption of the Dutch name Saint Nikolaus , and the present custom of putting small toys into stockings on Christmas Eve was introduced to Great Britain from Germany in 1840.

As children we were oblivious to the fact that our sitting room was usually chilly. The Christmas tree with its sparkling decorations and twinkling coloured lights, or candles, sent a glow to the room that overcame any discomfort we might have felt. Festoons which decorated the tree would sway in the draught, if anyone left the door ajar, casting fairylike shadows on the walls.

Parents have always watched the excitement of their children as stockings, parcels or even pillowcases were inspected. Whatever the cynics may say

Chapter 2 - Scenes from Childhood

– Father Christmas does bring much love and happiness with him. Only children accept the fantasy and magic as being true. It is a little make-believe world, far away from the trials and tribulations of this earth; a dream place to enter, sharing that which the aborigines call the Dreamtime. May the glowing message of Christmas live on through the ages, with its stories of love and peace beamed to the four corners of the world, irrespective of colour or creed.

Did the boy Jesus have the same problem as I had? Asking always the same question – to whom do I belong? For Joseph was not his real father, was he?

Prior to my starting school my parents decided to move. They found a cottage in Charroterie ,which adjoined a house call La Montage. This was 'high society' to us, consisting of a living room, kitchen, scullery, two bedrooms, an inside lavatory but still no bathroom or gas or electricity. Cooking was done on a Martin range supplemented by a metholated spirit primus, which was pumped to bring it to the right pressure before ignition. There were glass funnel oil lamps whose adjustable wicks controlled the brightness of the light and gave a feeling of warmth and cosiness, far removed from the coldness of modern fluorescence. Heating came from two round oil stoves on which one could boil a kettle or heat up a saucepan fuelled by paraffin, whose tang lingered in the room while in use .

As I write, my nose recalls the smell of the paraffin. Today we complain about such primitive living. The great thing for me with the move was the fact that I had my own bedroom. I was able to enjoy this luxury until Granny Blestel joined us. Her advancing years forced her to leave windswept Alderney and to return to her birthplace. Mother took her under her wing, until she evacuated in 1940. I loved this small, quiet lady of French descent; she spent most of her life in Alderney, where her life had not been easy. Her husband died and she was forced to look after five children with no Government assistance. She pondered about supporting her children; this was not easy for widows in those days. Finally, she saw an advertisement for the sale of a donkey and decided to go into the fish trade. She became the proud owner of Bijou the donkey, and with him came a cart which enabled her to become a fish purveyor. Purveyor sounds more posh than Hawker, I suppose. After all Granny had her pride.

The previous owner, whose motives were rather suspect, said to her – "You have a fine, young donkey Mrs Blestel. It breaks my heart to part with him. He's a bargain at half the price for which anyone else would pay double. Many a day I've said to my dear wife – who is hopefully in heaven now, and whom I trust, God rest her soul..."

He cast his eyes to the great beyond and crossed himself, making sure that his wife did not return to see the act he had put on purely for Granny's benefit. Granny took all his blarney with a grain of salt, then, armed with the tools of her trade, she set up in the business of hawking fish around that northerly Channel Isle. She tells the tale of the man who always wanted his mackerel cheaper. "How much is the mackerel?" he would ask.

"Fourpence each," she would reply.

"That's too dear, he replied . Granny answered Take three for a shilling," smiling broadly and thinking that he had won a bargain also that he had outdone Granny on price. But my Gran was no fool!

Larrikins often played tricks on the poor soul. One night her donkey turned into a zebra. Bonny Newton was a boy known for his pranks,and, with one or two other boys, they managed to paint the unfortunate donkey with black and white stripes. The islanders who lived in the vicinity of Buttes Show field could not believe their eyes when they saw a 'wild beast' wandering about, enjoying the pasture that Bijou usually ate. On another occasion, they stuck the cart shafts on the side of Granny's front gate at Braye Road, with Bijou on the other side. Stick in hand, Granny gave chase. "Wait till I catch you young buggers!" she shouted after them. Sadly, catch them she never did. I felt safe with Granny who never mentioned the fatal word – adoption.

I like to think that she classed me as her grandchild and so to me I was her grandson. Yet, beneath it all I was uncertain that this was so.

Soon after moving into the cottage at Charroterie I started kindergarten, which was attached to the Intermediate school. Here I spent the most

Chapter 2 - Scenes from Childhood

enjoyable time of my school life. The teachers were Miss Hazel, Miss Johnson, Miss le Page and sweet Miss Carre to whom I gave my heart, falling in love, hook, line and sinker. Love at that age knows no bounds. I like to think that she too loved me, that being nice was not just a part of her teaching job, though I must admit that she was a favourite of all the class.

On one occasion Miss le Carre arrived wearing her Salvation Army bonnet. She looked so sweet and told me that Jesus had entered her heart at quite a young age. Then she asked me if I had given my heart to Jesus, and, though I wanted to please her, I had no intention of parting with my heart. Such ignorance on my part.

A large sand tray stood in the middle of the classroom. It became a kind of fairyland in which we created scenes from stories read to us in class; a time when we made models out of paper maché with water, flour and paste. Here we were away from harm. We felt safe.

Our headmistress was Miss Nora Roughton, a kindly lady and a follower of the Arts. She was given the gift of music and often played the violin with her sister Winifred. The sound of both violins was always sweet to hear. They both encouraged the formation of a school band which proved to be great fun. We took great pride in our performances in front of the school and parents. The triangle was allotted to me.

Another highlight in the curriculum was the annual play, which would be performed for the parents. Mother set to work making a Red Indian suit, complete with feathered head-dress for the Hiawatha Production. Those early performances gave me a taste for the stage which has lasted all my life. Ultimately it led me to appear professionally on TV, stage and films.

I often wonder what happened to my early classmates like the Davidson twins, Beryl Ascot, Joan Maunder, John Mallet, Noella Hubert, John Baxendale, David Rich, Allen Mauger, Brian le Mesurier, Pat le Gallez, David Morgan, Ramsey Hubert, Allen Guppy, and Peter le Cheminant. There are many more whose names have been lost with time.

I was summoned to Miss Roughton's study one bright morning. Brian had made contact, with a toy mallet which was part of a children's carpentry set, to Beryl Ascot's head. I had received the set due to the generosity of Father Christmas. Because it was mine, I was called in. Miss Rroughton sat at her desk, and it strikes me now that her appearance was very different from that of teachers today. She wore a plain grey blouse with button sleeves, a black skirt, thick lisle stockings and brogue shoes. The room had that indescribable odour which seemed to permeate school classrooms the world over. It is a kind of pencil and graphite mixture, which is the best way I can describe it. The fireplace in her room was hidden behind a tall, vertical Victorian chair from which she conducted the school's curriculum and other weighty matters.

Coal burned brightly in a tiled peacock-designed grate sending a moderate warmth through the room, which was lined with bookshelves on which the books were arranged in alphabetical order. There were editions on child education and other volumes by distinguished authors; the classics themselves took up a large part of the bookcases and a large, brown filing cabinet sat on Miss Roughton's right. This contained the details of each pupil, both past and present. I remember almost photographically. Placed on the left side of the study was a Victorian whatnot, or small mahogany table, on which was placed a vase of sweet smelling mixed flowers. The flowers were picked at an established garden at the Vardes and lovingly cared for by Miss Nora and Miss Winifred, who replaced those that were withered each day. Flowers played an important part in the lives of the Roughtons. The whatnot was a piece of furniture cherished by the sisters. It had been willed to them by their late grandfather whose portrait, of a whiskered gentleman, sitting beside his wife, hung in a place of honour over their mahogany treasure.

Brian and I stood meekly before Miss. Roughton. "Gentlemen," she said in measured tones. "Do not go about striking young ladies on the head in whatever circumstances. This behaviour is simply not done."

"But Miss..." Brian said.

"There are no 'buts' in this case," interrupted Miss Roughton severely. "You will apologise to Beryl, and, if you appear before me again for a similar offence, both your mothers will be informed. I am sure that this would

Chapter 2 - Scenes from Childhood

cause distress and you have no desire for this to happen. Kindly return to your class now. The matter is closed. As for you, Bernard," she went on, turning to me. "This er...thing... what it is ... mallet?"

"Yes, Miss, a mallet," I whispered.

Then she picked up the mallet and she finished by saying, "This mallet should never have been brought to school." And she threw the offending instrument into the fire, whose dying embers were momentarily rejuvenated.

I left the study in tears, while Brian felt no remorse, as he skipped happily along the corridors. My thoughts were full of venom against the now not so sweet Miss Roughton. I did not dare mention any of this to my parents in case father punished me as well.

Life went on without the mallet, and in due course Miss Roughton was restored to favour. We remained happy until Brian decided to set fire to the school. He asked me to bring the matches and he would supply the newspaper. I am not sure why but the plot ended before the first match was struck.

Reaching the age of seven we were transferred to the main boy's school, leaving our younger pals behind. Things became rather different and I was glad that my best friend John Mallet (yes, he had the same name) joined me there. We remained friends for many years.

Chapter 3

More Treasured Memories

I spent the first ten years of my childhood on the beautiful island of Guernsey. Victor Hugo chose to live in exile in Hauteville House and wrote some of his greatest works, like Les Miserables and Toilers of the Sea there.

Years later, I got to know this house pretty well; it seemed massive to me. I remember heavy, carved furniture; big tables and carved cupboards and a door leading to a secret room, which I believed was used by the great man as a clandestine meeting place ,where he would embrace his mistress, Jullette Drouet. I remember tapestries and majolica and Delft china.

Supposedly, there was also a ghost in the house. Victor Hugo loved to commune with spirits through a new parlour game called, perhaps appropriately, Tipping the Table. He was introduced to this game by his old friend Mme Emilie de Girardin an ardent Republican, known to Victor as Delphine Gay. (More to follow later regarding the spooks in this strange, unique and wonderful house.)

Today, adding to the export of tomatoes and grapes, is the tourist industry. When the Normans settled in years gone by, their influence, including the patois still spoken here, and, therefore, created the special atmosphere which is still enjoyed. It is now predominantly English, though the French flavour still remains, together with old Norman laws.

My life went on at a peaceful unhurried pace. People had time to chat and crime was mostly caused through drunkenness. I remember only one murder. A housekeeper called Gertie de la Mare killed her old employer, cutting Mr. Brouard's throat for his money. This naturally caused a sensation on the island. The Guernsey Press and Star covered the trial from start to finish – news indeed! Nothing like it had happened for years. Mr Brouard and Gertie de la Mare were front-page news for years.

The film Pygmalion caused tongues to wag after Eliza Doolittle uttered the words "Not bloody likely!" – a forerunner to the more general use of four letter words. Things were changing. Young and old joined the yoyo craze and people decided to relax, casting off the depression blues. Big bands provided the carefree music enjoyed by the masses, bands like those of Paul Whiteman, Ray Noble, Duke Ellington and Glen Miller, playing the compositions of Cole Porter, George Gershwin, Irving Berlin and Ivor Novello. Among the most popular singers were Bing Crosby, Al Bowley and Rudy Vallee. Radio became a must in every home. The Charleston and other energetic dances were also favourites.

Little did the islanders realise that soon the peace of this sun-drenched isle had run its course to be replaced by a jailer, whose grip never loosened for five, long years.

Before Granny Blestel, or Bletel, as it was pronounced in Alderney, came to stay with us, a company which owned the Courier, a small boat, ran trips between Guernsey and Alderney. The captain of this gallant little vessel helped in the rescue of soldiers from the shores of Dunkirk. His name was Dan Ingroeule and he was a cousin of my father. During those pre-war years, our family often boarded the boat to visit Granny Blestel as well as my aunts, Alice, Amy and Lil.

Lil had earlier worked for General Booth, founder of the Salvation Army. There was also George, son of Aunt Mabel and Aunt Mim who lived in Reading in England. Aunt Lil and Uncle Robert Slade owned a butcher's

Chapter 3 - More Treasured Memories

shop at St Ann's. When on holiday I often helped in the delivery van with John Odoire, who was sadly killed later while on active service.

Holidays spent in Alderney were carefree; I often fed Bijou with a tasty carrot, sometimes allowed to hold his reins and leading him along the unlevelled paths. Is it my imagination, or did the sun seem to shine for days on end? As I enjoyed the company of my Alderney cousins, we seemed to be oblivious to the darkening shadows that were encircling us at that time.

Between 1940 and 1945 Alderney was turned into a concentration camp for slave workers, brought over from Europe, and more than a thousand died on the island as a result of that terrible oppression.

In the meantime, the warmth of the sun's rays, not known to be harmful in those days, filled me with joy. I loved to be in the company of my cousins as we roamed the island, unafraid of any danger that might befall us, for violent crime did not lurk around the corner as it does today. There was no TV to take up our time, no computers nor internet with which to scan the world. We listened to the wireless. Among my favourite programmes was the Paul Temple series; his adventures held us enthralled. There was plenty to amuse us like a variety show, the children's hour, a weekly educational programme and comics, including Jingles and Beano. And there was a children's newspaper -- Enid Blyton produced Sunny Stories, which was a small booklet telling us all about the goings-on at her home at Greenhedges, including the adventures of her two daughters and the misbehaviour of a scamp of a dog. Whenever we had the time, we made up our own games. School was thought of as a necessary evil.

We lived without much pressure, having the chance to grow up in a world that did not force us to become adult before we had the experience of enjoying our childhood. Though money was in short supply, we learnt to appreciate whatever was given to us, large or small.

Yet, there were times when I wished my father would curtail his temper, upsetting Mother. And, at the back of my mind lurked the word 'adoption'. One half of me wanted to know the truth, but at the same time I preferred a negative answer. I chose to live in shadowland. It was secure.

Once again it became time to move. This time to a nice house in Mount Durand, though we were still without a bathroom. Since Granny Blestel had come to live with us, she had occupied my bedroom, but the new house had three bedrooms so that I could once again enjoy one for myself. As well as having three bedrooms we had gas lighting, which was much better than the oil lamps or candles we had put up with before. The flickering flames of the gas lights cast a soft mellow illumination, which created dancing shadows on the walls, which were magic to me. And gone were the days when ablutions had to be washed away with a bucket of water – we had the luxury of a flush toilet! Plumbing in those pre-war days was inadequate on the Island, for it It took an armed conflict to improve sanitary conditions there. Nowadays, we take modern conveniences for granted.

During the summer months, picnics were arranged by Aunt Alice. Not only did she bring along her full picnic basket, but also a methylated sprite stove, which made it possible for us to enjoy hot tea on the beach. Popular venues to visit, included Fermain, Grande Rocque, Saints and Lancresse, all good bays for a day on the sands. When the time came for refreshment, Aunt would find a sheltered spot under some rocks and then she would light the stove.

After a short wait, the kettle, filled with water, would start to boil and Aunt busied herself making our tea, with three teaspoons, plus one for the pot, and it was left to brew. No teabags were yet to find cupboard space. Liptons produced a wonderful brew, and on those beaches the tea seemed better than it had ever been at home. Homemade cake and sandwiches, plus apples or bananas, completed the meal. There were times when gusts of wind brought sand onto our food, but who cares? A swig of Guppy's Cream Soda or my favourite apple juice would wash away the offending addition to our menu. Granny informed us that one had to eat a bushel of dirt before one died. She had many funny sayings.

We either walked or travelled by bus, according to the bank balance. These were modes of transport on those far-off sunny days and we thought nothing of it, whichever way we went. Cars did not feature in our lives till after the war, when the whole structure of life changed for all time. We only looked forward to joyous days, unaware that storm clouds and vicious

Chapter 3 - More Treasured Memories

time lay ahead of us; the politicians, those in power seemed to be unwilling or unable to have a clear vision of what was to come.

My first five years at school proved to be uneventful, taking a dramatic turn in 1939, as happened to so many. The mail boats like the St. Helier, St. Julian, Roebuck and Hazelmere sailed between the islands and England bringing newspapers. Other information came to us from listening to the wireless or by the use of the telephone. Smaller boats such as the Courier and Joybell served Alderney and Sark. The boats were our main link with the rest of the world. As we listened to the wireless, we heard of the death of George 5th, the much loved monarch, whose death caused a huge amount of grief throughout the island. And then we heard of the abdication of Edward for love of his mistress, Wallis Simpson, and this news was received with mixed feelings. Everyone seemed to settle down when King George 6th came to the throne with his wife Elizabeth and their two children. Newspapers told us of the rise of Hitler and the subsequent global involvement. In some way we felt geographically apart from what was happening, but this illusion would soon be shattered.

We were informed, through the wireless, that the clouds of war were now visible on the horizon. We heard that Neville Chamberlain had attempted to defer the inevitable on his trip to Munich – he failed, as we know too well. Hitler determined to conquer the whole of Europe. When he invaded Poland, England declared war on Germany, on the 3rd September 1939, another dark momentous shadow in history.

My mother received the news while preparing dinner. "Oh, my God, not again" she cried, as tears came to her eyes. "You did your share in the last lot, Charlie!" Then she turned to me. "Thank God, you are too young to fight," she said, speaking the words with confidence as she embraced me, kissing me gently on the forehead. How I loved to be embraced by my mother; the scent of her fresh dress together with the fragrance Eau de Cologne and Palmolive lingers still. The loss of my mother's brother Cecil and that of two brothers-in-law during that terrible conflit was surely enough for her to bear. Each year, on Armistice Day, the loss of her brother caused her to weep, and when she did, tears also came to my cheeks in sympathy. I could not bear to see her cry, and so I did on that awful day.

Bernard Blestel

I never knew what Father had experienced during the First World War: it was a closed subject, rarely spoken, but, as I brushed my own tears, I glanced at him and saw his lips trembling. Perhaps the memory of the horror of casting a cold steel bayonet into a body of a stranger came back to him.

After several moments I picked up the water can that stood near the kitchen bench and left my parents to discuss the situation. I passed a few people talking to each other across low garden fences. Their usual smiles replaced by sad faces, which showed their disappointment and anxiety.

I made my way down to the communal pump at Mount Durand. This pump sat on a cobbled platform with a lead insert which proclaimed that the pump had served the community from the early 1800's. Well water is refreshingly cool on a hot day. As I glanced at the garden opposite, it seemed that the flowers themselves were hanging their heads in misery. Pumps on the island were confiscated after the war, when, in its wisdom, the States Water Board decided that well water did not meet the standards for human consumption, much to the people's disgust. They enjoyed the water for years without ill effects.

As I continued to fill the can with cool water, the wail of the siren burst forth, declaring to us islanders that Great Britain and her allies were now at war with Germany. That dreadful sound heralded death and destruction and I would hear it again many times under many different circumstances.

Carrying the heavy can back home, my thoughts turned to Mother who would be facing a second war in her lifetime. How would the hostilities affect us? The unexpected answer came before many months had passed, though we first lived through the Phoney War, so-called because nothing significant was happening at that time. Many altercations took place quite quickly. Rationing was introduced and young men began to join the armed forces of their own accord. There was no conscription introduced on the islands. Men were eager to fight for King and country, perhaps their fathers had been involved in the previous 'Great War'?

They did not count the cost of the war to end all wars, in the hope that this time, perhaps, peace could be secured for all time. Once again these words had a hollow ring on government lips.

Chapter 3 - More Treasured Memories

Perhaps they believed, that, by crushing Hitler's youth, which had been brainwashed from an early age, they could force the avoidance of Hitler's ambition to rule the world?

The economic decline in Germany caused thousands to march against poverty and Hitler promised them that a new regime would be born, which would once again bring back a super race to the country. Who can blame those unfortunate youths from believing in a doctrine that ultimately led to disaster?. Many still live today with guilt.

At the age of nine I saw picture books extolling the glories of war, where the agony was superseded by the illustrious deeds of heroes. My father followed the progress of the war with great interest, which was a major reversal, as he had hardly mentioned the Great War at all. Suddenly, he began to talk about his own experiences in the trenches, telling of the terrors they brought to the young men who occupied those self-dug death traps. He predicted that – "Bombing from the air will win this lot." Unfortunately, he did not foresee the horror of the atom bomb.

My father had been blinded in one eye by a chip of granite whilst working in the quarry. There was, of course, no compensation in those days. A boyhood notion of mine believed that the injury had been caused during his time on the battlefield. It was a bit of a letdown ,when I later heard about the real cause.

Every Saturday, during the football season, Father and I would make our way to the Track, which was Guernsey's main venue. Two local teams would play for a place in the Muratti, the winning team then played against the opposing rival Jersey team. Having to go to a match each week brought out some defiance in me, and I ended up being put of the game altogether. Father would meet with his mates to discuss football or work, leaving me to become familiar with apathy, at its best. I would shuffle from one foot to the other, though sometimes the waiting had its compensations, when a coin was slipped into my hand by some kind soul, who undoubtedly saw complete indifference on my face. "Your old man can't half talk," he would murmur.

The only sports I enjoyed at school were cricket and tennis. The curriculum included a boxing class, which was a definite no, no for me.

Following the tradition of most schools, nick names were the norm for teachers, and our Intermediate School was no exception. Mr. Fulford became Fluff, our headmaster Mr. Warren was called Ticky, Mr. Williams became Taffy, Mr. le Pelley was Pellets, of course. Mr. Gibbons became Gibbo and Mr. Ross became Rosie. Miss. Jones was the only lady teacher at the school and she became Winni (for some reason) finally,Mr Paul, Paulo also Mr. Girarad was known as Pierro.

Discipline, though never harsh, was strict. Detentions and written lines were common ,and, though corporal punishment{Cuts} was administered at the whim of a teacher, we learnt to respect it. It all played a part in keeping us in tow. Things then were different from today's classes, when teachers all too often resign due to a lack of respect by their pupils.

Sometime, during the thirties, while we were still living at Charroterie, the Breisers, which was a French boat carrying wine, hit the rocks off the west coast of Guernsey near the bay of Grande Rocques. The sea was treacherous during stormy weather causing indistinct rocks to become death traps for captains who found themselves in unfamiliar waters.

A hole was torn in the ship's side and the damage was too great to save it; the sea gushed into the side, disturbing the cargo. As the ship broke up, large barrels of wine floated out to sea. Word got around quickly and the islanders managed to retrieve much of the flotsam and jetsam before the customs men arrived on the scene.

Whenever such a disaster occurred my father was one of the first on the scene, and, as a result, a large barrel of sour red wine found its way to our house to be hidden in the loft of the wash house The wine was only palatable when sugar was added, but the very fact of smuggling wine seemed to be a kind of adventure to me.

One reason why this adventure became exciting for me was that our landlord at the time, a Mr. L'Oiseau, who was a devious Frenchman, would turn any situation to his advantage, which included reporting us to the authorities

Chapter 3 - More Treasured Memories

– if there was money to be had. It therefore became a cloak and dagger operation in which the illegal refreshment had to be contained in all sorts of receptacles. On that occasion, my aunt filled an old-fashioned stone hot water bottle with the wine and nearly died, when, on her way home with it, she was accosted by a policeman. He touched his helmet as a mark of respect and said, with a smile – "Good morning Mrs Salmon." He was eyeing the hot water bottle as he went on. "On a cold morning like this, I'm glad that you're keeping warm." And then he went on his way. Needless to say, that was the last time Aunt Alice entered into criminal proceedings.

In spite of Mr L' Oiseau's financial interests, he and Granny Blestel, conversing in French, enjoyed each other's company. He showed her the shell grotto he had built in the garden with the Virgin Mary as a centrepiece beside a font with a crucifix adorned with Ormer shells and broken pieces of china embedded in concrete. These decorated the edges of the steps leading to the top of the garden. It was quite a climb up a bramble-lined path to the summit.

Once there, one could glimpse the saw mill with the timber piled high in the yard. I often saw a horse awaiting its driver to load or unload the timber trolley. I felt sorry for the poor animal carrying such a heavy load.

I remember collecting sawdust from the mill to make a Guy Fawkes to be burned on the 5th November. From the top of the garden one could see the town area of St Peter Port, incorporating parts of St. Martins. For me, this was always the pinnacle of the world. In another part of the garden, my father planted vegetables to feed the family, including cabbage, carrots, beans and onions.

One of the most memorable features of the garden were the three or four apple trees, which produced the sweetest apples I ever tasted. On odd occasions, Mr. L'Oiseau invited me into his storeroom to choose an apple. On opening the door one was greeted with an aroma only apples could yield.

Mr. L'Oiseau was a lonely man who received few visitors, which probably explained his grumpy moods. But he always appeared more cheerful, when Granny or I were in his company. He never discovered the wine in the loft. One day I caught him climbing up the loft ladder; on spying me he retreated quickly to the ground. After this scare, my father fitted a lock to the door leading to the loft.

In those days, milk came straight out of the milkman or woman's can and into your jug. Very few people brought bottled milk. Those were the days when a rich cream came to the top – and how delicious that was! And, of course, the powers that be, decided, much against the will of the islanders, that the milk should be gathered from the farmers, dairy and tested for TB at the States Dairy after which it would be bottled.

Grace, our milk lady, though otherwise nice enough, always passed remarks about how large my feet were for my age. I thought these comments were bad mannered. Surely other boys had large feet, why pick on me? Every so often she would ask my mother if I ever saw my father. Or – "His mother would have been proud of him, if she had lived. How are his brothers and sister, living with their grandmother?" Or, perhaps even more to the point – "This is better than if he had gone into a Children's Home, thank God."

Asking my mother why she would say such things Mother would say firmly, "Take no notice, dear. She is a silly woman." Father thought that she was talking about someone else.

Still, the question continued to lurk in my mind. Who am I? To whom do I belong? Wishing not to hear such things, I kept out of her way whenever the milk was delivered.

Mother always looked nervous, with a tinge of sadness, whenever people made reference concerning me. It was a look that I never understood, until I grew older. She had a way with looks, melting me into obedience when I misbehaved; there was no need for a smack. A glance from her deep brown eyes was enough to control any sensitive young boy or girl. Father, on the other hand, resorted to the strap as punishment for my misdeeds, which, fortunately, he only used on a rare occasions.

David Morgan was a school friend and a member of our gang. Shall I say a very special friend, because he had access to cigarettes? His father kept a large linen chest on the landing, which was full of Sunripe cigarettes.

Chapter 3 - More Treasured Memories

They were produced by Buckrout in their Cornet Street factory, and, when passing the premises, the tang of tobacco would fill the air. Every so often David would purloin a packet of fifty to distribute among his friends. In those days, the danger of smoking was unknown; our only fear was to be caught by our parents or teachers. Like children everywhere we would smoke in the toilets behind the school. Then we would suck on Uncle Joe's mint ball. which dear Miss. Poidvin supplied out of my pocket money.

On one occasion a number of us were smoking in the Regal cinema, when, unfortunately, Reggie Lamb was working as an usher, came up to us and threatened to report us to the headmaster. On another occasion, John Mallet, my friend from school and for many years to come, and I hid behind some bushes near his father's vinery having a quiet puff. Suddenly a gunshot rang out over our heads! It turned out to be a fool of a man who thought we were wild ducks. We quickly retreated, running like hellfire with our hands above our heads to the safety of the vinery, leaving a bewildered gunman shouting – "You young buggers! If I catch you here again I won't miss!" No comment.

Many a time Father forgot his lunch and it became time for me to take it to him at his work. The quarry was an hour's walk from home and when I arrived, I would stand on the edge of the huge hole and peer down. Far away, the workers looked like the dwarfs out of Disney's Snow White. I half expected to hear them singing "Yo ho, yo ho, it's off to work we go!" Instead, the crane driver would shout out from the wheelhouse – "Okay Bernard, up you come and hold tight!"

He carefully lowered the rusty, muddy skip (called Blond), so that I could board it. My hand gripped the twisted metal rope which was attached to an iron hook, and clambered into the skip. Even though I enjoyed this as a kind of adventure, as it swung precariously over the side and descended into the guts of the earth, butterflies roamed around in my stomach. If the wind caused it to sway, I was more than thankful when the rig reached terra firma.

Father was the foreman in charge of the explosives. It was dangerous work, but he never showed any fear, as he climbed the rocks to set the charges which would explode to send the granite to the floor of the quarry. Due to his toughness, he was given the name of Iron Man. He often brought home sticks of dynamite, removing them from his pockets and depositing the lethal bundles under the bed, till he returned to the quarry. He told us that the only safe place for dynamite was away from naked flames. If, by any chance, contact was made, then goodbye Guernsey, hello Heaven! My poor mother really lived on her nerves, having to put up with having the stuff in her home.

From an early age I attended Trinity Sunday School. Trinity was the church in which my parents were married and they chose it for my christening. They preferred me to be brought up in the Protestant faith, where I learnt all about leading a good or a bad life. Wicked boys went to Hell and good girls to Heaven. This sounded good for the girls, but the boys never seem to have a chance. Was something wrong there?

The Sunday School superintendent was called Miss. Steadman. She was dressed in the style of by-gone days with a high-lace collar around her neck, a hat trimmed with mauve net. This was entwined with a spray of artificial flowers, held together by two hatpins with bulbous pearls on the smooth end, and a sober coloured coat and dress, which reached down almost to her ankles. On her nose were pince-nez glasses. Dear Miss. Steadman was an upright Christian soul, as someone once remarked; she was an unclaimed treasure. She never seemed to age and was tireless in her work, spreading the Gospel and seeing to the needs of unfortunate souls in a practical way.

Our Minister, the Rev. F. Carpenter, like Miss Steadman was held in high esteem. He was a man of vision regarding the young people of his congregation and started a Youth and Badminton Club, which I joined after the war. It was there where I met my future wife, Mildred. Her lovely smile captured my heart, and, as she always laughed at my jokes, it was inevitable that we fell in love – with a capital L.

While Mother insisted that I must go to Sunday School, it sometimes went against the grain as far as I was concerned. And then, after school, we would also scatter in snake-like fashion on our way to the Church with Miss Steadman leading our happy band of pilgrims. We would pass an

Chapter 3 - More Treasured Memories

old pump, where horses drank from a trough and rested before climbing up the hill to pull their heavy load of timber to De Guerens mill. I think I have already mentioned that the mill was the source of sawdust for the making of a Guy Fawkes for our celebrations on November 5th each year. All of us children collected sawdust from De Guerens for the same purpose, and there were times when saw dust from the horse drawn carts blew inadvertently came into the church. Though we were exuberant about our coming effigy adventure, we were soon quietened by Miss Steadman who believed that God's house did not tolerate idle chatter of the young. And so we sat quietly, gazing at the tablets over the communion table on which were inscribed the Ten Commandments. I thought, as I read them, that only a saint could keep to them and there was little chance of my ever becoming a saint.

A few years later, after the war, the boot was on the other foot, when I was approached by Miss Steadman to become a Sunday School teacher.

Across from the tree-lined square was an old-fashioned shop, which was opposite the church. It was run by Miss. Renouf and her sister. They sold everything from tea, coffee, soap and cheese, but most mouth watering of all were the glorious sweets. No wonder that we spent time in that shop, enjoying the wonderful odours and delicious confectionery. The shop has sadly long since gone. Today's supermarkets do not impart those enticing odours, or the personal touches of the Miss Renoufs.

I learnt hymns and stories of Jesus' love without really understanding the implications of His devotion, just believing in the wonder of Heaven with a child's simplicity. I was ever thankful that my mother saw fit to send me to Sunday school, even though I sometimes rebelled against its discipline. I believed in God who lived above the clouds then as a child, and I still do this day. It is a faith that became steadfast in later life.

One of the highlights near Christmas was a dinner organized at Ebenezer Church. Nellie Vaudin was a friend of my mother and invited us each year to the church dinner, which included turkey, honeyed ham and roast potatoes, plus all the trimmings. No turkey dinner is complete without cranberry sauce. It was pure delight as far as I was concerned.

The Vaudin family were neighbours in Charroterie, which consisted of Nancy, Doris, Barbara, Peter and Molly, who later became a missionary. Barbara, who was a year older than me, became my childhood sweetheart, or so the family thought. In fact we were just good chums, attending the Ebenezer church at times with their family.

When I attended Trinity, there were camps and picnics. For some reason I was never allowed to go to the camps. The picnics were wonderful during the summer months. We would take bus trips to Lancresse Bay, with its white sands or to the Green Common, where games of all sorts were played with gusto. This was fun time. The Guernsey motors would make their way along narrow lanes, passing cottages and farmhouses, built in traditional Guernsey style with four windows on each side of an ornate front door beneath a stone lintel.

On the hard surface the stonemason had chiselled the year in which the house had been built. There were five windows upstairs, two on each side and one in the centre. Around the farmhouses were green fields with haystacks, built in the autumn in the shape of cottages, ready as winter fodder for the animals. The famous Guernsey cow was seen busy chewing the cud or being milked by hand. In those days the cows were tethered to a rope, which made sure that the pasture was eaten evenly. Sometimes, as we drove on, we would watch as the farmhands gathered up the hay for the stacks and I clearly remember that special smell of the fresh hay. At other times the bus would stop on the side of a particularly narrow lane to allow a horse-drawn cart, laden with vraic to pass. Vraic was a fine fertiliser, gathered from the shores of the sea. During the early part of the century it was used in the making of iodine on Lihou Island. At last we saw the open coast road ahead, our streamers flying out through the windows and passers--by waving with smiles and cheering us on.

With such encouragement, we kids stood lustily, returning the waves. Our favourite songs included 'Paddy wack, give a dog a bone', 'Ten green bottles hanging on the wall', 'One man went to mow. Went to mow a meadow,' which was particularly popular. Miss. Steadman led choruses like 'I am H.A.P.P.Y.' or 'Zacceus was a very little man as he climbed the sycamore tree.' And there were many more, sung off the cuff.

Chapter 3 - More Treasured Memories

Our bus driver entered into the fun, singing along with us, as he drove us to the Grassy Common by the sea shore. Miss. Steadman, who always seemed to be prim and proper to us children, relaxed a little, though her style of clothing never altered. She became like us as we stood in awe to watch her, as she wielded a cricket bat like Don Bradman.

Alighting from the bus in boisterous anticipation we were greeted by the warm salty breeze, mixed together with the smell of yellow thorny gorse. I clearly remember the seagulls screeching, the lapping of the gentle surf onto the sandy pebbled shore, children licking flavoured ice creams and men and women carrying tomato chip crates put to a different use as picnic baskets, which had been loaned to carry purchases bought at Le Noury tea rooms. This was a haven, where everyone gathered for a mouth-watering feast which included mixed sandwiches, sticky buns, jelly and ice cream and a piece of famous Guernsey gauch. This feast sometimes had dire results from over indulgence, but it was certainly worth it. Games and races were all part of the afternoon fun.

Then there were sand castle competitions, rounders, an egg and spoon race or tug of war. The three legged race was always popular bringing with it much laughter whenever someone stumbled. Bathing costumes were at the ready for a dip in the briny or an exploration of the rock pools or just a paddle in the shadows. The fun ended with a treasure hunt and the giving of prizes to the day's winners, like bags of sweets to munch on the way home.

Finally, tired but happy, we would sing to the driver who had become our friend – 'For he's a jolly good driver and so say all of us', 'Ten green bottles hanging on the wall', 'It's a long, long way to Tipperary' and 'Show me the way to go home'.

Arriving back at school we would be met by our parents with Miss. Steadman and other teachers offering a prayer of thanks for our safe return. Those happenings are as clear in my mind as if they were only a stone's throw away. Yet they are gone, gone never to return again.

Will today's children be lucky enough to have such happy childhood memories? Or has technology taken over, confining them to a computer, restricting their ability to switch off and to enter a world where entertainment is self made?

In pre-war days celebrations for the King's birthday took place at Fort George, a fortress built in the 18th Century, which housed the Guernsey Militia, in barracks, together with the English Sherwood Foresters Regiment. They were there to guard the island against potential French foes. Little did we know that there were other latent foes ready to pounce on our Island home. The granite fort has since then been given over to a housing estate for the rich, seeking a tax haven. I believe that it was a foolish decision, which desecrated tradition such is the greed who allowed the sale .

The sun always seemed to shine on the pomp and circumstance of the event. Both the servicemen and women and the onlookers frequently succumbed to the heat and required the services of St John"s Ambulance.

The Troops, Boy Scouts, Girl Guides, Brownies and Cubs, all fell into formation, awaiting inspection by the Governo,r who looked resplendent in his ceremonial uniform, complete with a white plume distinguishing his headwear and seated on his chestnut horse, especially trained for such occasions.

Men in scarlet uniforms presented a striking picture against the azure blue of the sky, the sun glistening on well-polished armoury, and then the strains of the National Anthem halting the general chatter of the crowd ,as the Governor approached, returning the salute.

The sound of a bugle playing a command began a display of mock warfare enacted on Belvedere, a large expanse of land which overlooked Half Moon Bay. The ever imposing Castle Cornet with Sark, Herm and Jethou were visible in the background.

The crowd, in holiday mood, focussed their eyes on the spectacle about to commence. Canons and shells exploded; soldiers in sham combat fought against the enemy. Grey smoke, tinged with blue arose from the explosions; mock hand grenades created by the wizardry of pyrotechnics were pitched to impede the advancing infantrymen.

Chapter 3 - More Treasured Memories

To us young boys, the essence of this excitement made us feel, that, as men, we would be in the midst of it all, serving King and country on the battlefield. Little did I know that this whim would become a terrible truth for many. The floating clouds of war in the guise of nonaggression were deviously travelling to us to engulf our island.

Mr Del La Rose made his way through the crowd, carrying a red and white ice box supported by a strap around his shoulders. Inside this Pandora's Box were ice creams of many different, delicious flavours. On hot days he was assured of a sell-out.

Once the carnival was over, family and friends intermingled with the dispersing crowd, wending their various ways home to enjoy the rest of the day. Alas, the spectacle will only be replayed in the memories of those who were fortunate enough to actually witness yet another important part of Guernsey heritage. The Guernsey Militia were disbanded after the Second World War, which caused great disappointment for many islanders. Many volunteered to join the English forces during both wars. There was no compulsory conscription at the time.

As I return to my eighth birthday, a pleasant surprise in the form of a cuddly, mischievous black and white puppy greeted me. I have no idea how we acquired that bundle of joy, but I do recall a cousin of Mrs. Toms, a lady who became a neighbour of ours later and who worked at the Grange Hotel, whose proprietor wanted homes for his puppies. My puppy was called Rover, a black spaniel who made his presence known very soon. By taking a liking to the kitchen table and chair legs,-- thinking they were bones useful for exercising his jaws. My mother and father were disgusted, but he soon found refuge under my bed, and, as an only child, he took the place of a brother. He would sit on the floor with his head to one side, probably listening as we conversed, though he also responded with little yaps, begging me to give him a bone or throw a ball. Yes, dogs do speak.

A shadow entered Rover's life, when he suddenly became prone to fits which left him rather aggressive, particularly towards my father. For no apparent reason, on the day that we left Charroterie for a new abode at Mt Durand, poor Rover, decided to bite father on the leg. This proved to be poor Rover's undoing, because it was now father's turn to become aggressive. "No bloody dog is going to bite me," he said, smacking the dog on the back. Rover turned to me for comfort, but this was short—lived. Father picked up the now docile animal and promptly took him to the vet, thus ending the companionship between the wretched dog and me. Needless to say, tears flowed in bucket loads from my eyes, as I implored Father to spare the life of the poor beast.

"That dog's done enough damage to the furniture, let alone biting me on the leg!" my father stated grimly. "Biting is the last bloody straw!"

And so, after just one year, Rover joined his ancestors. The departure of Rover caused a sullen mood in me. This was only ended when cousin George (Mabel's son) arrived from Alderney. This northern cousin was just one and half years my senior. Yet, surprisingly, he already knew many worldly ways of life. Smoking, for example, came as second nature to him, as he instructed me on how to inhale, so that I would get the full benefit of mother nicotine. And girls! Well! what he didn't know was not worth knowing,

George seemed to know everything. "Girls are different from boys down below. We have a dick and they haven't. Girls have a post box; if you want a baby you put your French letter in her post box."

If anyone else had imparted this information I might have queried the facts, but George knew everything so I accepted it, without reservation.

George encouraged me to fish, so we armed ourselves with fishing lines and dug for worms on the Salerie beach, trusting that our worms would survive in a cocoa tin packed with seaweed. We set off on our journey past the Carrning yard where, at high tide water polo was played. Or we stopped to watch the dockers unload from the coal boats in the old harbour.

One day, I recognised a man on the ship's deck; he had been introduced to me as Uncle Charlie when he and father met. As I watched him, a shadow appeared in my mind. How had this man become my uncle? I looked away from him, not wishing to become involved at that stage.

Chapter 3 - More Treasured Memories

George whistled, a feat I never seemed to manage, accompanying him in his merry tune by humming. It was a good life as we continued with our walk without a care in the world. The shadow faded, the sea was blue, the sun warmed us and our lunch would be delicious, prepared by Mother. And there was companionship. What more could we want?

We reached Castle Cornet and made our way to the end of the breakwater, sitting on the stone steps beneath the lighthouse. We threaded our worms, those which were fat and juicy onto the hooks, and cast the lines into the blue lapping sea. The smell of ozone was in our nostrils and life was good. We left our parents to do the worrying in those times of depression. We fishermen just sat and waited, sometimes for an interminable length of time, trusting our dangling worms would entice the fish to bite. We hoped for a tasty meal; if we were unlucky we would go hungry. George, who was known as Georgie by his family, never tired of fishing, lucky or not.

George's father owned a small boat which he handled as if this was second nature to him; he never understood why my father did not own one also. On his second day in Guernsey he befriended one of the local lads who owned a rowing boat. By means only known to himself, he managed to acquire the boat for the whole duration of his holidays. My mother was sent into fits of worry every time we left the house, telling us to be careful or we would be drowned. As soon as we were out of earshot, George said that we should never have told 'the old girl' what we were up to. That 'old girl' was, of course, my mother.

George handled the boat around the harbour as if he had been a sailor forever. He rowed in and out between small yachts and hailed those on the larger vessels in true seaman like fashion. Sometimes he allowed me to take the oars, but being no match to his masterful strokes, I soon returned them to him, much to his delight.

The holiday went without a hitch until we left our shoes on a rock while inspecting the surrounding pools. The old saying – Time and Tide wait for no Man is certainly true, because we lost all sense of time, as we inspected the pools and clambered over the rocks. The tide came in – and we lost our shoes, much to Mother's annoyance, when we heard about it.

The rest of our time together was uneventful. We spent our days on the beach, in the boat or climbing the rocky cliffs. Surveying those same rocks much later I wonder that we were never killed. Georgie Redhead returned to Alderney. During the following months, war raised its ugly head and I never saw him again. He was lost in time and space, as so many people when circumstances change for us all. I thank you Georgie, wherever you are. Perhaps we'll meet again in the land above another blue sky.

Chapter 4

Menacing Clouds

1939 changed the lives of many people in England, but it did not immediately effect us in Guernsey. It was, after all, known as the Phoney War. It was only when Germany advanced towards Normandy and Brittany that the waves of fear began to swirl towards Guernsey.

Early one Monday morning I was lighting the fire for the copper in the wash-- house. It was June 1940. Suddenly, I heard what I thought was an explosion in the distance. I later learnt that it was gunfire near the French coast. Having no idea of what lay ahead, I proceeded down the garden path, when one of the Veron boys who lived next door shouted – "The bloody Germans are coming! Did you hear the gunfire?!" I told him that I heard something, but wasn't sure what it was. By this time the rest of his family appeared; Roy, Norman, Kath and Len who was in the last stages of TB and died a few months later.

"Yes, it's gunfire," they echoed. Apparently, their Uncle Dick who worked at White Rock loading tomatoes, had said that the enemy was getting closer and could be in Guernsey very soon.

I ran to the house and promptly told my mother what I had heard. "The island is too small," she said. "The Germans won't come here. Off to school you go." She certainly had misgivings about what she had just said, but I was not aware of them at that stage.

As soon as we arrived at school Mr. Fulford ushered us all into the main hall. We wondered why he called us in before assembly but we soon found out.

"Due to the Germans now being very close to the Islands, the States have let us know that evacuation may be necessary, so I am calling a meeting of all parents at seven o'clock tonight." Then he dismissed us.

Father, who had already heard the news of the evacuation, left work as many others did, and came straight home. He found my Mother in tears which I quickly followed, reducing her to sobs. Father suggested that he and I should go down to the harbour to see boats perhaps arriving from France, or we might hear more news of the situation there. We hurried down Mount Durand and met many people with the same idea, making their way to St. Peter Port.

Emergency meetings were called by the State, which had not resolved the situation regarding what the British Government intended to do about the Island, whether or when Hitler decided to invade us. The British Government had not made direct contact with the German Government ,which meant that Guernsey was not yet declared open Island . Did that mean 'neutral'? Whatever. The island received a bombing attack on the harbour, causing loss of life and breaching the Geneva Convention. The Convention stated that if a country had been declared 'an open town' then it is immune from bombing and open warfare of any kind. But, due to the bungling of the governments, the island was bombed and lives were lost. However, this was yet to come.

As we wandered through the town, we heard stories of what might happen. On the far horizon towards Alderney black smoke was already covering a large area of sky and the distant sounds of rumbling left no one in doubt as to its cause. Small groups of people stood together and wondered whether to go or stay. This was probably the most serious decision they would ever

Chapter 4 - Menacing Clouds

make during their lifetimes. Father did his best to offer advice, though he himself did not have any answers.

The old harbour of St. Peter Port had never been so crammed with boats of all shapes and sizes. Tired, drawn faces greeted us as we approached the slipway. Many aboard the boats were exhausted by hunger and lack of sleep. They had taken the risk of dodging the minefields to escape the terror of war. It's a miracle that any of the vessels ever reached safe haven. Families were huddled together, children were crying and then there were the elderly, whose tired faces underlined the desolation they felt, forced into a situation once again of horror beyond their control. Being French, they encountered a language they hardly understood, making it more difficult when they needed to buy the basic necessities of life. Many did not have passports or visas, distinguishing friend from foe--- The right, or not, to land.

To my young mind all this held the essence of some kind of adventure; I had no understanding of what it meant. Father spoke to many of the refugees, trying to determine what was happening in France. He said things like – "Don't panic. Guernsey is your home now. Stay put." And he advised the Guernsey people he met to stay put also.

Guernsey people are known as Guernsey donkeys, because they show the same stubbornness as the animals. Placards Don't be Yellow were posted outside the Constable's office telling people to stay. But they made up their own minds. Even though the sun shone brightly on that June afternoon, the warmth faded to be replaced by cheerlessness, which enveloped the crowd that had gathered to hear what news they could.

The picture of a young girl comforting her grandmother remains in my mind. I watched as the girl gently kissed the old soul on the forehead, wiping away the tears and dust. "Don't cry, Grandmere," the girl whispered. "I won't leave you."

The old lady looked up and managed a smile and uttered, in a voice charged with emotion, "God bless you my child. God bless you." Then she stroked the face of her granddaughter with hands that were lined with the story of the hard life she had led, probably in the service of others. I learnt that she had suckered six children; two of them had been killed in the Great War. No wonder that she feared for her future. Misery and fear surrounded me on that sunny day in June.

"How old are you now, Sonny?" asked a friend of my father, whom we met at the Town Church square. This was a venue that we children hated, because our parents would chat endlessly, while we flitted from foot to foot, wishing that their conversation would end. Our efforts proved useless, as on and on they went, telling us to keep still or we would wear out our shoes.

"NIne" I replied.

"A fine lad for his age," the friend said. "His mother would have been proud of him. So its nine, years since she died. It doesn't seem possible,anyway, you've got a good Mum and Dad now," he said, patting me on the head. He wished us goodbye, not knowing what turmoil he had caused within me.

On the way home I questioned my father about what had been said. He ignored the issue saying, "It's time to get home. We'll be late for the meeting otherwise." It was a curt reply to a question to which I never got an answer.

Nobody at 65 Mount Durand ate much dinner that night. Mother remarked, as she cleaned away the dishes, that she need not have bothered cooking Father's favourite meal of roast pork.

The pork was supplied by Grandma's sister and her husband Harry Falla, who reared pigs. Before one was to be slaughtered Grandma journeyed to the north of the island to help in the cutting of the unfortunate creature. Salt was used to cure the carcass for the winter,and the sausages made by Grandma's sister, Alice were simply out of this world. I have never tasted their like again. When Gran returned, pork was on the menu for many months. Sausages, chidlen (offal) or pork roasts, which, when cooked, supplied us with dripping for our bread. Three cheers for Gran's sister and Uncle Harry!

Refugees continued to pour into the island, destined for England or any other country that would take them. These war torn people were tired and desolate; their possessions had been ravaged or looted. They came with nothing. As a child, from seeing all this as some kind of adventure, I was

Chapter 4 - Menacing Clouds

suddenly brought to reality at the sight of a young boy, about my age, lying in a boat with bright red blood seeping through a dirty oily rag which had been used as a makeshift bandage. His mother and two men attempted to stem the flow of blood. His breathing was irregular and his ashen face showed signs of bewilderment and terror. One of the men cried out for help, but none came; no one wanted to be involved. Then, as if the people were suddenly emerging from a dream-like trance, a shrill voice shouted out that the boy needed help and for someone to quickly call for an ambulance. But it was too late. The boy died in his mother's arms.

A cold shiver went through my body, and, as I clutched my father's hand, I felt a reassuring squeeze, assuring me not to be afraid. This was one of the few occasions when I felt truly close to him, as his squeeze relaxed my doubts. As we slowly left that terrible scene, I tried to hurry my father away from a world I did not comprehend. My tenuous security was about to be shattered entirely. Half turning I glimpsed smoke covering the sun on the coast of Normandy. Soon the Channel Islands would be enveloped by the sounds of gunfire. And here I was, grasping a hand for security from a person I yet needed to prove as being my father.

Chapter 5

Exodus

The scene at the harbour remained in my mind, as I told my mother what I had seen, then, in a voice filled with emotion, she turned to me and asked – "If God loves us, why does He allow such suffering?"

At that moment neither my father nor I could supply an answer. I am sure that she found an explanation much later, when she herself suffered from cancer. With the help of our minister at that time, God became more real to her. I believe that we learn to put our trust in Him, when we are close to suffering, and that He will assure us of His love. There are so many things in life that we do not understand, but much will be revealed to us if we have faith.

The time came for us to go to the school meeting; mother stayed at home. The walk to the school in Brock Road took half an hour and we encountered many parents going the same way. The atmosphere in the hall was filled with foreboding and some excitement, as we waited to hear what Mr. Fulford would say. The staff sat on the stage behind the headmaster, as he announced, that, due to the imminent proximity of the enemy, the time had come for a total evacuation of the children, in their best interests. Amidst mutterings he continued to inform us that those, who had decided to leave must be at the school at 7am on the following morning, complete with gas mask, identity card and a small suitcase containing a change of clothes, toothbrush and paste, soap, towel and face washer, plus anything else that might be required.

Needless to say, a shock wave passed through the hall. Fearful parents wondered whether, if they kept their children at home, they might live to regret the decision. Most people did not believe the war would last that long.

Mr. Fulford intimated that Canada might be our final destination and a ripple of surprise touched everyone. In my imagination I immediately conjured up a picture of Mounties, resplendent in their red uniforms and mounted on their magnificent horses, riding through snow and ice to get their man, though I was quickly brought back to reality, as I saw a young mother holding back her tears, so that she would not upset her son in her anguish. Father mixed with the adults, while I joined my friends as we discussed what Fluff had said. Canada sounded like adventure to us; it spelt Shangri-la. We decided that it would be a great holiday. How wrong could one be.

On the way home Father suggested that we should go to see Granny Penny to say goodbye. Though I liked this softly spoken elderly lady, who often gave me half a crown when we visited her, I saw no logical reason why we should visit her. I asked my father what the reason might be and he told me that it maybe the last time that I would see her. I did not consider that this was a happy answer.

At Paris Street we found Grannie in a worried state, not knowing if her three teenage grandchildren would have to leave the island. As things turned out, neither Gran nor her grandchildren left. They stayed put. Gran did not seem surprised to see us, offering us a chair in the small, neat sitting room.

"Terrible times we are living in, Charlie," were the first words she said, as we entered. Willie and Fred came from the kitchen to greet us. I had seen the two boys on various occasions and they fascinated me through their lack of hair. I thought that baldness only happened to old men, a theory I found to be untrue when I reached their age.

Chapter 5 - Exodus

Father explained that I would be going away with the school. Granny Penny hugged me and wished me good luck, slipping another half crown into my hand as she did so. As we left she turned to Father and said - "His poor mother would be broken hearted if she was here." I thought that this was another odd thing to say as we walked home asking Father what she had meant. He hesitated for a few moments before he replied saying - "Old people say funny things at times. I suppose she thought your mother had not heard the news from Mr. Fulford, as she had stayed at home. We'd better get back home You've got an early rise in the morning." I never knew if he was going to say anything more.

A loud voice greeted us from across the street. I instantly recognised Granny Penny's son Uncle Charles, who was another mystery to me. Whenever I asked about how he had become an Uncle to me, I was imformed that any friend of the family, either male or female, would be called Uncle or Auntie. One thing that worried me was that I did not think that he was a great friend of my family. "Hello, my son," he said, patting my head, bending over me. "I hear you are going away. You are a lucky boy," he continued. His breath smelt of alcohol as usual. As he turned away, he put half a crown into my hand. Two in one day, I thought. The Germans should come more often. I had never before had so much money. Then he bent over me again and gave me a hug. "Your mother would have been proud of you," he mumbled.

Twice in one evening my mother had been brought into the conversation! It sounded as if my mother had died, or was away somewhere. A pang of fear engulfed me and I tugged at Father's hand, urging him to get home quickly.

"Keep still!" Uncle Charlie said. He turned to look at my father. "Both you and Lena have done a a good job in bringing him up and I Thankyou he said wiping tears from his bleary eyes. I did not   understand why he had thanked Father; grown-ups say funny things, don't they?

Sleep did not come-easily to me that night and Mother thought that I would be better off sharing their double bed. A thousand quandaries flashed through my mind as I tried to sleep. Has Mother packed my suitcase ready for an early start in the morning? Then I heard a plane circling overhead.

Could this be a German plane ready to descend on Guernsey with its bombs? The very thought sent me under the covers in a false search for safety. Had Father brought home any dynamite? Surely this could only make matters worse. No Canada or no more Guernsey! This thought caused me to bend over the side of the bed and to feel underneath, as my hands delved into every inch of the floor there was nothing there. The lethal bundle was safe in the bowels-of the quarry. Or was it!

Settling once more into the warmth of the bed, my brain worked overtime thinking that in a very short time I would be leaving the security that I had known for the last nine years, embarking on a journey that supposedly led to Canada. Would I ever find out the true relationship between myself and my mother and father? Did I want the truth? Deep in my heart the answer was no. Twisting and turning I offered a prayer as my mother had taught me from an early age. I am eternally grateful to her for teaching me to pray to Jesus if I were troubled. So, in childlike belief, I asked Him wherever He was to take care of me and my family. They say that Jesus lives in Heaven above the bright blue sky. I hoped that my plea would reach Him, for I needed Him badly at that moment. Oh, I nearly forgot - please take care of Granny Blestel. She is an old lady Jesus, and she won't be able to run fast from the Germans, so please help her. Old or not, Granny was a survivor, because she managed to live to the age of 95. I like to think that prayer did help her and that she did not have to run.

The night wore on till Mother woke me at 5.30.am, With breakfast over, plus a thousand instructions from her, she hugged me close, tears welling in her eyes and said quietly - "Behave yourself and write as soon as you get to Canada, if that is where you are going. "She straightened my tie, adjusted my school cap and kissed me goodbye. "Are you sure you have everything?" she asked again. It had been decided that Mother's farewell would take place at home, but, true to form as women often do, she changed her mind at the last moment. No sooner had she kissed me than she turned to Father saying - "I am coming to the school, Charlie".

My father simply said - "Make up your bloody mind or we'll be late." This was a statement I thought could well have been left unsaid, but that was

Chapter 5 - Exodus

Father. Sometimes he said things without understanding how hurtful his words could be.

I picked up my small suitcase and flung my gasmask, attached in its box by a string, over my shoulder. My father had acquired the suitcase without payment from a shop, which was already empty, as the owner had left Guernsey for England. He had left his premises open for everyone to help themselves to his stock. There was a note pinned to his front door which said - "Please help yourselves." He had been in a hurry.

Trust my father to find a bargain. Every now and then, as we made our way through the town we saw similar notices left by shop owners, who had departed in haste.

The three of us made a sorrowful trio as we trudged down Mount Durand and very few words were spoken. We passed others who looked equally glum and there was little talk, just a nod of recognition; everyone dreaded reaching the school, knowing what the final outcome would be.

As we reached Brock road, in front of us, one of our teachers in company with his wife was walking sedately, without hurrying. This caused my father some annoyance, setting a speed and expecting us to follow. He always arrived everywhere on the dot, or before time, and hated anyone being late, "This is not a race, Charlie," my mother remarked. Mother had always been more liberal with time, sometimes having to rush at the last minute. I think I take after her in that respect. To me time was made for man, not man made for time, a quote not appreciated by everyone.

The school hall had become a hive of industry with parents filling in forms and informing staff about their children's special needs. Tommy is not fond of vegetables, John may wet his bed if he is upset, make sure that David washes behind his ears or Bobby is inclined to become constipated, if he was not given enough fruit. The poor teachers had to memorize all the do's and don'ts which had to be implemented, while they were in charge of the children in their care. Mr. Fulford announced that a boat would arrive during the day to take us to England on the first part of our journey. No one knew if or when this boat would dock; it became a matter of patience. In the meantime, the boys had to remain at school, until a phone call would summon us to the White Rock. Some parents left soon after the announcement. These were mostly farmers, whose cows needed milking or had thousands of things that needed to be done on their farms. Others stayed. Mother and Father left, promising to return later. As for me, I spent the time with my friends, discussing the latest developments.

The day wore on without any further news of the boat and many thought that the Germans would arrive before the boat ever got to us. All day long the rumbles of war continued and the constant smell of smoke mingled with fine dust, polluting the air from a continent that was being torn to pieces by a maniac overlord. No need to bring to mind how near the enemy was to our shores. The islanders knew that it was just a matter of time before the sound of jackboots echoed on the cobblestones, on an island that had maintained its independence for a thousand years.

On that sunny day in June we little realised that it would be five long years before we returned. Some never made it back. As we waited at school, we chose to treat our departure as an adventure into the unknown. It became an experience that we would never forget.

During the early part of the evening word came through that the Batavia, a Dutch ship from Dunkirk, had anchored in the harbour, ready to take us on board. My parents had returned to the school by this time, wondering what should be done next. While most boys thought of this as a sort of picnic, the parents took a more serious view. Mr. Fulford announced that in fifteen minutes everyone would have to line up, ready for departure to the boat. And so, the painful time had come to wish our parents goodbye. For some, this was the breaking point in their emotions. Mother and Father did their best to compose themselves, making light of the situation and hoping that tears would not betray the depth of their emotion and anguish. Then came a final wave as we made our way, through the school gates. My mother held a white handkerchief high, now wet with tears, making sure I caught a final glimpse of her. Then we were off.--- a crocodile stream of boys on our way to Elizabeth College to collect more pupils from both colleges

The passersby saw a long line of boys and girls, making up 800 in all. We made our way down St. Julian's Avenue, which already bore little resemblance to

Chapter 5 - Exodus

its pre-war state. At the Weighbridge clock building, a barbed wire fence stretched across the road, preventing unauthorised people from entering the harbour. Placed along the fence were sandbags to shield the soldiers, if the enemy came too close. The soldiers stood by on guard, as we arrived, to let us through the double steel gates, with our teachers leading the way.

In company with other parents, my mother and father hurried down to the weighbridge, in the hope that they would catch another glimpse of us. Turning around I searched for a glance of them, and saw the white hanky, still held high, and being waved frantically, as she stood beside my father. If I had felt any doubts about who my true parents were, up to this moment, they would surely have been dispelled by this show of devotion. The word adoption, which I had learned to hate and which should never have been put into my mind, should now be dispensed with. At that moment, those two people, waving a tear-stained hanky were my mother and father. My true Mum and Dad. And would always be. Somehow this revelation made the parting even harder.

As we got closer to the ship, my mind was working overtime. I realised that, from now on, I would be alone. There would be no mother or father to guide or comfort me in times of distress. No more family gatherings, no more visits to Aunt Alice, no more picnics on the beach - and no more fits of temper to upset me. From now on, all my battles would be fought alone. I glanced at some of the other boys with whom I now shared these circumstances. While I was shy by nature, and the thought of this dramatic change to my life frightened me, it was all I could do not to run back to the barricade. But I had to be brave. And I was aware of the shame such an act would bring, before my friends brought me back into line.

So I tried to think of the positives. The thought of Canada excited me and more or less managed to push those other thoughts from my mind. The closer we got to the vessel the more the apprehension left me. This is the beginning of a new life, I told myself. A real adventure on a real ship to a real land. But if we expected a P& O Liner, our hopes were very quickly dashed. The S.S Batavia was a cargo ship and made no secret of this fact, as halfway up the gangplank the smell of guano overtook us. Many a child fell sick as a result. However, the Dutch Captain who stood at the foot of the gangway was proud of his ship. He smiled, as he told us that she was very fast. Fast or not, it took many hours before we reached Weymouth.

As we sailed away through the Pier heads, no lights were visible on Guernsey; a total blackout had already been observed. Likewise, as we huddled together below decks, we were in almost total darkness. We used our suitcases as pillows, fighting the discomfort of the cork lifebelts, which had been strapped to our bodies. We were told that we had to wear them, because they were designed to keep us afloat if at any time the ship hit a mine or was hit by a torpedo - and sank.

Earlier, as I stood by the ship's rail for a moment, I knew that somewhere on that now blackened island parents would be grieving for their lost children. In an act of faith, mothers and fathers had entrusted their children to teachers, who did not have the slightest idea of where we were going or how long we would be away. Many tears flowed that night.

Isolated below decks, we boys had no idea of the dangers that faced us, beyond the discomfort and the bad smells. Above us, the Captain had plotted a safe passage through the minefields, which was a time-consuming operation and delayed the progress of his 'fast' ship. Then, at one point, an alarm went up that a submarine had been sighted off the port side. A deathly silence prevailed ,until the Captain was able to establish that what had looked like a periscope turned out to be the mast of a sunken boat. With that scare behind them, the Captain and his crew steered the ship on its way with a gentle roll on a calm, moonlit sea. Many succumbed .to seasickness due to the oily fumes coming from the engine rooms of this courageous vessel. The splashing of the waves against the sides of the ship and the throbbing of the engines were the only sounds we heard.

Most of the travellers tried to sleep on that seemingly endless journey. With the break of day, without land in sight, there were murmurings of 'I am hungry' which spread through groups of boys and girls; many of whom had not eaten for hours. My mother had had the foresight to pack a few sandwiches for me, but even so, my tummy began to rumble. This was no luxury liner, and neither food nor drink would exist until we hit terra firma. I can still hear the cry that we made, as Weymouth came into

Chapter 5 - Exodus

sight. Although we were weary, we surged to the rails to catch our first sight of England. It was the first time for many. We landed eventually and were taken to the Alexandria Gardens, where we received some light refreshment. After that we were moved on to a theatre in which a long, winding staircase was reminiscent of the one in Gone With the Wind. At the top, a doctor and nurse examined each one of us. We were told to say Ah, with wide-open mouths, and our throats were scrutinized after which a stethoscope was run over our chests and we were pronounced fit. This diagnosis applied to me also, though I landed up in hospital a few days later.

How strange everything seemed to be on that dismal day. I didn't know when, or if I would ever return to the safety of my home in Guernsey. I felt terribly alone. I wanted to give way to my feelings, but, in doing so, who would reassure me? I wanted to sob my heart out, but there was no mother here to hug me and to tell me that all would be well. Despite my being in the company of the whole school, apprehension surrounded ,me because I had no idea of what the future might hold. Surely this whole experience was a dream. At any moment I would wake up in the safety of Mount Durand. I realised that the future was in my hands - oh, how those shadows encircled me. Yet, what did it matter whom I belonged to? Somehow I concluded, though I was still a child, that I would survive.

As we stood in groups and waited for our teachers to tell us what would happen next, we chatted among ourselves. Where were we going? Would Canada be our safe haven? Where is the boat? We asked our teachers, but they seemed to know as little as we did. It seemed that nobody knew anything and the damp, rainy weather did nothing to improve our spirits. Everyone appeared to be exhausted; the hustle and bustle of the last 24 hours had left their mark, which showed on all our faces. Our escape had taken its toll.

At long last, and impatient to be on our way, we boarded a train. Many of us clambered to the windows to view the countryside. As we sped along, teachers pointed out famous landmarks on the way to an as yet unknown destination. Coming from an island of only 25 square miles we were overawed by the apparent vastness of the land around us.

People gathered at various sidings and passed food and drinks to us through the windows. We never knew how they had discovered that the train contained refugees; their kindness filled many empty tummies. There was no dining car on this train. On and on we sped, still not knowing if Canada was to be our final destination. Many of us began to lose our sense of adventure, and homesickness took over. I listened to the language of the wheels, which seemed to say - "Here we come, clickety click. Here we come, clickety click." It was a mesmerising sound. As this latest engine of mercy hastened towards an unknown destination, a deep fear clouded my thinking. Will I ever hear the clump, clump of my father's boots on the cobblestones of Guernsey again? The repetitive clickety click of the wheels seemed to take me ever further away from the ones I loved.

Sitting by a half-opened window I stared out at smoke-grimed houses, black cows, factories, graffiti scrawled on hoardings ,displaying a word only used by the lowest of the low, or so we had been led to believe. Sleep overtook us in fits and starts. There was very little room to relax in the train which was filled to capacity.

At some point, a boy sitting next to me awoke with a start saying that he could hear an air raid siren. Everyone strained their ears to hear the sound, a warning that became all too familiar during the next few years. The windows and lights were fitted with special blackout precautions and so we spent our nights in semi darkness. The windows were shut tight, and I hoped that no-one suffered from claustrophobia. After nearly two days on the rails our hygiene began to suffer. Whew! Who said boys don't wash? We longed for a bowl of water and soap, the stuffiness being oppressive.

Over a period of time, I suffered a series of stomach pain which were later diagnosed as being a kind of a consumptive bowel, and no treatment was offered. It was considered that I would grow out of it. During that train journey I put it down to the cramped conditions.

If only Mother was here to reassure me. Not only did we not know where we would end up, but we also did not know how our parents had fared. Did they escape? Were they safe? I longed for the nightmare to be over. Any sense of adventure had long since passed. Prayers my mother had taught me

Chapter 5 - Exodus

came to my lips. "Please, gentle Jesus, take care of Mummy and Daddy and make my tummy better."

It was a long time before I knew the whereabouts of my parents, or, if they managed to escape. Mother did, but Father lost his freedom for five long years, during which time he lost his connection to me, from nine year old to adolescent. As for the tummy, that's another story.

Dawn broke, and still no one seemed to know where we were going. Our route had been long with many diversions, along many country roads and through borders into Wales, to avoid bombings. On and on we travelled, until at last the shrill whistle of the train brought us to our journey's end.

Alas, we were not in Canada but on the out skirts of Manchester. We ground to a halt at Mumps Station in a cotton-spinning town in the county of Lancashire. Many of us would spend the next five years in this smoky environment. I ended up in Oldham. The town boasted that it enjoyed two fine days, followed by a thunderstorm and then the summer would be over. It was a place of peculiar dialects ,like that of Gracie Fields, and entirely unfamiliar to all of us. But it was also a town whose people had hearts of gold, because they received us with warmth and love.

When we first asked the guard the name of the town, he replied - "Oldham, and God help you. This is a town of coal pits and slag heaps and snow in winter, not like the sunny island you come from." Then he smiled. "But the people are champion. Good luck." With these few words he made off along the platform, flag in hand and singing 'You are my sunshine', perhaps to cheer us up and hoping for a change of the bleak, cold weather. He gave us a wave and vanished from our lives.

All that he had predicted came true, and, yes, the people were 'proper champion'. There was neither snow nor sunshine on that grey June day as we huddled together outside Mumps Station. The teachers sorted us into groups, making sure that no one was missing ,and we were ushered into waiting buses which drove us to Hills Stores. Though short, the journey lasted long enough for me to take stock of the identical, row on row lines of grimy brick houses. A couple of windows, a front door and no gardens; with only a short footpath separating each one from the road. Their sad similarity bore no resemblance to the green fields, cottages and farmhouses that we had known in Guernsey.

Wiping the condensation from the windows, each one of us was keen to see what we could of our new home. Hill Stores turned out to be part of a co-operative complex situated in Huddersfield Road. Imagine our new host's surprise ,when a large group of grubby boys and girls arrived. The staff had been misinformed. There was confusion, because they had been told to expect and prepare for young babies! They had collected high chairs, cribs, feeding bottles and of course, nappies. When reality set in, all this vanished, and single mattresses appeared through the generosity of Slumberland Inc., which was a worldwide company whose products, according to their advertisements promoted a good night's sleep for everyone who bought such a mattress. Unfortunately, three boys sharing two of them soon found out that this was not necessarily the case. Still, it was better than lying on the bare floor.

Mr. Fulford and all the staff did their best to make us happy. The Hills Stores staff provided good meals for the ever-open mouths and arranged visits to concerts. Despite the lack of news from our parents in Guernsey, we fared well. After our third day at Hills Stores foster parents arrived to choose whichever pupils appealed to them. We lined up like cattle at a show,while the good folk walked up and down the rows selecting the child that might fit best into their family environment. Needless to say, an element of fear dwelt within us. If one of us wer, chosen we had no option but to go with whoever had made their choice. And who do you think the first chosen boy was? Yes, it was me. Mrs. Ethel Neal clasped my hand gently. She was a softly spoken lady whose face showed a tinge of sadness as she asked me what my name was. "My name is Mrs. Ethel Neal. Will you come and live with Mr. Ellis Neal and myself?"

The answer came painfully slowly from my lips."My name is Bernard. Thank you. May I bring a friend?"

Mrs. Neal replied by saying, "I'm sorry, but I only have room for one boy as my aged father lives with us. And even then, until another bed arrives from a friendly neighbour, I'm afraid the bath will have to be your temporary

Chapter 5 - Exodus

bed." What could I say? The bath offered more comfort than three on a mattress? Bidding my friends and the staff farewell, I collected my worldly possessions ,and, then, fighting back tears, I turned my back on that latest place of refuge.

Shortly before this selection process began, Mr. Fulford had told us to present ourselves as sensibly and intelligently as we could, and look happy. Fear of the unknown had been with us for some time and it was still within us, yet, somehow most of us were taken in by strangers. The Government had decided to award each foster parent ten shillings a week - for our keep. Is this why they agreed? Not in my case, because the Neals never accepted payment.

Mrs. Neal took my hand with a reassuring squeeze and we made our way to 87 Redgrave Street. As we walked, she told me that a few years earlier their only child, a son, had died and she had been told that she would have no more children. As she spoke, the shadow of loss was evident in her eyes, but both she and her husband had decided to adopt a boy if one could be found. If we established a good relationship, perhaps I might be that boy. Yet again, that word adoption came into my life. No, I thought, it's not possible for them to adopt me,because I already had a mother and father, didn't I? But no news had arrived from them. Perhaps they were dead!? In the midst of all this I remembered a conversation I had overheard shortly before leaving Guernsey.

"His mother died and Lena took him in as her own son. His father drank heavily and was incapable of having him. " 'Poor' little devil."

And now someone else had taken me and once again I asked – to whom do I belong? A hot, panicky wave passed through my body. It tightened the muscles in my throat, choking me as I was breathing my last breath; the anguish and torment of the last few days overcame me, only to be released by uncontrollable sobbing. The little suitcase fell from my hand and lay on the footpath. I stood and gave way to my inner feelings. My world was tumbling down around me and I could not control my feelings any more. In the midst of all this Mrs. Neal produced a handkerchief which we shared as her tears mingled with mine. "Don't worry," she said. "No one will hurt you." Little did she know that for too long I had carried that hurt inside for many years.

Chapter 6

A Lancashire Hot-Pot Mixed Stew

When we arrived at the house in Redgrave Street, Mrs. Neal opened the front door and we were greeted by her husband. Ellis Neal welcomed me with a warm handshake and a friendly smile, which quickly won me over. Any other apprehensions faded when I met Ethel Neal's father, Mr. Broadhurst. He was a pharmacist who still worked, as most of the younger men had left to join the army. I sensed that I was among good people again.

On the right-hand side of the small hallway was a sitting room, furnished in the style of the late twenties with a carpet on the floor. We had never owned a carpet at home! Further down the hall was a cosy living room in which a fire blazed in a black range; the coal behind its bars sent out a glowing and flickering warmth on this cold, damp day. The range also provided heat for the oven in which Mrs. Neal baked her delicious cakes. Upstairs was the main bedroom looking out over Redgrave Street and a back bedroom, which was occupied by Mr. Broadhurst. He was known as Pop and his room overlooked a brick air raid shelter in which we spent many nights. Next to this was the bathroom, which became my temporary bedroom. The house smelt of Lavender Polish, because Mrs. Neal kept the furniture and floors spotless.

For the first time in many days I knew I would be safe with these good people, though there was still no news of home. Mrs. Neal wrote to my mother assuring her that I was safe and sound. On a wall in the living room hung a portrait of a curly-haired boy of about my age, dressed in a school uniform. As she gazed at the photo, Mrs. Neal touched me gently on the shoulder and said in a voice filled with sorrow, "That is our son, John. Such a lovely boy. We miss him so." He died during a diphtheria epidemic. Once she had finished laying the table, I found myself sitting next to Pop who encouraged me to eat up. I grew to love this man as the aged grandpa I never had.

A wonderful meal was laid out on the table and included homemade bread, a speciality of Mrs. Neal, eggs and bacon and sliced tomatoes. We finished with strawberries and cream and fruit cake. The strawberries and tomatoes had come from Mr. Neal's allotment, which piece of land was loaned by the Government and was a part of the war effort, encouraging many people all over the country to grow their own food.

At the end of the meal Mrs. Neal placed three large mugs, known as pint pots, on the table - one for both the men and one for me. "Our John loved his pint pot," she said softly, as she poured tea into each mug. There were two heaped teaspoons of tea and two of sugar, and, though this was all a bit much for me. I dared not refuse, since it would desecrate John's name. So I accepted the mug without knowing whether or not I would be able to swallow such a large amount. Here goes, I thought. I'll make it my war effort giving up sugar. It wasn't much of a sacrifice and I soon became addicted to my pint pot.

"We are lucky to have Ellis's veggie plot," Mrs Neal said, as we finished our meal. Her husband promised to take me down the next time he went to 'dig for victory' and I looked forward to it. Mr. Neal asked me if I had seen some of the slogans the Government had posted on various billboards. When I said that I hadn't, he recited a few –

Eat carrots to help you to see in the blackout

Chapter 6 - A Lancashire Hot-Pot Mixed Stew

Be like Dad, keep Mum. The walls have ears

Wear something white in the dark, so that the cars can see you.

"I am starved, put some wood in the hole, please lovey," Mrs. Neal said. When I told them that I had no idea what she meant, Mr. Neal explained - "Starved means cold," he told me. "Put wood in the hole means shut the door." Such was the language in that part of the country, so you can see that I had a lot to learn.

During that first evening at the Neal's, 87 was a busy place. Neighbours called with the excuse that their visits had to do with air raid precautions as Mr. Neal was an air raid warden. But Mrs. Neal had other ideas. She said that they came to see what a Guernsey boy was like, making sure that I was not a cannibal for example. All of this seemed very different, the people spoke differently and Oldham itself was strange. A mill town with no beaches. Tall, smoky chimneys, brick houses, damp weather and constant cold. As time went on, it continued to be alien to me. There were no beaches with gentle breezes, no cliffs with yellow gorse, mingled with wild flowers. But Oldham did reveal beauty outside its walls. I well remember the Pennines with their long stretches of moors over which I enjoyed many a ramble in later years. And, of course, snow in winter, which was a rarity in Guernsey.

Yet,, I realised that I must not play one against the other. Guernsey is Guernsey and Oldham is Oldham. How different they were and how strongly my private shadows remained within me. Though the Neals were very kind and did their best to make me feel at home, for which I was thankful, I still lived with the fear of loneliness with no parents to care for me. If only I heard from them then this uncertainty might leave me. Suddenly, my childhood had ended and I would have to fend for myself. Yet, my childlike emotions remained. The fact that I was tall for my age made people expect a lot more from me, perhaps too much.

It was time for bed and Mr. Neal made the cocoa, a job he had done throughout their marriage. "Get this down you lad, then off to bed," he said in a gentle voice. "With a bit of luck we may hear from your Mum tomorrow." But we never did.

"News will come, love," Mrs. Neal reassured me. "In the meantime Ellis and I will adopt you," she added.

Again the word 'adoption' haunted me. Ethel told me that if I needed the toilet during the night, she had placed a chamber pot beside the bath for my use.

So this was it. My first night's sleep inside a house after so many days. They both hugged me and gave me a kiss and I was grateful to them for their kindness. But tears came to my eyes again, as I mounted the stairs. As I looked at the made up bath with its warm blankets and hot water bottle, I decided not to sleep with my head under the gas geyser. This was just as well, because the wretched thing began to drip during the night and remained unnoticed, until I awoke to find my feet wet. A wave of fear went through me. Had I become a bed wetter? I quickly felt the lower part of my body and breathed a sigh of relief when I discovered the culprit.

Then we heard the sound that was to become so familiar to us, the siren that told us the enemy was on its way to bomb Manchester. Ellis Neal opened the bathroom door and hurried me down to their air raid shelter. Fortunately, it was just outside the back door. It was built of brick with a concrete slab roof and an iron door which would protect us from the bomb's blast. There were meagre, basic comforts inside. A concrete slab ran along the whole length of the bunker serving as a seat or bed; torches, candles or an oil lamp provided light. Heavy rain sometimes entered, leaving a few inches of water under ones; feet, making for wet feet if unsuitable shoes had been worn. The houses ,that had gardens, had Anderson shelters built underground. Redgrave Street lacked this luxury. Their back yards consisted of cobble stones on which sat the coal shed and lavatory.

Life spent in these 'safe havens' brought out the best in people. They shared each other's problems, carrying out a barter system for food and other goods in short supply. At times, card games were played, if there was enough light, or there was a sing-song, which cheered us up when explosions were heard in the distance. We were left to guess if the bomb blasts were close enough to hit our streets or houses. "That's a bloody close one," was a comment that was often heard. Once the All Clear siren was heard, we felt able to return

Chapter 6 - A Lancashire Hot-Pot Mixed Stew

to our beds or to work, because many raids lasted throughout the night. Daytime raids meant no school. 'Hurrah'.

A Mr. and Mrs. Greves lived in a nearby street and had fostered a school friend of mine called John Tostevin. Two days after I came to live with the Neals, John and I took off to play in the nearest park. All went well, until suddenly a terrible pain hit me. I was unable to walk and John had to carry me home, fortunately without damaging him. As soon as we got home, Mrs. Neal called for the doctor and he diagnosed a Strangulated Hernia. This was serious. I was rushed to hospital immediately.

For the second time since coming to the Neals, I asked myself, if this was really happening to me. On the way to the Oldham Infirmary Mrs. Neal told me that my stay there would be short. It turned out to be six weeks. Lying in my bed after admission and trying to cope with the pain, I looked around the ward and saw that a number of beds were occupied by children of all ages, most of whom were asleep. The boy lying next to me asked if the lady who had come with me was my Mum. I replied "Sort of", being in too much pain to explain further. The mention of my mother sent waterworks tumbling down my cheeks and I buried my face in my pillow. My sobbing was noticed by the boy in the next bed. He jumped out and came over to me, and, putting his hand on my arm, he said - "Don't cry. It's not too bad here, they give you ice cream." As if ice cream would be the answer to all our problems. Then, back under his warm covers he whispered - "I'll say a prayer for you," After which he promptly fell asleep. I was never able to thank him or discover his name, because a nurse moved him to another ward during the night, as he lay sleeping. I wondered if I would ever see him again, but I never did.

The night nurse returned to give me an injection saying, "It will only be a little prick, don't worry." Then she turned me over and pushed the needle into my bottom. A little prick maybe, but it was still painful. Sleep came quickly after that, but I became half awake some time during that first night. It took some time for me to gather my thoughts together, until I finally realised that I was in a hospital. I cried out for my mother, but she never came. Was she still alive, or had the Germans killed her already? The thought sent me once more into uncontrollable sobbing, silenced suddenly by the wail of the siren.

The ward quickly came alive, as nurses wheeled beds out of the room. I was placed in a cot which had been standing beside my bed, containing a two year old female child. I spent that night lying next to her in the shelter, which was cellar of the hospital, as the bombs blasted away above us.

The following morning Sister McGill, the charge sister, came to tell me that my operation would be undertaken that morning. Detecting a look of fear on my face, she said in her soft Irish brogue -"There's nothing to be afraid of. Dr. Brown is a very good doctor and you will feel no pain." They had once again transferred me to my bed in the ward. I still could not come to terms with my situation, so much had happened in the last weeks and I pined for my mother. At that moment, the chance of ever seeing her again appeared to be nil. And so, still clinging to my faith, I prayed to God, in the hope that I would gain His attention. The trolley was brought back by a young student nurse ,who was assisted by Sister Crawford. I developed a schoolboy crush on her and longed for her return whenever she had a day off. Lying on the trolley once more, I was carted away through a corridor with green painted walls, seeing nurses busily going to and fro. I heard the swishing of bed pans and smelt the strong odour of carbolic. Patients returning from operations passed by, complete with dangling tubes and oxygen masks on deathly white faces. A shudder went through me, as I saw a man's hand, covered in blood from a severed finger, as he held his hand over a tray. An ambulance man supported him on his way to the Casualty Department.

The trolley crashed through double doors and came to rest under a glaring light. Assisting nurses wore the kind of dust caps I had seen on my Aunt Alice. Oh, how I wished that she was here! A nurse took my hand and said quietly - "Just a little prick. It won't hurt." Then she gave me a pre-med which did not seem to work for me as my eyes fixed on a frosted glass door and I wondered what lay beyond it. The thought had no longer entered my mind, when the door opened, and, as it swung shut behind him, I saw a robust, balding man wearing a red, rubber vulcanised apron coming towards me. He looked every bit a butcher, complete with knife. Hang

Chapter 6 - A Lancashire Hot-Pot Mixed Stew

on, I thought. This must be the Doctor Brown to whom I have entrusted my life. As my trolley was moved closer to him, I lay in anticipation of the next move; my eyes scanned the room taking notice of the paraphernalia set out in an orderly fashion around the room. The last time I had endured an operation was for the removal of my tonsils and circumcision. I asked why this operation was necessary. I was told It will keep you cleaner when a man. To which I replied childlike," Will not a Bath do the Job" In those days adults gave only the barest facts; at the time I was too sleepy to notice anything. But, on this occasion I wanted to remember everything, so that I could tell my friends about it later. Dr. Brown placed a mask over my face, and it smelt strongly of chloroform. I took hold of the doctor's wrist in an attempt to release the mask, but to no avail.

A nurse rushed to his assistance and held my arms down. Then, in a commanding voice, Dr. Brown told me to count backwards from ten. Nine, eight, seven, six, five, four, three, two, one. As I attempted the count, I felt as if I was rushing from a great height to earth. Then came oblivion.

I awoke back in Richardson Ward. The operation was over. My beloved Sister Crawford was holding my hand, speaking softly with her Scottish accent - "There now, it's all over." As she spoke she wiped my face with a cool, perfumed wipe. The oppressive smell of the anaesthetic still lingered and caused me to feel nauseous. I dreaded being sick, because the hurt of such an action would bring the pain back to my tummy. Sister Crawford took care of my every need and I made up my mind at that tender age that I would marry her some day. Oh, the innocence of a child's love!

The headmaster and the Neals visited me; apparently, I had caused quite a stirl when Mr. Fulford announced my predicament at the school where he now worked.

Still, no news of my parents. On June 28th we heard over the radio that Guernsey had been bombed and 35 people had been killed. Of course, the worst fears grew within me. Were my mother and father still alive? Please, I begged God, let me have news soon. But none came. Sister Crawford kindly supplied the details of the collapse of the Islands, but I never knew how she came by them. And she assured me that everything regarding my parents would be alright.

Other children in the ward also shared her love, but my ego allowed me to think that I was her special patient, because she was telling me what was happening in Guernsey. Then the terrible news came through that the Germans had landed in Guernsey. It transpired that many islanders believed the British Government had deserted them by not defending the Isles.

Unbeknown, to me Mr. Fulford had contacted a minister in Stockport who knew that some refugees had been diverted to that town. On the off-chance he got in touch with the council to see if my mother was in that group. The council suggested that I should write a letter to her which would be sent on if her whereabouts could be found. After a week I heard that she had been found along with Auntie Alice and Uncle Bill. They were renting a house together. My father had been unable to escape and was now trapped in Guernsey under German rule.

The first news received by my mother told her that I was having my stitches out. This came as a shock of course and she and Aunt Alice visited me as soon as they could. It was a tearful but wonderful reunion and the shadows began to fade.

Due to our enforced departure to England, many things changed for us. Mother found employment with Mr. and Mrs. Johnson as a housekeeper, and Uncle Bill was employed as a storeman at John Williams' grocery chain. He stayed there for a few months then left and joined a chemical firm, which was closer to home. He remained with the firm throughout the five years of war. Mother also changed jobs. After working for the Johnsons for a short time she found work with the Moss family, where she established such a good relationship that they asked her to stay with them after the war.

As for me, after six weeks in hospital I returned to the Neals. Mother visited me whenever she could. The School Education Department of Oldham had found accommodation for our Intermediate School under two rooves; the juniors at Hollins in Hollinwood [not Hollywood] and

Chapter 6 - A Lancashire Hot-Pot Mixed Stew

the seniors at Hulme Grammar. This arrangement worked well until the end of hostilities, when we returned to Guernsey. The Neals were very kind to me, treating me as a son. Ellis was a great bowls fanatic and introduced me to the game, which was a novelty at first, but, because he played nearly every day, I lost interest and the alternative of rugby was suggested.

Alas, after watching Oldham play I realised that there would be no scrums or rough and tumble for me, and Ellis came to the conclusion that sport was probably not my metier. A young woman called Norrie lived next door with her baby and mother, whose brother had composed "I'm forever blowing bubbles." Norrie's husband was a German, who had owned a handbag factory, but who was now interned with all other aliens for the duration of the war, in case they might be spies. Karl was a peace-loving person, who only wanted to continue with his business, but his factory was shut down during those five years. Once a month Norrie visited her husband with their baby. I spent many happy hours playing with Norrie's baby.

The Cuncliffs were also neighbours and their son Keith became a friend along with his sister and other children. Together we formed the Redgrave Street gang and enjoyed playing all sorts of games for many happy hours. Tilly was one of our members, and, as a twelve year old, she was rather promiscuous, attracting boys in spite of having a harelip. She managed to use this fact to her advantage. Those who savoured her kissing skills always went back for more, but she never went beyond the kissing stage. She was the best kisser in the street and I must admit that I too sampled her charms and enjoyed the sensation. Though puberty was dawning for us, we would have liked to pursue the adventure with her. Tilly never allowed it.

There was never a shortage of visitors at No.87; the kettle was always on the boil for tea or coffee. The house was a meeting place either for a chat or for the more serious ARP meetings.

One of the lasting impressions I have of Oldham is the weather. It was so different from that of Guernsey. In Lancashire snow was on the menu every year, but on the Island snow created a special occasion, and a treat for us kids to build snowmen, and, of course, there was the fun of snowballing.

But the snow soon melted and the fun was short-lived. In Oldham we kids made winter warmers consisting of an old round cocoa tin with a hole in the lid, filled with lighted cotton waste. It was a wonderful invention, which kept our hands from freezing and a particular help in the air raid shelters. Many nights were spent huddled together, wrapped in blankets with our feet often wet, when rain flooded the floors. Some people used to remark - "If bloody Hitler don't get us, bloody pneumonia will!"

The memories still live on---- Listening to the bombs falling and exploding nearby and all over Manchester------ Wondering anxiously if the next one will come down in your street, destroying houses and perhaps even the shelter, which was supposed to afford everyone some safety from the horror falling from the sky.

Mrs. Neal and some of our neighbours busied themselves knitting scarves and balaclavas for the servicemen during those long dark nights. Then, finally emerging after the All Clear had sounded, we would find the sky aglow from the flames, which were devouring homes shops offices. Also, there would be the smoke-filled air with its acrid smell of burning wood making you catch your breath. The fire engines would ply hoses to quell the infernos created by a Dictator, who thought he could control the world at any price. And I remember the ambulances conveying the dead or injured to hospitals or morgues, and workers with picks and shovels digging to rescue those unfortunates, who had been buried under the rubble. This was the scenario of modern war. Then, in that other war to end all wars, there were the horrors of the rat-infested trenches and the mustard gas. This was war brought to your doorstep, killing loved ones in their castles; homes built by scraping and saving during times of depression in the hope that no landlord could evict them. And the sounds of the weeping and the tear-stained faces of the bereaved. The recollections live with me to this day, and, in those far-off days, they forced me to make the transition from childhood to a sort of pre-adult limbo.

In spite of everything that was happening around us, school life continued at a steady pace. If we were not given a detention for misbehaviour, there were trips to the cinema on Thursday afternoons or to the Oldham swimming baths in which the water smelt terribly of chlorine. Three boys

Chapter 6 - A Lancashire Hot-Pot Mixed Stew

were selected to play for Oldham Athletics; Sylvester Rabey, who was later killed while on active service, Roy Martin and Bill Spurdle. Bill went on to; play for Manchester City. And there was cricket or boating in the park during summer. Every so often we enjoyed a night out to hear an orchestra at the Hill Stores or at the Town Hall.

All this added to our enjoyment during those enforced years away from home. We never really knew what was happening in the land of our birth. Changes were taking place on the islands, which would affect the structure of governments in post war years. One important change was in the foundation of better working conditions and wages. The power of the Unions was partly brought about by those who had evacuated to the mainland. If the occupation had not taken place, things would probably have remained, as they had been for many years.

October 12th 1941 was a night to remember for all the school. Just after midnight the sirens began to wail. John Laine, one of the pupils, was about to go to the shelter when he heard a bomb screaming down. That's a close one, he thought, and then there was oblivion. He remembered nothing more, till he awoke to find himself buried under the debris of the house. The bed ,which he had shared with the son of his foster family, had crashed through the floor landing downstairs. Except for being able to move his hands, he was trapped and around him was a strong smell of gas. "Oh God," he thought. "Will they ever be able to find me before I'm gassed?" He stretched out his arm to feel for the boy lying next to him and asked if he was okay. There was no reply or movement, and, as John removed his arm, the dreadful realisation overcame him that the boy had been killed by the blast. A cold numb feeling spread through him and he wondered again ,if he would ever be found. After what must have seemed like an eternity, firemen found him and he learnt that his foster mother had also been killed. Needless to say, this incident sent shockwaves throughout the school. Sometime later two more boys from the school died. But this was not due to the war. One of the boys died from tuberculosis and the other from meningitis. Three more ex-pupils were also later killed while on active service. All of them were far away from their loved ones and would never again see the green islands of their birth. Our stay in Oldham was not without sorrow and shadows.

As I write, a school photo taken all those years ago lies before me. As I glance at all those happy, smiling faces I wonder how many are left to tell their stories of those far-off days. In the blink of an eye it only seems like yesterday. Letters were not allowed to be sent between countries that were occupied. The only news from Guernsey was a twenty-five word message, which came through the Red Cross via Geneva. Most of the letters were censored, though some were cleverly worded to avoid it.

Mr. Broadhurst with whom I shared a bed, because the loan bed did not fit into the bathroom and the bath not being a suitable bed for me over time, began to feel unwell and found it difficult to swallow. Cancer of the throat was diagnosed and Mrs. Neal decided that, after twelve months, another home would have to be found for me.

Mrs. Martin, who lived opposite number 87, was willing to take me temporarily. She already housed a boy from Guernsey, whom I hardly knew. Kenneth Cleal. The Martin family consisted of Mr. and Mrs. Martin, Kathleen, their daughter, who was a Joe Loss fan - the Joe Loss band was very popular during the forties --- and plus a lodger named Joe, a carpenter by trade . With sadness on both sides I left the Neals, staying with the Martins for six months. The atmosphere during that time was not like that at the Neals, where I had been happy.

Like many other foods, sweets were rationed. Once a month Mrs. Martin sent me over the moors for sweets in a village called Delph. The village was a few miles from Oldham and a family friend in Delph always gave the Martins more sweets than were allowed by the rationing. The most exciting part of the journey was passing a prisoner-of-war camp. One could actually see the Germans and Italians walking behind the wire from a hilltop nearby. One day a prisoner escaped, sending shivers down everyone's spines. We were all told to keep a lookout for this potential killer. One evening, as shadows began to fall, I returned from a sweet buying excursion and saw a figure lurking in the gloom. He wore a long black coat with the collar turned up. His head hung low and one hand was thrust into his pocket,

Chapter 6 - A Lancashire Hot-Pot Mixed Stew

probably holding a knife, ready to cut some poor soul or to slice it quickly across a throat, bringing out a rush of blood and silencing the unfortunate victim who had stood in his way.

This must be the escapee, I thought, as my neck tingled and my blood ran cold. My feet were glued to the damp ground. I knew there was no point in screaming for help, because no one would hear me on this deserted moor with the wind screeching as it gained force. My imagination worked overtime and I expected that I would be found - eventually - blood stained after an all night search, with the sweet rations clutched tightly in my fist. The boy, who had escaped from Guernsey, would be found stabbed and alone. All this went through my mind in what seemed to be a lifetime.

Then slowly, as I watched, the figure raised his free hand then leant down to pick up what looked like a very heavy sack. Suddenly he called out, beckoning to me. Oh, how I trembled! Could my ears be playing tricks on me? But the sounds that came from his lips were not those of the guttural Germans. They had the lilt of Lancashire. "You're the young evacuee who lives with the Martins, eh?" He peered through the gloom as he went on - "I promised the missus some spuds I grew from my allotment. Ask her to send Joe around tomorrow with a sack. Don't forget. Now you best be getting back, it's getting dark and that German could still be around these parts."

Not knowing whether to laugh or cry I took off like a spitfire, the little wonder plane that helped to win the Battle of Britain by guarding our skies. When the prisoner was eventually caught, it turned out that he was quite harmless, only wanting to return to Germany to see his newborn baby. When I heard the news, I began to think that perhaps the Germans were not all bad. He just wanted to be with his family and so did I.

War and peace give rise to different standards. Killing a fellow human on the battlefield, someone who has never harmed you, classes the killer as a hero. Yet, when someone kills another in peace time, this person becomes a murderer. Depriving any soul of life is murder, whether in peace or war. Thou shalt not kill. But mankind bends the rules to suit itself.

Time at the Martins ran out and my next stay was at the home of Mr. and Mrs. Kay. Once again this was a temporary home of only a few months. Esther Kay had a lovely singing voice and I always went along to hear her. One night, due to an air raid, I had to sleep on a billiard table at the club, where she was singing. Living next door to number 32 Percy Street, where the Kays lived was a 23 year old called Ada. Her husband was in the Air Force and he was stationed overseas. One day Ada asked me to help her undo the door of a china cabinet in her house. As I went to fix the key which had got stuck, Ada came very close to me and began patting my head saying - "What a tall boy you are. How old are you? Have you got a girl friend or ever made love? Do you know how babies are made?"

Somewhat naively I wondered why she was asking me these questions and when Mrs. Kay later asked me how my day had gone I told her of my visit next door. She sniffed and a quizzical look came to her face, indicating that - 'all was not well in the state of Denmark.'

"Bernard, please do not go in there, unless I am at home," she said firmly.

When I asked her why not, her reply was very short. "Because I said so," she said.

Later, I overheard her talking about it to her husband. "What do you think about that young madam inviting Bernard into her house Fred? Using the cabinet as an excuse. My guess is that was not the only thing she wanted. Bernard is a big boy for his age, so I'm taking no chances. He knows he's not allowed to visit her unless I am here."

"You did right, lass," Mr. Kay responded. "She is a fast hussy and had her eye on me. Touched my leg in the air raid shelter." "Go on Fred," she said, laughing. "You can't half spin them. Mind you give her, her money's worth next time!"

"Time for bed, Casanova," she called out to me. Mounting the stairs to the bedroom my thoughts returned to Ada. Oh, boy, maybe she really wanted a shag? As schoolboys we had often talked about shagging, though none of us had experienced it. But there was one boy, who instructed us

Chapter 6 - A Lancashire Hot-Pot Mixed Stew

on the why's and wherefores, boasting that the girl next door to him had experienced his charms. Whether or not this was true we never knew.

Young Leslie, the Puritan of the group, listened with a look of disgust, and, shaking his head, took it upon himself to quench the fire of the conversation saying-"Dirty! There's no such thing as shagging!" When the boy who had boasted remarked that even dogs shag, the unbeliever shrugged his shoulders, still unconvinced. I sometimes wonder, if he ever found out the truth. I never visited Ada again, although she approached me on occasions. Secretly, I would have loved exploring her charms, but Mrs. Kay's vigilant eye saw to it that I remained pure.

One day Mrs. Kay took me to the Mill with its tall, black-smoked chimney reaching to the sky, belching out its foul smoke. This was a forerunner to the pollution about which we hear so much today. My first visit to her workplace was interesting. The floor on which Esther worked held about twenty machines. I watched as the looms wound the spun cotton on to their bobbins with one machinist working each loom. All this activity created a terrific noise. The woman wore clogs, similar to those worn by the Dutch, which protected their feet from the constant vibration of the floor caused by the continuous motion of the machines. The spinner sometimes developed Spinners Cancer, due to the oil used on the looms, which left the hands with cancerous sores. Mill workers had to start early in the morning and paid sixpence a week to the Knocker Up, a man with a very long stick that reached to the upstairs windows. Attached to the end of the stick was a piece of metal or wire, when sounded against the windows, woke those inside. It was a sort of human alarm clock. I was pretty fearful, when I first encountered this traveller of the night, thinking that we were about to be burgled or worse. Mrs. Kay had forgotten to warn me about this worthwhile service. Because of the black smoke puffed into the atmosphere by the tall chimneys, many people suffered from asthma or bronchitis, but, on the whole, the Mill folk were a happy crowd.

They looked forward to Wakes Week, a holiday usually spent by the seaside at Blackpool or St. Anne's or perhaps further afield. Lancashire people were warm and caring, and our school was fortunate to be billeted in Oldham, even though the scenery was not like that of beautiful Guernsey.

The time came for another move, because my stay with the Kays had always been temporary. Unfortunately, my stay with the Knotts was far from pleasant. They owned a hairdressing business on Huddersfield Road, but they were unhappy people, and we were constantly exposed to it. The meals were always meagre, while they continually reminded us that we ate too much, considering the fact that there was a war on and food was rationed. However, Mr. and Mrs. Knott's plates were never short at mealtimes. Hunger pains were always with us. When things did not go her way, Mrs. Knott would complain of a heart turn - which never became serious.

Another Guernsey boy called Ken de Moulpied was already living in the house and he shared my feelings. I think that they had accepted us, because each foster family was paid ten shillings a week by the Government - for our keep. I never complained to Mr .Fulford, because billets were hard to find and, anyway, It would have been useless. It would have been our word against the Knotts, who appeared to be very nice people outwardly.

I suppose that at that time in my life my hormones were producing a pretty restless boy, functioning between child and man, while subconsciously I was still trying to find the answer to the adoption question. I understood the word by this time, but I did not wish to accept it as applying to me. As a result of this confusion my emotions between myself and others were mixed. When I visited Mother on odd occasions, I did not broach the subject in case the bond between us was broken, without realising that a mother's love is not so easily severed. Yet always, at the back of my mind, was the question - 'to whom do I belong'? '

The question remained unanswered for many years, and, then, in an unsuspected way, I learnt the truth.

One Thursday evening Mrs. Knott had one of her turns, caused by a misdemeanour by either Ken or me. I decided that enough was enough and that the only response to this woman's tantrums was to run away. Action was required, and leaving was the best solution, but going where? Certainly not to Mother in Stockport, because she would have sent me back to the Knotts. A plan began to form in my mind. My secret desire was to go on the stage and then into films. Perhaps this was the moment, when I would

Chapter 6 - A Lancashire Hot-Pot Mixed Stew

turn dreams into reality? I would do the deed on a weekend, when I was due to visit my mother. I would usually leave on Friday and return to the Knotts on Sunday evening. So, if I left on Friday, no one would miss me till Sunday. If I did not return, I would be far away and lost for all time, until my name appeared on the silver screen as the discovery of the year! I identified myself with George Cole (later a star in Minder) ,who was a youngster not much older than me making his debut in a film 'Cottage to Let'.

Friday dawned - I had spent half the night awake - and I knew that silence was golden, if my plan was to work. I caught the bus to school and bid goodbye to the Knotts as usual. Then I spent the day at school, until stage one of my plan was about to begin. The only capital in my pocket for this Great Adventure was the huge amount of three shillings, and that was for food. Smuggling myself on to a train could be difficult without a ticket, but, with a bit of luck, buying a platform ticket would get me through the gates, where the London train stood ready for departure.

School over, and still in my school uniform I caught the bus to Manchester, using the free tokens, which had been issued to students, allowing us to go to and fro from home to school. The bus eventually arrived at Piccadilly Square in the centre of Manchester. I saw the bomb damage to the city for the first time.-- Whole buildings torn in half, crumbling wall areas cordoned off for safety with ARP officials clearing the rubble and men digging, perhaps searching in the hope that they might still find survivors. The air was filled with the smell of burning or still smouldering charred wood--- a thick blanket of dust entering throat and lungs, causing many people to cover their mouths and noses with scarves or handkerchiefs, which supposedly trapped the pollution. They stumbled about on the rubble, not knowing what they would find. On grimy and often tear-stained faces was the constant look of despair. Their shoes were wet and muddy from stepping through the puddles left by the firemen, who had plied their hoses on the blazes, which had enveloped the city night after night.

Dodging large holes I made my way to London Road Station. I realised that this was truly war on the home front ,as had been predicted by Winston

Churchill. No one can escape the terror of modern warfare. No one can escape the murder of innocent women and children, while death was hurled from the skies, finding its mark on the unsuspecting hordes below.

Behind a glass window in the pay office sat a middle-aged man who demanded to know my business. "One platform ticket, please Sir," I said. He asked me how old I was, and, when I told him that I was nearly eleven, he looked doubtful, telling me that I was big for my age, but he gave me my ticket, leaving the change on the counter. He had to remind me to pick up the change; I was in a hurry to get away from him in case there were any more questions. I hurried through the barrier to the platform, where passengers were already waiting to board the London train. Some people were already alighting the train, and I realised that I had not needed to buy a platform ticket at all, because the platform was overcrowded with men and women in uniform, who passed unheeded through the barriers.

The train was due to depart at midnight, so I had quite a few hours to wait. As the pangs of hunger descended on me, I paid threepence for a buttered muffin at the cafeteria. It was certainly better than nothing. I mingled with the multitudes, walking aimlessly, trying to be as inconspicuous as possible in case someone recognised this runaway boy. I was killing time but feeling very uneasy, yet aware of what was around me.

A group of American soldiers sat on their kitbags and called out - "Hi, kid!" They gave me a wave and beckoned me to join them. "Like some gum, chum?" they asked, offering me two packs. "You kids don't get much candy these days, what with rationing. In the States we're not hit like you guys here. Stick around, buddy." And so began a friendship that lasted to the end of my getaway to London. I've often thought of Buck and his mates Joe and Wilbur. Did they make it through the war returning to their loved ones or were they killed or maimed? I will never know. War is like Russian roulette; the players in the hand of destiny either live or die.

Thanking them for the gum, I accepted their invitation to stay with them. Anglo-American relationships. I sat down beside Buck and he asked me where I was going. "It sure is late for you to be travelling on your own."

Not wishing to give too much away I merely replied - "London."

Chapter 6 - A Lancashire Hot-Pot Mixed Stew

Joe went on to say - "Watch out for those Jerry bastards. They're sure giving old London Town a pasting."

To tell the truth, I never thought about the bombs on this escapade. I believed that anything was better than the Knotts. I had never been to London and it held a fascination for me, wayward and homeless or not. My new-found friends joked among themselves, until a pretty girl appeared and caught their attention. They called out to her - "Hi Babe! Come and see what Uncle Sam has got for you!" They produced a pair of nylon stockings ,which were not obtainable in England at the time. The bait usually worked; what girl could resist such a temptation? Several girls came up to the group, received their nylons and left after a quick kiss. The three Romeos were disappointed, when the girls left, but laughingly took it in good part. "So much for British hospitality," they mused. Sitting on one of their kitbags my tongue never stopped asking a hundred and one questions. Had they seen action, did to they have girlfriends, what was America like, had they met any film stars and what was the Stage Door Canteen in New York like?

"You sure can ask questions," Buck said. "I guess we should take this kid back to New York, eh Wilbur?" He winked as Wilbur nodded his approval.

As the night wore on, the four of us had coffee and sandwiches at the American Service Canteen. Buck had become a sort of older brother to me, making certain that I was never hungry. I earned my keep by carrying his kitbag ,which certainly was heavy.

Everything around me seemed to be chaotic ,as we struggled through the crowds, jostling to find the right platform again in the arid atmosphere of smoke, with the blowing of whistles, passengers hurrying to board the fast filling trains, young children, way past their bedtime clutching their parent's hands, and whimpering for attention. It was chaotic.

Standing near the London train was a collection of men, women and children, shedding tears amidst the laughter, as they wished their loved ones farewell. This was no ordinary parting, for the anguish within their hearts told of the uncertainty ahead. Soon these brave men and women would face the incongruous reality of the battlefield to be revered much later as heroes. Would that be enough to quell the ache in the hearts of the bereaved? Such thoughts did not enter my mind at the time; it is only now that I can reflect on the drama played out during those hazardous years. I stayed close to my mentors and noticed Joe passionately kissing a young girl he had apparently met at a local dance. She too succumbed to tears, leaving with two pairs of nylons.

Suddenly, a sound that we all knew ,halted the milling crowd for a few seconds. Some people quickly changed direction and made for the nearest air raid shelters. Others continued on their journey, pushing and jostling to board the hissing steam juggernaut, which, in the dimmed light seemed to me to be unwilling to move, until the danger was past.

My new companions made for the underground shelter with me in tow. Just as we approached the steps leading to a safe area of the station, a terrific explosion shook the building. While sheets of flame lit the place up, we were forced to hit the ground. Wilbur, the quiet one of the trio, only uttered - "Holy cow! Gee, that nearly blew our asses off!" Lying there I heard the explosion of the bombs around us and wondered if the next one would be a direct hit. But as suddenly as it started it ended and there was silence. It was broken by the screeching brakes of fire engines and ambulances and the shrill whistles of the firemen.

As I scrambled to my feet, I muttered - "Never been so close to a bomb." It was an experience, which was repeated for me during those war years. It must have been clear that I was terrified, because Buck put his arms around me saying, "it's alright Kid." I pushed him away so that I would not be regarded as a sissy, though I was grateful for his concern. Had I not made up my mind to survive on my own, relinquishing childhood to be replaced by independence? But, not to seem ungrateful, I shook his hand, while my voice still held a trace of fear as I uttered, "Thanks Buck."

The raid on Manchester was pretty heavy that night, and when we emerged from our shelters later, we noticed a large hole in the station's roof. The stars twinkled through the twisted girders, but the heavens were as yet untouched by mushroom clouds.

Though the station was covered in debris, it did not stop people from boarding their trains, which had not been damaged by flying fragments.

Chapter 6 - A Lancashire Hot-Pot Mixed Stew

From a kind of apathy came determination. No bloody bomb will break the British spirit! Britannia rules the waves - and she also rules the skies!

As he looked around him, Buck said--- "You British sure got guts. If this bloody war ever reached the United States, only God knows how we'd handle the situation." These sentiments were also shared by Joe and Wilbur. We successfully found an open carriage door and clambered aboard. The overcrowded compartment was filled with smoke, suitcases, kit bags and hand luggage, precariously stacked on the overhead racks.

While we were confined deep down in the shelters during the air raid, we had no idea how much damage was being done to the city. We could only guess at the havoc, until we again reached the street and saw the flames lighting the blacked-out surroundings. A huge, red glow in the sky told us how severe the inferno was raging in the once peaceful city.

A wave of tiredness overcame me, though the excitement of the day made sleep impossible. I sat, squashed between Buck and Joe and shut my eyes, trying to avoid the smarting cigarette smoke. Then I heard the hissing of steam and the whistle of the guard announcing the departure of our delayed train. Doing kangaroo hops, which became a more purposeful momentum, our journey began at long last.

My three uniformed companions were bound for an unknown destination, but I was heading for London and, hopefully, freedom from an unhappy environment. Drifting between sleep and a drowsy awareness my mind turned to my mother. She had no idea of the whereabouts of a son, who should have known better than to embark on a journey that was doomed from the start. Like Dick Whittington, I hoped to find the streets of London paved with gold!

Needing the toilet, I carefully got out of my seat and jostled my way to the very crowded corridor, finally reaching my goal, only to wait endlessly and uncomfortably for my turn. I finally squeezed into an unlit, wet floored and terribly malodorous lavatory. This was certainly no first class train. Groping in the dark to find the toilet seat,I sat down carefully, oblivious of what was beneath me and the, search began for the toilet roll. Of course, there was none. Fortunately I remembered a part of a newspaper, which I had retrieved from a station rubbish bin, and, which for some reason, I had put in my pocket.

A wave of nausea overcame me, as I left that stench-ridden enclosure and I vowed to never again enter such a place. I pushed and shoved my way back and settled down between Joe and Buck, who were asleep and snoring loudly by this time, as were many others in the compartment. As I tried to ignore the noise made by my companions, a thousand and one thoughts went through my mind.

Sitting in the train, which hurtled towards the capital city of England, I glanced at the person opposite, reading a newspaper. A clear, remembered picture formed in my mind of a pair of scissors, a pile of newspapers and me, sitting at the kitchen table in Mount Durand cutting up squares of news or tissue paper, then carefully inserting a hole with the aid of a meat skewer for a piece of string, which would hold the bundle together. Those were the forerunners to the modern toilet roll. In those far off days, only the rich could afford the luxury of an Izal or other scented loo roll to adorn the lavatory wall.

Suddenly, a loud explosion nearby shook the train, throwing us to the floor. "Jesus Christ! Bloody Jerry is after our guts tonight! Fucking Hell!" called out a sailor, as he fell. Then came another loud bang which shook our trusty steed to a stand-still, its brakes sending out a deafening screech, which more or less drowned out the four-letter words on many lips.

"Fuck me!" said a soldier as a kit bag fell off the rack above him, hitting him on the shoulder. I wondered what the bloody hell was happening. "Bugger those Jerries! Fucken Hitler!" I heard four-letter words I had never encountered before. This was surely the start of my education into the adult world. Luckily, no one sustained any injuries. In this moment of confusion we had no idea where we were. The wail of the All Clear sirens finally came after a delay of over two hours, during which time we had several near misses with no shelters to go to. Our only option was to stay on the train, which offered little protection, and we would have endured a massive loss of service men and women, if there had been a direct hit. The carriage became full of dust and smoke and other smells, which caused

Chapter 6 - A Lancashire Hot-Pot Mixed Stew

many of the occupants to cough. A small child awoke and was comforted by its mother, and an elderly lady offered the fearful child a sweet, which immediately sent the child into a screaming bout. As the mother tried to pacify her child, a woman voiced her opinion in a loud tone.

"Bloody Hitler! He should be ashamed of himself upsetting that poor little mite!"

Any further opinion was cut short, when the hissing of the steam and the rattle of chains caused by a series of jerks told us that we were once again on our way.

The all too familiar sounds of ambulances, and, fire engines, and a red glowing sky-greeted us, as we eventually came to Stoke Station. Somewhere in the background a radio was blaring out Vera Lynn's so appropriate "We'll meet, again some sunny day". Joe made his way to the canteen and brought back a sweetened coffee for me, while Wilbur and Buck found a girl who greeted them like long lost friends. They made their way to a darkened end of the platform, where she doubtless received nylons as a token of Anglo-American friendship, and perhaps for services rendered.

It was the time, when everybody lived for the moment. There was no guarantee of a tomorrow and people's popular morale was boosted by radio shows like Itma, Workers Playtime, Forces .Favourites or Happydrome. Stars were introduced, like Tommy Hanley, Arthur Askey, Wilfrid Pickles, Vera Lynn, Jack Warner, Elsie and Doris Waters, Richard Murdoch, Anne Driver, Sandy McPherson, Reginald Fort, Ann Shelton, Carol Levis, Ben Lyon and Bebe Daniels and Suzette Tarry, who appeared in a weekly show as a charlady. Her catchphrase was - 'Can I do you now, sir?' then bursting into song like 'Red Sails in the Sunset'. These were just a few of the performers whose talents were heard weekly over the air waves. It was all a part of the war effort to lift us from the shadows of those uncertain times.

And, as a further boost to our morale, Hollywood produced films, and musicals, comedies and dramas, and all those memorable stars like Bette Davis, Betty Grable, Rita Hayworth, Tyrone Power, Van Johnson, Robert Taylor, Deanna Durbin, Spencer Tracy, Errol Flynn, Katherine Hepburn, Judy Garland, Bing Crosby and Mickey Rooney, to name just a few. The films were made to lift our spirits in a world fighting for freedom. British films also contributed in their own style like In Which We Serve, Lady Hamilton, The Wicked Lady, Henry Vth, The Man in Grey and Brief Encounter, with such fine English actors as Laurence Olivier, James Mason, Margaret Lockwood, Noel Coward, Stewart Granger and Vivien Leigh.

I was an avid picture-goer in those days, paying three pence admission— Quite, often even going to different cinemas every day, such was my enthusiasm. Hence the reason I was on that train, heading for London, to visit Gaumont Studios in Lime Grove with the hope of acting in films myself. If George Cole, at the age of fifteen years, could act in such films as A Cottage to Let, then so could I. Some years later this did happen, but that is another story.

We arrived in London in the early morning. The train stopped at a crowded platform and the first part of my expedition was over. It was time to say goodbye to my travelling companions, a sad moment, and I wondered if I would ever see or hear from them again. I never knew what the future held for them, as they wished me luck and departed into the madding crowd. A backward glance and a wave was the last I ever saw of Joe, Buck and Wilbur. Onward Christian Soldiers, I thought, Marching as to war. My hope was to find fame and fortune, Their's the fight to live.

War is a terrible puzzle. Men fight to live or die, so that peace will reign on earth; paradise found - then lost. Will Man ever learn? This was not the time for emotion, so I elbowed my way through the crowd towards the Underground Tube, which was being used as an air raid shelter by thousands of Londoners day by day.

Here I was alone in London and many miles from Oldham. Once again the warning sirens could be heard and at the sound the truth of my situation hit me. If I was killed through enemy action, no one would ever know what had happened. Shadows of fear overcame me, as I pushed forward to the overcrowded lifts, which would descend to the bowels of the earth.

Making my way along the crowded platform I managed to find a seat, next to a young boy of about my age. He sported a mop of red hair, which reminded me of the story Just William, only his name was Tim. He was

Chapter 6 - A Lancashire Hot-Pot Mixed Stew

a real cockney by birth, and, humorous introductions over, he asked me where I was from. I wondered whether to trust this chubby redhead or not. Perhaps unknown to me my photo would appear in some newspaper under Missing Persons ,and, if he recognised me, might inform the police and my hopes of stardom would be over before they began. But he seemed friendly enough and I decided to pour out my whole story. I shook his hand and told him that my name was Bernard Blestel, and told him how I had escaped from Guernsey, because of the imminent German invasion.--- That the boat to Weymouth had finally docked and I had arrived in Oldham, from where I had eventually decided to run away to seek my fortune in films.

Tim took in every word. "Phew," he said, "How exciting. The only thing I ever done was stopping home from school for a week. I told my mother we was on holiday for a week. She boxed my ears for telling a lie. Mum went off with a sailor and left me and my sister with our Nan (Pot and Pan). My Dad's a prisoner in Germany and Mum thought he was dead, but he turned up later in a POW camp. By this time Mum had gone off. My Nan had a lot of love for us, but I still love me Mum, because she's my Mum."

At the mention of his mother, I thought of mine; pain and guilt overcame me again. Yet, though I had no idea of what lay before me, my only care was in getting to the studio. Oh, the excitement of it all! Here I was in London. As we walked along the platform, we passed a kiosk and Tim stretched out his hand and grabbed two chocolate bars. He thrust one into my hand and instructed me to 'run like hell!' Instinctively my feet took flight, while we purtsued by the irate shopkeeper, who was waving his arms in the air and shouting abuse. All of it for just two small bars of Cadbury's Fruit and Nut.

Tim spied a policeman and quickly changed direction, making for stairs that would take us even further down. As we breathlessly reached the platform, a pile of suitcases was sent sprawling, much to the disgust of a porter who was trying to get them onto a trolley. 'Bugger!' the porter yelled and I raced on. I lost sight of Tim and thought that I was once again alone, being chased by a heavy-breathing policeman, and no help in sight. And then, through yet another milling crowd I saw Tim, bent double, trying to get his breath back.

A cool wind that seemed like fresh air arrived as the train came towards us through the darkness of the tunnel. Tim lost no time boarding and beckoned me to follow. We got in fast and the doors closed. Tim found a seat and was soon enjoying his ill-gotten gain. I sat beside him and we moved off, seeing the red-faced policeman shrugging his shoulders in defeat as we sped away.

I must say that the chocolate tasted very good in my near to starvation condition. "In this war you've got to look after yourself, or you'll bloody well starve," proclaimed Tim, as he swallowed the last bit of his Fruit and Nut. "Stay with me Bernie, and I'll show you the ropes. You have to be quick on your plates of meat (feet) or the filth'll catch you and you'll end up in reform school or suchlike." he said seriously.

My introduction to crime, though exciting, filled me with apprehension at the thought of reform school. Tim's life, like mine ,indicated turmoil at that moment, and I knew that we would have to part. I wished him success on whatever chosen path he embarked on. "Come on Bernie," he said. "Stay with me and with a bit of luck we'll both end up as bleedin' stars." I don't think he understood my reason for refusing his kind offer. My fear was that the only stardom we would achieve would be a spell in prison, if today's escapades were anything to go on. I alighted from the train at Westminster Station and waved goodbye, as the train proceeded on its journey. Even though he smiled as he returned my wave, I detected a look of disappointment.

Alone once again, I followed the crowd to the exit, trusting that no one would ask for my non-existing ticket and luckily no one did. To my surprise hordes of people seemed to be coming into the entrance, with very few departing. Outside at last I was greeted by warm sunshine and my first glimpse of Big Ben. As I looked at this grand monolith it burst forth, bellowing out the hour of eleven. I pinched myself, making sure that this was no dream. This was the sound I had heard so often over the radio and also at the cinema, advertising the start of London Films made by Alexander Korda. This was no fantasy, this was real.

Chapter 6 - A Lancashire Hot-Pot Mixed Stew

However, my thoughts were soon shattered by yet another explosion, and I did a right about turn and rushed back into the station with hordes of other people all- bent on making their way to safety below. As Big Ben tolled the final stroke of eleven I reached the stair way, descending into the catacombs like those of old.

Churchill memorably said - "I have nothing to offer you but blood, toil, tears and sweat." Indeed these words were true when Britain stood alone. One of the pleasures attributed to the time we spent in shelters were the conversations between people, who would otherwise never have met. War brought closer friendships between the rich and the working classes; there seemed to be few barriers between the classes during those long hours shared in the battle for survival.

In retrospect today ,my thoughts are different from those I had at the time, when my concerns focussed on my very existence. I had made a vow to myself, with no father or mother to guide me, that I survived as well as possible. This caused a certain independence earlier than it would have done had it not been for the intervention of war, and accounted for a degree of selfishness regarding the decisions I made. Hopefully, I was able to overcome them later in my transient journey through my world.

Not owning a watch, I had no idea how long the raid lasted. Eventually A.R.P. wardens spread the news that the All Clear siren had sounded. Once again the crowds gathered up their belongings and made their way to the stairs or elevators to confront whatever fate held in store for them. Life would be very different for many. There would be the loss of homes and workplaces, and, most terribly, the loss of loved ones, perhaps even whole families. This was a time of deep sorrow, of never-ending tears. Yet ,through it all, there arose an indomitable spirit, facing the odds come what may, and it was undoubtedly this spirit that became the weapon with which the enemy was defeated. Though shadows encircled every life, people had to focus to the light, or, if not, be consumed by shadows, from which there was no escape .

At the beginning of the war I remember my mother, overcome by the brutality of it all, asking - "If God loved us, why did He allow such cruelty?"

I believe the answer came to her many years later, when she had to face the horror of cancer. Through her suffering I believe that she came closer to God. Each one of us is given the chance in our suffering to move nearer or further away, from the light, dispensing with the shadows. It is how we use our time during the journey that counts.

As I emerged from the station once again, the sunshine appeared to be even brighter after our enforced sojourn down in the shelters. Everything seemed different to me here in London.

For example, the way people spoke, often with a Cockney accent, which was so unlike the warm north of England dialect which I had grown accustomed. The mingling of servicemen and women from different countries, just an apparent natural part of the civilian panorama. I stood uncertainly at the station entrance, not knowing which road or train would lead me to my place of fulfilment, namely the film studios at Lime Grove.

Faces attached to bodies hurried past me, all knowing what and where their destinations lay, while my feet remained locked to the pavement, as if in fear of taking the wrong direction. I was again in a well of loneliness, not knowing or recognising anyone, as they hurtled past me. " Please God, help me" was the prayer on my lips. Whether it was the prayer or the shove I received from a dark-skinned man doing his best to pass me, I will never know, but it broke the imaginary chain that was holding me in place. "How do I get to Lime Grove, please," I asked him.

"Catch the train to Notting Hill Station. That is, if the bloody Jerries haven't knocked it to shit!" was his response. He vanished from my sight and I walked back into the tube station.

There was no directions board inside, a precaution due to the war in case the enemy landed. I went to the ticket office to ask and was sure, in my uncertain state, that the man knew I was travelling without a ticket by the way he looked and spoke.

He asked me what I wanted. "Please, which train do I catch to Lime Grove?" I asked rather timidly. He looked at me over his thick, horn-

Chapter 6 - A Lancashire Hot-Pot Mixed Stew

rimmed glasses with eyes that seemed to burn into my very soul, stroking his ginger moustache.

"Why are you going to Lime Grove?" he asked in a voice that was almost a whisper.

"I want to get to the film studio," I replied in an equally quiet voice. He broke into loud laughter.

"Trying your luck as a film star?" I nodded and the interrogation seemed to be over. "Change at Ravens Court for Shepherds Bush and good luck Mickey Rooney" he said smiling.

Boarding the next train I alighted at Ravens Court and caught the connection to Shepherds Bush. Once there I found my way to Lime Grove without too much difficulty.

Gaumont British Studios was a windowless, grey, cement rendered building, which looked somewhat forbidding. I had, after all, come all this way in the hope of finding a Shangri-la! Could this unimposing building really be the birthplace of so many movies?

I made my way to the entrance, and, ignoring a 'Strictly Private' sign I walked across the foyer to a small office. Photos of stars still under contract to the studio hung on the walls, intermingled with stills from various films, including The 39 Steps, which was one of my favourite films. Robert Donat looked down at me, handcuffed to a disbelieving Madeleine Carroll, and beside this, was a photo of Alfred Hitchcock, wearing his usual air of nonchalance. He had departed to America by this time, to direct the very suspenseful Rebecca. A whole batch of photos caught my eye ,ncluding that of Laurence Olivier, Vivien Leigh, Will Hay, Flora Robson, Dame May Whitty, John Gielgud and Charles Laughton. .

I dug my nails into my leg, drawing a spot of blood to make sure that I wasn't dreaming. Head up and shoulders back I reminded myself that if George Cole could do it as a boy then so could I. Inside the office sat an elderly grey-haired little man. There was a twinkle in his eye as he greeted me. "Top o' the morning' and what brings you here?" he asked.

Summoning up all my courage I replied - "Please tell me what I have to do to get into films." My heart missed a few beats, as I waited for his answer, wondering if this kindly man thought this a foolish question. As it turned out I need not have worried. Tilting his head sideways he smilingly gave me words of encouragement.

"If you are really serious, write down your name and address. Do you have a photo? You must have one for an audition."

"I am afraid, sir, that I did not bring a photo," I told him. "

Never mind," he said, with a look of slight disappointment. "Bring one when the Casting Department sends for you."

The idea that I would be summoned filled me with hope. He began to search for a pencil, which he finally found behind an ear, then in another search in he looked for paper, finally finding a small notebook and tearing off a sheet. He offered me the paper and pencil. I duly wrote down my name, and, with an little uncertainly, my mother's address.

This is unbelievable, I thought. Here I am at Gaumont British Studios and giving my name to a man I am sure will help me. It must be a step in the right direction. Finally, he shook my hand and wished me well, promising that if a part came up that would suit me, the director would get in touch. Leaving the studio I made my way back to the station to continue my ticketless life of crime. I shall always remember this first visit to London,where the flower girls sat around the statue of Eros in Piccadilly selling their small bunches and wiring button holes for those who still felt the spring in their veins. I am stil waiting to hear from Gaumomt British Studios. "What an opportunity they missed!" Some one said they were bombed, perhaps losing my address in the confusion.

On and off trains and buses, without paying fares, I travelled, determined to see as much of this great city as I could. Buckingham Palace, Marble Arch, Trafalgar Square, St.Paul's Cathedral,which had already suffered much damage to the north transept. The Dome remained intact, a sentinel watching over the city throughout the centuries,as people gathered daily

Chapter 6 - A Lancashire Hot-Pot Mixed Stew

in the act of worship. Sir Christopher Wren's masterpiece stood the test of time and change.

I learnt and saw much during my illicit trip. A familiar sight were the billboards with slogans like 'Careless Talk Costs Lives', 'Be Like Dad, Keep Mum', 'Wear Something White at Night' if going out in the blackout, 'Eat Carrots to see in the Dark' and 'Dig for Victory'. The hoardings were displayed everywhere, including those pasted to the sides of buses, which stared at you as you passed by.

Long queues formed outside shops, as people hoped for special treats like bananas, oranges, peaches or grapes, if they were ever available. I myself never tasted any of those treats during wartime. Pangs of hunger descended on me once more; with very little money in my pocket I knew I had very little chance of getting a square meal. Things were looking bleak, as I crossed over Westminster Bridge. A van stood near the Abbey, with a sign which announced in bold letters - 'Hot Chips'. Spiros' hot chips would keep out the cold the sign informed us. The smell of hot coffee drew me closer in the hope that food would be in the offering.

"What you want, sonny?" asked the keeper of the van, whose voice betrayed a Greek accent. "You a sandwich or cake boy or do you want chips?" he asked, shaking a basket of chips into hot sizzling fat. "You will not taste better in the whole of London. That great man Winston Churchill always stoped for twopenny worth of chips on his way to Parliament." He crossed himself. "On the graves of my departed grandparents it is true!"

"So that's what's helping win the bloody war, good old Winnie, all on two penny's worth of chips," said a rather fat man, as he issued forth a loud belch. "Pardon me," he went on. "Your bloody chips upset my guts. Let's hope old Winnie don't get the shits, while giving Adolf the lowdown."

"Take no notice, son, it is difficult with the fat on ration, but I still do the best chips," Spiros said firmly. "Today is your lucky day," he went on, handing me a large bag half filled with chips. "You see, Spiros gives the best chips."

In fact, at that moment, anything would have tasted good, as I had not eaten anything during the day. Further to his generous spirit, he handed me a mug of hot chocolate which, with the chips, was truly nectar from the gods. I finished my drink and returned the mug, thanking him for his kindness. I bade him farewell and wandered off along the street. I was oblivious of the passing crowds, my path leading me to unfamiliar locations, just walking wherever my feet took me over the uneven pavements. A slight rain began to fall, chilling my body. The benefit of the hot chocolate had long gone, leaving me shivering and damp underfoot. Oh, how I longed for a snug place to sleep, a cosy pillow, a welcoming blanket and food in my ever hungry tummy. I now lived in this vast city without knowing a soul. I had become just a number in a cosmopolitan circus, neither cared for nor belonging to anyone. An awful feeling of loneliness and self pity drifted into my uneasy, troubled mind. There was no cash in my pocket. I had nowhere to stay, and, worse of all, no food.

Suddenly, my feelings about my situation changed, as I became aware that people were hurrying past me, oblivious of the rain, as the wailing of sirens pushed them towards the underground. There was the sound of explosions and the drone of engines in the planes carrying death in their undercarriages. I quickly joined the throng, as- down, down we went in overcrowded lifts and on stairs, returning to the bowels of Westminster Station for self preservation. While waiting, for the All Clear to sound once more, people chatted, sang and told risqué jokes, which I absorbed, so that later, if I ever returned, I would be able to recount them to my schoolmates.

Sitting with my back against the tiled wall, once again a thousand thoughts crossed my mind. Had I been reported as missing? What would Mr. Fulford say? Would I be expelled? That thought really worried me. One of the older boys, the son of a vicar, had been expelled for penetrating a girl, or so the story went. I had no idea what it really meant. I remember asking my friend Peter, who like cousin George, knew all about such matters. He told me that the boy had been expelled, because he had shagged her when she shouldn't have been shagged.

I had no idea of the importance of shagging, though I was slightly interested and suitably shocked. Mr. Fulford kept the situation low key and told

Chapter 6 - A Lancashire Hot-Pot Mixed Stew

us at assembly to take no notice of any rumours. But a friend of the boy told a friend, who insisted that it was true, and he spread the news, which circulated like wildfire, in spite of Mr. Fulford's warning. The whole school was envious of the boy in question. What the vicar thought about the return of his son will never be known. At least I hadn't penetrated anyone.

A rather robust lady sitting next to me interrupted my thoughts, as she offered me a Spam and garlic sandwich. "Go on, take it dearie, it'll keep you warm and purify the blood ,and, if bloody old Adolf should drop in, your breath will kill the bastard." She noted my look of surprise at this outburst. "Sorry dearie, but I get heated up at the mention of his name. Him and his bloody raids! Why don't he leave us poor buggers alone? I got to get home for my Fred's dinner. He likes his dinner on time, Hitler or no Hitler. The only people he goes late for is our dear King George and his lovely lady. God bless them." With these patriotic thoughts she burst into song. 'There'll always be an England!' Though her voice was no match to Nellie Melba, she managed to inspire others to sing along with gusto, the accent strongly on the words 'And England shall be free.' A host of popular songs of the time followed. No one ever believed that victory would not be theirs. That time in the shelters gave me memories that will stay with me forever.

A mother feeding a young baby caused me to stare, having never seen a baby being breast fed in public before. Seeing me interested she said - "Hitler or no Hitler, the little mite needs his food. Have you seen your mother feeding your brother or sister?"

"I haven't got a brother or sister," I replied. "But I have seen young calves feeding from their mother back in Guernsey."

She smiled. "Oh yes, that's where those lovely brown and white cows come from not black ones like ours. Guernsey is in the Canary Islands. My Auntie went to Jersey for a holiday and said the Canary Islands were very pretty."

This lady, though right about the cows, did not know where Guernsey was on the map. I felt that I should enlighten her. "I had to escape from Guernsey,because the Germans occupied the Channel Islands."

"Ah, you poor boy, fancy old Adolf occupying those Canary Islands." she said sadly. At this point, I realised that it was useless trying to explain further. "Never mind," she went on. "Hitler won't kick you out of dear old London Town, not while George and Elizabeth are at Buckingham Palace with those dear little Princesses. God bless their little hearts!" Then, perhaps as an afterthought, she asked me whereabouts in London did I come from.

Yes, where did I live? I quickly endeavoured to change the subject by asking how long she thought the raid would last. "Gawd only knows and he ain't tellin' us, it could go on for hours. Where did you say you lived, darlin'? If your Mum is not in the shelter, you'd better get home quick when it's over, or she'll be worried."

When she asked again where I came from I replied -"I don't 'live here, I'm on holiday."

"Anyone who comes to London for a holiday is either brave or mad," she said and at that moment, fortunately for me, the baby started to cry lustily. Gathering herself up she began to pace up and down the platform, rocking the baby. The comings and goings and the chatter almost made sleep impossible.

The air raid finally ended after what seemed like an eternity. Though I had slept spasmodically in the shelter and still felt hungry and thirsty, I walked out into the fresh air with hundreds of other people. As I wandered over the bridge, I had no idea what my next move would be. I slowed down then stopped and leant over the rails to look into the water. I gazed at it and the picture in my mind changed. The water below was no longer the Thames, but a golden seashore with a boy walking along the sand. There were gulls pecking at the scraps left by the uncaring, which could become pollution mixed into the crystal clear water. I saw the tide advancing, obliterating my footprints, washing and shifting shells and pebbles on their repetitive travels. I saw a sunny day, the sky a vivid blue with a thin wisp of candy floss cloud - when you are young, you only remember sunny days, and the scattered rocks, which received the waves impeding their journey to the shore, sending salt spray into the air, the pattern never to be repeated,

Chapter 6 - A Lancashire Hot-Pot Mixed Stew

although its travels continued a thousand times. The beating of the waves against the rocks and the ebbing tide created the music of the sea. It is a tone today which is the same as when God composed the universe.

Soft, warm breezes fanned the bay, holiday makers and locals enjoying a perfect summer's day, mothers keeping a watchful eye on their paddling youngsters, the older ones racing and diving into the deeper, cooler waters. Some people hired Whoopee Floats to paddle further from the shore, giving a sense of adventure, alone on the high seas. Two or three sailing boats anchored offshore, the crew either swimming or fishing, others preferring to sunbathe. Buckets and spades were carried by children to explore rock pools, while they collected winkles or knocking limpets off those age-old rocks. Also, boys were picking up a selection of flat pebbles, skimming them over the top of the water. Children built sandcastles or played rounders, or just sat reading their favourite comics while others carried chip baskets, originally made to contain tomatoes and now used to hold the refreshments bought from the nearest kiosk.

Tears welled in my eyes, as the scenes from my childhood faded, replaced by the murky waters of the Thames. It was not the air raids that frightened me, but the sense of not belonging or being cared for at that moment. Here, in the heart of London, how could anyone give me the love that I craved for, when no one even knew where I was? I had accomplished my mission and it was now time to return, asking the silent question "To whom do I belong ".

Unknown, to me at the time, another member of my family was feeling the same pangs of hunger. . My father had failed to get away before the Germans arrived, and, like so many others, he knew what it was like to go to bed without food. Although the occupying force did not commit the atrocities which were taking place on the Continent, the islanders certainly had stringent rules and regulations imposed upon them. There was strict punishment, if the rules were broken.

Hitler, in his madness, decreed that the Channel Isles were to be a part of the Atlantic Wall, an impregnable fortress to stop shipping getting to

England, the Island acting as a stepping stone for his troops to invade England.

A great number of slave workers were brought in from far and wide, and forced to work in terrible conditions, as they built the concrete bunkers as fortification. Pieces of sacking wrapped around their feet served as shoes, and with little or no food these poor souls grew thin and weak, and many died far from home., Their relatives never knew what became of them. They were just buried under the mass of cement, entombed forever without a prayer or Mass spoken in their final moments. The operation was known as Operation Todt. All this was to construct an Atlantic sea wall. This mania of Hitler which led to the death of many.

They lived in requisitioned housing devoid of creature comforts. One such house was near the home of a Mr. Cecil Langlois, who, with his elderly mother and father, together with Linda and young daughters Mildred and Delma, witnessed the suffering of those poor fellow humans. The Langlois were to play an important part in my life at a later date.

And so I made my way back to the station and asked when the next train would leave for Manchester. Finding that I had two hours to wait, I filled in the time by having a last look at the city that endured so much bombing, yet never lost courage. England's Royal Family stayed put in what was known as the Heart of the Empire.

Then, as I slowly wandered along the platform awaiting my train, I wondered what the Knotts would say, when I finally returned to Oldham. Hopefully, they would have thought that I had been with my mother in Stockport. A great burden was removed from my shoulders, as I believed they would accept my explanation.

I found a seat, and, though pretty tired and very hungry, I managed to relax, till unexpectedly, out of the corner of my eye I saw Tim. He too was sitting on a bench, and, as usual, he was munching a piece of bread. Our eyes met and he instantly recognised me and greeted me like a long lost brother, rushing to sit beside me.

Chapter 6 - A Lancashire Hot-Pot Mixed Stew

"Hi, Bernie! Are you the next Mickey Rooney? Have you signed a contract yet? Can I be your agent?" He asked a hundred and one questions about the studio. Did I see any stars, how much are they paying me... and so on. I was sorry to shatter his dreams after relating what had actually happened at Lime Grove. "Never mind, Bernie," he said. "They will send for you." At least one person had faith in me, I thought gratefully. Then Tim told me of his past and latest adventures.

He began rather quietly and I had to listen closely to understand everything he said.

"My Nan went down with pneumonia and was very ill in hospital. The doctors prescribed a new drug penicillin, or some such, which had kept her alive, so my skin and blister sent me to live with my aunt, but me and her don't get on, so I stayed in Nan's house in Paddington. Auntie Glad sent the cops, but I scarpered" he looked at me as if to make sure I was still listening," She lives with Bert 'n he chews tobacco, has a terrible cough 'n spits in the grate. He used language, that my pot 'n pan would box my ears, if I was to use it." He noticed the quizzical look on my face. "Course where you come from you've never heard the Cockney slang. It's the proper English. Pot and pan means my old man, my Dad. Skin 'n blisters is my sisters. Stick around Bernie, you'll soon learn the King's English." He smiled and leand a little closer. "Bugger or bloody is allowed, but fuck's a no no. Uncle Bert uses it a lot." He went on to tell me that he had used the word in front of Bert once and Bert had boxed his ears. "Don't use that fucken language in front of me, boy," he yelled. Adults are funny people, Bernie," he said, shaking his head.

Tim offered me another bit of bread from a rather stale loaf he carried under his shirt. He then told me how he had spent hours in the shelters ,where people gave him food ,and the time spent in the railway toilets or bathrooms for his basic hygiene." That was pretty basic, Bernie, and left a smell I could well do without." He sat back and we both munched the stale bread. "Sometimes I went hungry 'cos old Adolf didn't always send his planes over at meal times, so I'd go to a baker's and ask for something in the back. When they disappeared, I'd scarper with a loaf. In fact, you've just eaten a piece from a shop in the Strand, where all the toffs buy their bread and cakes. On a good day I manage to be a real tea leaf - there I go again, sorry, a thief, nicking a cake. Today's 'n off day, sorry I can't offer you cake. Have a fag instead. Some silly bugger left them in a toilet. Come on, Bernie, have a Willy Woodbine!" As I took: the unfiltered weed it brought back memories of my smoking days back in Guernsey. Oh, happy days. Tim lit up, warning me not to throw the stub away. "I keep 'em 'cos they help make another ciggie." Then, looking happy, in true cockney style he got up and sang and danced, as if he were doing the Lambeth Walk.

"You are my Woodbine

My only Woodbine,

My twenty Players,-

My CravenA, my Senior Service

Please don't take my Woodbine away!"

A pretty good take' off of You are my Sunshine.

Laughing as he sang, he encouraged me to light up. Reluctantly I lit up with visions of whereabouts in the toilet he had found this noxious weed.

"Inhale, Bernie, like this!" And he drew back smoke, expecting me to follow suit, which of course I did, at the expense of feeling ill, never having inhaled before. The hot smoke brought on a fit of coughing, which left Tim in fits of laughter.

"Go easy old cock," he laughed. "Don't Tom Dick all over your school uniform or the headmaster 'll give you three of the best on your Aristotle. I reckon you'll get at least six of the best for running away." He stopped laughing and sat beside me again, suddenly looking a little serious. "Stick with me, Bernie. We can operate together," he said earnestly.

I was silent for a moment. A picture of Fagin's den flashed into my mind, but it took another moment or two before I was able to respond to his request.

"Thanks all the same, Tim," I replied finally. "But I have to return in case the studio phones."

Chapter 6 - A Lancashire Hot-Pot Mixed Stew

"Go on, stay," he said urgently. "Don't be yellow." It was a moment of decision for me and once again many other images came into my mind.

Outside the walls of this station platform was a city butchered by bombs, far from the shores of Guernsey, yet, once again I saw the streams of children marching down St. Julian's Avenue. Some were laughing, others given to tears and all pondering about what was before them. Each step was taking them towards a ship, bound for an unknown destination.---- Mothers trying their best to control their emotions, so that they would not upset their children--- parents still wondering whether or not they had made the right decision in letting their children go. Those words "Don't be yellow," which were displayed on notice boards outside the Constables Office, those words stuck in their throats. At that moment, while reliving the past in the heart of London were scenes I would never forget. Mean while, children meandered aimlessly. The hand of friendship had been extended to me by Tim. I had to decide whether to stay or return to the Knotts. I considered his invitation as the act of a true friend.

"Please stay, Bernie," he said, speaking in a tone while trying to hide his true feelings. "I want you to stay," he repeated.

Writing this today, I realise that I had at last found a friend, who needed me as much as I needed him. I understood how lonely Tim really felt. I will never know what happened to him after I left. He lives on in my mind, as I imagine what might have been if I had stayed. We parted just as the renewed wail of sirens sent people scurrying back down to the shelters. At the same time we witnessed a dog fight in the skies above us, between our Spitfires and the might of the Luftwaffe. As I looked skyward, I caught a glimpse of a German plane hurtling to the ground, its swastika torn in half. Hooray for the RAF!

Since those far off days, I have come to see the futility of war. To slaughter ones, fellow creatures is not the answer. Though Tim was gone, I still searched for him among the masses with misty eyes. Now that he was gone, I once again experienced the shadow of utter loneliness, even though I also knew that I had to go back, whatever the consequences might be. The raiders passed and the All Clear sounded.

I boarded the train without a ticket once again. Every carriage was packed and reeked of smoke in spite of the disinfectant that had been used to disperse odours> I found half a seat on a trunk next to an elderly man wearing a clergyman's collar. He was engaged in conversation with a rather large lady. As we moved off, the sound of her needles joined in chorus with the wheels of the train. Clickety click, clickety click, and on and on they went, rhythmically together.

"I consider this to be my war effort," she said." As I knit every stitch of these balaclavas, I say a prayer for the poor soul who wears it on the battlefield. God bless him, Vicar."

"Quite so, dear lady," the Vicar responded. "We must pray without ceasing. Your labour is not in vain, as you keep some mother's son warm. If it be the Lord's will that he be taken in battle, at least he will have died in comfort."

The lady looked shocked by the Vicar's words. "As I said, a lot of prayer goes into this labour of love, so I don't expect him to be killed by one of Adolf's lads. Where's your faith, Vicar? That's the trouble with some of the vicars today, as I said to my Ernie. Give me an old-fashioned vicar any day, and Ernie would agree, though he never set a foot inside a church. Still, he was a good man, better than some who goes." She continued with both her knitting and her speech. "God bless him and I hope to see him in Heaven. He passed away ever so sudden, eating fish and chips, while we was on holiday in Blackpool, watching the Big Dipper. Too much excitement, I thought it was caused by a fish bone. He gave a big cough and his face turned blue, no, a kind of purple. It was his heart., It just stopped, so the doctor said. I still think it was a bone. Never had much faith in the doctor, but Ernie did and what was right for Ernie was right by me. God bless him. Do you think Vicar, even though Ernie never went to church, he went to Heaven?" The minister was a kindly man with a look of compassion on his face.

He took her hand and responded," Our dear Lord forgave the man on the cross for not obeying God's rules. You ask a difficult question. Did your dear husband repent of his sins before he passed on?"

Chapter 6 - A Lancashire Hot-Pot Mixed Stew

She had stopped knitting. "I like to think so, Vicar, but on the other hand the poor bugger didn't have a chance before the bloody fishbone got him." She composed herself and went on with her knitting. "Sorry Vicar, I get carried away. Ernie often told me to restrain my language."

"Your Ernie sounds quite refined," the Vicar said.

"Oh yes, he was," she concluded. "But there were times,when he gave out with the odd shit or bugger. But never the f word and it's just as well he didn't use it. I can't abide it myself."

Though I was half asleep, I followed the conversation which seemed to help me from feeling so hungry. The Vicar gave a little cough, blew his nose on a patriotic red white and blue handkerchief and changed the direction of the conversation. He was obviously embarrassed by what he had heard.

"As I already said, your question was a difficult one. It will be answered in the sweet bye and bye, but we can take comfort in the words of our dear Lord. In my House are many Mansions. Who knows?"

"Oh thank you for those words. They must love you in your church!" she said.

"I have not got a church as such," he replied. "You see, I am an Archbishop."

"Oh, my gawd!" the woman uttered, almost dropping her knitting. "Please forgive me, your Grace." Then, more cheerfully, "Fancy me talking to an Archbishop. Wait till I tell my neighbour Flo, She'll be tickled pink. Fancy, a Archbishop!"

Their voices drifted away, as I fell into a fitful sleep. Suddenly ,I was woken up by the sound of the conductor asking for "tickets please", as he inspected the rest of the compartment. I made a quick exit into the crowded corridor and proceeded to the toilet, which, of course ,was occupied. I pushed further along the corridor, till I came to a cubicle. I hoped that the guard had already inspected those travellers' tickets. Peering into each compartment, I looked for an empty seat. Finding a space for a criminal on the run reminded me briefly of Robert Donat in the 39 Steps, Richard Hannay did escape from the police, didn't he? Finally, after much pushing and shoving, I secured a place between two dogs, who immediately insisted on licking my face. As they licked me and pawed at me, I tried to ignore them, not wishing to draw attention to myself in case the guard came past.

The owner of the dogs was a middle-aged woman of masculine appearance with short bobbed hair and a deep voice, which seemed to suggest that she was a heavy smoker. "Down girls!" she commanded, but they took no notice. In fact, they continued to lick me, as if I was providing them with a hearty meal, while I tried to extricate myself from beneath the bodies of those two large Alsatians. At this point, the owner tried to pull them apart by pulling on their tails, but she tripped and fell on top of them. I felt as if my very breath was being squeezed out, as I somehow managed to scramble to my feet and fled from the compartment.

This proved to be my undoing, because I fell straight into the arms of the ticket collector, knocking him sideways into the toilet's door, which had been unlocked. He hit his head against the window latch causing both his cap and his glasses to fall crashing to the floor. Escape was impossible, because, through this whole episode he kept one hand firmly attached to my coat. To make matters worse, the toilet was already occupied by a rather obtuse lady about to do her ablutions. She let out a piercing scream which confused the poor man even further. While fumbling for his glasses on the floor, he came into contact with the woman's leg. Having found his glasses eventually, and muttering an apology, he dragged me back down the corridor towards the guard's van. "It's all your fault my boy, and where is your ticket?!" he asked harshly. Then, with one final tug at my coat he shoved me into the van. Retreat was impossible leaving me entirely at his mercy.

He pointed me towards a wooden bench, and, as if giving orders to the Alsatian dogs ,he said "Sit, boy, sit!" Nervously I sat on the uncomfortable seat, in real fear of this character. His thin, veined face had a bluish tint and a nose that was bulbous, resembling the beak of a budgerigar with deep-set eyes that bored into one's very soul. His menacing voice suggested that untruthful answers would receive no mercy. I likened him to a Dickensian character. Pointing his finger at me, he asked me to produce my ticket. He must have seen the fear in my eyes, because he went on - "Ah ha, you got on without a ticket, didn't you? Well, we send boys to Aldernley Edge, if they

Chapter 6 - A Lancashire Hot-Pot Mixed Stew

are caught. In case you don't know what Aldernley Edge, is, it's a home for criminals the likes of you. Bad, unrepentant boys like you."

By this time, the very fear of God had come over me. "What station did you get on?" he asked, his eyes on me, watching for my reaction. Not wishing for some reason, to say London, I hastily I said Crewe, thinking that, if that station was closer to Manchester, I might get a lighter sentence. He broke into laughter, which dissolved into a twisted smile.

"So you boarded at Crewe, and on what day may I ask?"

"Today, sir," I whispered, not sure if I was giving the right answer.

"Well, well," he went on. "You must be a magician as well as a liar. Are you sure it was Crewe?" I knew immediately that I had given him the wrong station. "I'm sure that Alderley Edge will find a place for you, seeing as how we haven't reached Crewe yet. Perhaps you will wave your wand to end my shift Mr. Magician. Well, I've wasted enough time with you. Meanwhile, stay here, under lock and key till we reach the city, and if a bomb hits the train it could be your lucky day." He seemed to take a sadistic pleasure in tormenting me. A cruel smile added more fear to a heart already beating overtime. Findley he left banging the door.

Cold, tired and hungry I sat on the wooden seat opposite a very large packing case. Glancing at the writing on the front, my heart missed a beat at what I saw there in bold letters. J. S. Entwhistle, (Undertakers) Express Delivery, Perishable Goods. The chest contained a coffin! Goose pimples became the order of the day and I tried to get out, but the door did not give way. I crouched in a far corner of my prison, as the wheels beneath me sang just for me - "Silly boy, silly boy, silly boy." My eyes closed tight and I dozed off for how long I had no idea. I .was woken by my Dickensian jailer.

"Time to get up, boy, to face the music in the Stationmaster's office. I forgot to mention that you were not alone in here. I'm afraid he wasn't much company.--- some poor chap killed in a raid, being despatched to Yorkshire to be buried by his family. You're lucky. I've seen as many as ten boxes in here, still, you could have sat near a better box in Alderley Edge, I suppose." His voice betrayed his obvious enjoyment at the power he had over me. "It's a reform school. 'Cos that's where you're going to end up," he concluded. Passing the pine crate, shivering at the thought that a cold corpse was inside, I suddenly remembered my kissing the marble-white face of Mrs. Simms. Oh, to be there, safe with my mother!

But there was no time for memories, as the guard hurried me along the platform of the great Manchester station and up a flight of stairs, while I wondered if this was to be my last walk before my final execution. "Oh God, help me," I prayed. "I say my prayers every night. I promise to be good. Please help me and don't send me to Alderley Edge."

Whether my prayers were answered, or if it was due to the kindness of the Station Master, I don't know. But they allowed me to return to Oldham on the next available train, but not before the kindly Station Master had interrogated me about my parents, school and so on.

On this particular night, Mrs. Moss, my mothers employer, had decided to give her a treat by taking her to the local cinema. I learned later, that, halfway through the film which both were enjoying, a notice appeared on the screen asking for Mrs. Lena Blestel to come to the office, where an urgent message awaited her. The stationmaster had phoned Mr Moss, who told him of mothers' were about Mother, fearing the worst, hastened to the office with Mrs. Moss close behind her. My mother was told that her son had absconded from his foster home and made his way to London, but was caught on the way back, without a train ticket. He was safe and sound in the Station Master's office at Manchester Station and that he would be returned to Oldham that night.

Mother reacted with tears swearing to 'kill the little devil...' I am sure she meant 'a stronger word . Mrs. Moss, on the other hand, thought it was an act of bravery on my part, facing the bombs of London. She further suggested that Mother should not try to quell my adventurous spirit, but that I should tell them when another adventure was in the offering, so that it did not clash with their cinema arrangements. This information I gleaned later from a not too happy mother.

Eleanor and George Moss lived in a lovely early Victorian house, complete with stables and orchards. There were fruits of all kinds, including my

Chapter 6 - A Lancashire Hot-Pot Mixed Stew

favourite delicious pears and blackcurrants, gooseberries, plums and damsons. All were made into preserves and jams, through the wartime skills of Mrs. Moss with assistance from my mother. Chickens provided eggs to supplement the rations. My contribution was to grind coarse bread into crumbs to make sure that the .egg shells were not brittle. Another job assigned to me was the making of butter pats for the table at mealtimes.

Barber, the gardener, provided the family with fresh vegetables. His prize blooms won praise at the district flower show. This ivy covered house had a sundial placed to catch the sun, away from a tall monkey puzzle tree, whose branches provided shade for the first floor windows. Beside a rockery on the front lawn was a small pool containing multi-coloured goldfish, darting beneath white and pink water lilies, providing shelter from the ever vigilant cat, its paw skimming the surface to claw at unsuspecting prey. Steps had been carved out of a large Felstone boulder leading to a lower lawn, where perfumed flowers and bushes created an Enchanted Garden.

It was truly enchanting for those, who sat on the garden bench under a spreading chestnut tree, its leaves fanned by a cool breeze, as they watched birds bathing in a marble bath and enjoying the seed clusters hung by Mr. Moss. He was a true English gentleman in the true sense of the word----. ----Quiet, unassuming and gentle, whose disposition saw no reason to anger when others caused annoyance, devoted to his wife Eleanor who he had married late in life. It was here, during school holidays, that I learnt to appreciate the finer things in life. The Moss family treated me as one of them and it became a real joy to spend holidays at Green Bank. It was situated in Heath Bank Road, Cheadle Hume, a lovely suburb of Stockport, as yet untouched by the ravages of war. Steam-powered trains puffed past on their way to their major junctions, opposite the house. I first saw King George and Queen Elizabeth waving to residents lining the track, wishing them both God speed, as they returned from inspecting bomb damage in Manchester.

One of the many good things that happened to me at Green Bank was meeting Stuart Woodland, a second cousin of Eleanor. He was three years older than me,but we became firm friends, the friendship lasting many years and only ending with his death. Stuart lived at Northampton with his mother Dorothy and visited Green Bank several times a year. Both Mrs. Moss and Dorothy had a flair for cooking. They produced meals that you would only get at top restaurants, meals I had never tasted before in our working class home. How they did it on their meagre rations, I will never know, but I suspect that they bartered fruit, vegetables and eggs with the butcher or grocer for the ingredients they needed.

Sitting in the train on my return journey, I wondered what my reception by the Knotts would be. But I was lucky. They had not been told about my escapade, assuming that this was my usual monthly visit to my mother. Both Mother and Aunt Alice came poste haste the next day. Sorting me out, Mother gave me one of her looks, which told me that she was not amused by my behaviour. Aunt Alice remained silent, indicating that she was not pleased either. Mr. Fulford, however, had plenty to say, even asking me how much longer I had at school ,and, when I told him that I had another two years he groaned, "Not another two years," he said, and the way he said it did nothing to improve my morale. "I believe you are not happy with the Knotts," he continued. "And perhaps the Knotts would like you to be placed in another home. Where, I have no idea. The novelty of taking in an evacuee has worn off, so your placement may be difficult, especially since this latest episode."

Standing in the school hall in front of the Headmaster, with Mother and Aunt Alice listening to my pitfalls, was certainly not the best way to spend a morning. Giving me another of her meaningful looks, she asked in a voice that matched her expression, "Why did you go to London, of all places, with all that bombing going on? You could have been killed!"

I burst into tears, as she reminded me that I might have been killed in London. The tension was released as I cried. Not wishing to tell her my real reasons, for fear of being thought stupid, I replied, "To see London." I will always remember the look on Mr. Fulford's face. He was amazed.

There was a moment's pause before he responded. "So you wanted to see London. I trust you were content with what you saw. While that was going on, you had no thought about the distress you would cause your mother

Chapter 6 - A Lancashire Hot-Pot Mixed Stew

and me. Any more nonsense such as this will require drastic action. You may like to ponder about this," he concluded sternly.

Recalling what had happened to the minister's son, I realised that there was no point in pondering. It could only mean expulsion. Mother brushed away her tears, borrowing a handkerchief from her sister. "You left in such a rush that you forgot the handkerchief as well as your bag," she said. "This just shows how worried I have been," Mother said; "It's a good job your father is not here. If you carry on like this, you'll have me in a mental home," she said dramatically. This was a tactic she often used to draw pity and ultimately, repentance from me, and she nearly always reduced me to tears. There was no exception in this case. Following further conversation with the headmaster regarding my welfare, both women departed, after extracting a promise from me that I would behave in future. They kissed and embraced me, and left feeling humiliated, because of the publicity of the display.

Life at the Knotts remained the same. They learnt of my adventure through Mr. Fulford who assured her that I would be moved as soon as another home could be found. A temporary change of heart came over Mrs. Knott. "Why move Bernard, we love him as our own," she said. She turned towards me and said - "You are happy here?" I failed to reply and fortunately the phone rang at that moment. As she went to answer it, she failed to see that I was shaking my head. During the rest of my stay on Huddersfield Road Mrs. Knott never failed to remind me of my indiscretions. She constantly reminded me how 'ungrateful' I was and unable to appreciate such a good home. Wicked and Wilful were the words most often used to describe my personality. Homes for refugees became harder to find, as time went on.

Mr. Fulford finally found me accommodation at 13 Hargreaves Street which was behind Tommyfield Market, situated in the grimy, smoky centre of Oldham. A poorer area of the town became my next home. It certainly was not luxurious, but there was love in this house. Mr. Fulford introduced me to seventy year old Mrs. Mary Howarth. She suffered a lot of pain throughout her body from arthritis. In spite of this, her eyes and voice displayed kindness. I instinctively knew, that, unlike the home of the Knotts, I would find happiness in this house.

It was a typical brick terrace house consisting of two bedrooms, a kitchen and a living room, which had been turned into a bedsitter, due to Mrs. Howarth's .ill health. There was no bathroom, no garden, and a cobblestone path led one to the outside communal toilet, which was left dirty from time to time when others used it. The corrugated iron roof leaked whenever there was rain, which proved to be very unpleasant, when the pitter-- patter of raindrops landed on one's head, shortening one's stay considerably. Each user supplied their own toilet paper, or, occasionally, some squares of newspaper, such as I had cut from newspapers in Guernsey. A sooty kettle rested on the hub of a black-leaded range, its coal fire burning brightly to give a cheerful warmth to those in the room. When visitors arrived, Mary Howarth invariably made them welcome with a pot of tea brewed from that ever hot, sooty kettle.

The Range oven cooked most of our meals, even though a gas cooker was housed in a damp, distemper-walled kitchen, adjacent to a pine table. A white enamelled bowl sat on the table. It was used for washing our dishes and beside it a jug always filled with water for the sooty kettle. The one and only tap was situated near the back door. Plumbing was limited in this house. Bars of Sunlight Soap took the place of today's detergents. Apart from the washing of dishes, the soap was also used to bath On the day that I scrubbed the kitchen floor and the toilet, I used Carbolic instead of the usual Sunlight. Mary insisted that an air of freshness permeated the place. She often said -"We may be poor, but we are clean. A clean house is next to Godliness." A sweet lady.

I asked Mary what had happened to her husband. With her voice betraying some emotion, she told me that he died of neurosthenia. "Eh, lad, it's a sad story." She saw that I did not know what neurosthenia was. "It's a bad nervous breakdown, my lovely," she went on. "My poor Sam committed suicide in that gas oven. The poor darling was only forty-six."

This news sent a shiver down my spine, as I often used the stove to cook a dinner. From then on I closed my eyes, whenever I had to place food on the nearby shelf, in case I saw the ghost of poor Sam Howarth. Through a lack of funds, the offending instrument was never replaced. The country had faced hard times with hunger marches and strikes, and then the war came.

Chapter 6 - A Lancashire Hot-Pot Mixed Stew

In a way, Mary loathed the thought of having it removed, deriving comfort from the thought that this was the way her dear husband chose to end his life, ending his earthly pain. A lovely thought but bizarre. In her mind the gas stove became his shrine.

Due to Mary's ill health, I cleaned the house and did other domestic duties. I should mention that the oven was black not through lack of cleaning, but, simply, in those days the working classes could not afford enamel stoves. Stainless Steel ovens were yet to come .

This dear Catholic lady shared her house with two paying lodgers, both men; it helped to eke out the pension. Frank was a middle-aged ex colliery worker, now employed in the office of J. Higginbottom & Sons, Coal Merchants. They were reputed to be fine, upstanding Christians but a shadow of doubt was cast when J.Higginbottom Senior fathered a child to eighteen year old Sissy Russell. She was generally described as flighty by the local gossips, who muttered that it was a wonder that she was not 'up the spout' before. You can't blame the boys, they said, when they were led on by being shown this week's knickers. And on and on it went. If she was mine, I'd tan her arse, she was terribly spoilt, if you play with fire you must expect to be burnt and she got what she deserved.

Mary Howarth was not one to condemn those who fell in misfortune. She often remarked that God had given us tongues to speak with love, not to wag with unkind words. Many thought that getting the girl pregnant was a black mark for Christians.

Frank's sturdy body, prone to overweight, moved slowly and silently, catching you unaware when you least expected him. His voice lacked warmth and he only spoke, when it was necessary. He dressed in black trousers, a grey shirt and a dark cardigan, topping this with a long dark coat, which almost reached his ankles. He was clothed in this fashion day after day. His very presence was frightening to me; he seemed to depict a character from a horror film and I was truly thankful when he departed for work. He spent most evenings in his bedroom, smoking and reading the newspapers, only emerging to brew himself a mug of tea on the ill-fated stove or emptying his chamber pot on rainy days, throwing the urine over the backyard instead of in the toilet. He spent Friday nights in the local Horse and Hounds, returning at closing time a little the worse for wear.

I would hear him climbing the stairs and muttering to himself, as I lay in bed, wondering if he would make it to his room or enter mine by mistake. Anxiously, I would retreat under my bed clothes for safety. Bed clothes are a children's safety net I say my bedroom, but this should have been our bedroom, because I shared a double bed with Jimmy Walsh, a twenty-three year old Irish coalminer, engaged to Betty. Jimmy, or James, as Mrs Howarth insisted on calling him, was the complete opposite to Frank. He always had a smile and a cheery word with jokes that were pretty near the mark, some needing laundry treatment. We became the best of pals and he was very sympathetic, when he heard about my having to leave Guernsey. He understood how I felt, because he had had similar feelings about leaving Ireland and coming to Oldham for work. He was exempt from the military, because mining was regarded as an essential service. Not long after, Jimmy became one of Mary Howarth's lodgers 'She regarded him as a third son, along with Joe and Sam and her daughters Alice and Agnes. Both daughters owned public houses, Alice the Sly Fox and Agnes the Royal Hotel.

Mary had her fair share of tragedy. One dreadful night, at around 10pm, there was a knock on the door, and, when she opened it, she was confronted by a policeman standing on the whitened donkey stone step. Since it was too late for the usual callers, it could only mean bad news. The policeman entered carefully after establishing that this was Mary Howarth, careful not to let light escape due to the blackout. Harry Entwhistle had been in the force for some time, and among his duties, all too often, the need to deliver bad news to families. His superiors knew how well he conducted himself in these circumstances and often sent him out on these sad errands.

"It is with great regret that I have to divulge the sad news that your son in law has passed away," Entwhistle told Mary. The colour drained from her face, as she asked in a hardly audible voice how and when had this happened.

"I am not sure of the details, Madam," he replied. "And I am not at liberty to divulge all the facts, but since you are related to the deceased, I will tell

Chapter 6 - A Lancashire Hot-Pot Mixed Stew

you what little I know. I understand that a bottle of disinfectant, Lysol, was consumed, as the poor soul sat on the toilet. We have not established a motive and murder has not been ruled out."

The word 'murder' sent a chill through my body and Mrs.Howarth drew her breath in sharply, a look of horror spreading over her face. She began to sob, crying out - "Not murder! It's too horrible to behold! Poor Alice, poor Alice, poor Alice," she repeated again and again. P.C. Entwhistle raised his hands, as if he were about to bless or calm her.

"As you know, he was a large man and the effect of the Lysol caused him to swell, Unfortunately, the lavatory door had to be removed before the body could be brought out. The firemen did an excellent job with reverence." He paused for a moment. "A sad case, a very sad case," he said finally.

"Dear Mother of God," Mrs.Howarth cried, becoming agitated. "Poor Alice. I must go to her immediately! By all the saints in Heaven, a second suicide! May the dear souls rest in peace!" As she searched for her rosary beneath her eiderdown, P.C. Entwhistle gently restrained her.

"It is your daughter's wish that you stay home till morning. Nothing could be achieved by your going out at this late hour."

Poor Mrs. Howarth's pitiful sobbing turned my thoughts to Mother, when my father's unkindness and temper reduced her tears. I instinctively went to Mrs. Howarth and put my arms around her to comfort her. Though I was determined to put on a brave face in front of the policeman, it was a wasted effort, as my own tears began to flow.

Mrs. Howarth's tears slowly subsided as she grasped my hand. "Thank you my dear," she said. "Now kindly make a cup of tea. It's the least we can do for P.C. Entwhistle, arriving at such a late hour." This was typical of her, as she was always concerned for others. The constable accepted his tea, realising that this simple chore would ease the atmosphere in the room, even though the tea was the second brew, due to rationing.

Sleep did not come easily after the constable left. Bed was out of the question for me, so I dozed in a chair next to her bed in case she needed anything during the night. Frank had very little to say as he left for work at 6 o'clock next morning. He made a cup of tea and prepared his sandwiches and left the house, merely saying "Morning, Missus." as he departed. Jimmy arose an hour later, bright and breezy, not knowing what had happened the previous night. Mary left it to me to break the news to him. He immediately went to the bed to comfort her, but Mary apologised for not fixing his breakfast. The thought of having forgotten this trivial duty meant that she was once again reduced to tears. Drawing Jimmy close, she gently kissed his cheek. He hugged her, telling her that it was indeed a sad business. Then he dried her eyes with the top end of the bed sheet.

I often wondered what became of Jimmy, after he left us to get married. It was through him that I really developed an interest in sex. Having retired early one evening, I was almost asleep, when Jimmy returned from seeing his future wife. He wished me goodnight. I did not answer, as he searched for the candlestick in the darkened room. I watched through half-closed eyes, as he adjusted a candle and tried to get it alight without success. After a moment, he decided to do without it, and he undressed by the sliver of light that came through the side of the blind. It was enough for me to see his naked body, as he undressed and got into bed. In my childish curiosity I could see that he already had an erection. He lay down on his side of the bed, quite unaware that I was watching, and pulled the covers over him. The minutes ticked by from the old fashioned alarm clock, which sat on a table close to the bed. The tick, tick, tick of the clock broke the silence. Suddenly, Jimmy's hand located the area on his body that was called 'private'. His breathing became uneven and the blankets rose and fell in rhythm, as his performance gained momentum. Finally, he let out a gasp as he reached a climax, a gasp of satisfaction. An experience, as yet unknown to me. The ruffled sheet became warm in that cold night, due to his movements and perspiration. Stillness resumed and I hardly heard the ticking clock because my head was thumping, sending up my blood pressure at what I had just witnessed. Wiping the sweat from his body and organ, both had sought therapeutic relief. At the time I lay still, hoping that I would remain undetected from what had gone on. Yet, in retrospect, I think that I received enjoyment.

Chapter 6 - A Lancashire Hot-Pot Mixed Stew

My boyish curiosity had led me to a state where childish innocence no longer existed. My eyes were wide open by this time, and Jimmy sensed that I had seen the whole business. Facing me, he said - "Please don't say anything about this to anybody. It's the first and only time I've done it with anyone in the room." Poor Jimmy didn't want to upset me, or for me to feel badly about him. I assured him that there would be no mention of any of this to anyone from me. He gave me a hug, and, as he did so, I experienced a warmth not just from his body but from his whole being, as if we were united in the act he had just performed. This was a night that I never forgot. It was the first time I had been hugged by a man. My father had never hugged me, and at that moment I felt that we shared a real bond. Lying next to Jimmy, I realised later that he was the one, who had put me on the threshold of understanding emotions.

No other conversation passed between us and I slowly drifted off to sleep with his arms still around me. For the first time in a very long while I did not feel lonely. Jimmy in no way abused me.

Morning finally came, and Jimmy had already left for the colliery, when I awoke. Pangs of remorse came over me at having intruded into a very private life and these were particularly strong, as I faced Mrs. Howarth and prepared her breakfast. I placed the tray beside her bed within reach, she sat up painfully and touched my hand. "Eh lad," she said, smiling. "You are proper champion spoiling me with breakfast in bed. I've said it before you're a second son to me." I had never understood this, as she already had two sons, Sam and Joe, but it was nice of her to say it. If she had known anything about the night's episode, she did not mention it. My only moment of concern came, when she asked if I had slept well. I nodded, rather than giving an answer. I managed to avoid eye contact, as I ate my own breakfast of Cornflakes, washed the dishes, brushed the lino, shook the mats and emptied the chamber pots. The fire in the grate had gone out through lack of attention, so I filled a coal bucket from a shed in the yard and coaxed the still warm embers back from black to yellow, and finally to red, emitting new life to the fireplace and to the room. In some way I likened the reawakening of the fire to a new beginning for me, due to what had occurred during the night.

"Lovey, would you be so kind as to pour a drop of cold water into the basin? I nearly burnt these poor old fingers, the other morning, not that they are of much use, these days with my arthritis. God is still good to me. He sent me you."

I poured water into the china hand basin, that had reportedly bathed her newly born mother. As I poured, I listened to the history of this heirloom.

"Lad, this here basin washed the blood from my dear mother, as she came from her mother's womb, God bless her. When I pass on to my eternal resting place, this precious basin is willed to my granddaughter Hazel. May God grant her children to bathe in this precious bowl. You know love, I've seen heaven. Such a lovely place."

Dear Mary retold the tale so sincerely, that it was impossible not to believe that she had peeped into her future resting place.

"It's like this love. Pneumonia struck me down in one of the coldest winters I've known. Dr. Wild called, shook his head and said 'the infirmary for you Mary'. I decided to stay at home against his wishes, even though he tried his best to change my mind. He gave in, in the end, supposedly because he thought that if I were going to die in hospital, I might as well pass away in my own bed. Double pneumonia developed, with my dear family sitting near me waiting for each breath to be my last. Bernard, it was such a comfort to have my family near."

As she spoke, her voice lowered. Some people die alone. I thought, how sad, how very sad. Then on her face the shadow lifted to be replaced by tranquillity.

"I felt at peace," she continued. "To face whatever happened. Gazing up to the white-washed ceiling, which I have looked at for many years, suddenly a strange thing happened. It vanished, opening to the most beautiful garden, so tranquil, so serene. A coolness came over me, not coldness but a warm assurance. A voice spoke, its tone so gentle and loving. I stretched out my hands to grasp the distant, radiant figure clothed in white. I heard our Agnes say - she's gone Sam. I sensed in her eyes a well of tears. At that moment I felt so close to my family, so near yet so far away. I only wanted

Chapter 6 - A Lancashire Hot-Pot Mixed Stew

to tell them not to weep. Even though I walk through the valley of the shadow of death, I feel no evil. The presence of the Lord was very near me. My feeble words went unheard. Disappointed by the changing scene, my body was shaking, as I watched the beautiful garden slowly disappear, replaced by the white-washed ceiling.

Funny, it seemed cleaner and whiter 'Not yet, Mary. Go back.' The kindly voice, unheard by my family, spoke directly to me. Then silence. Oh, how I longed to listen again to that sweet voice, to feel His presence."

Retelling the experience, tears rolled down her cheeks "Oh, I did so want to stay. You can live too long Bernard. You may remember my words when you get to my age."

"My family thought I suffered hallucinations. No, my brain was as clear as a bell, So real and as genuine as I am here. It might seem strange, but from that moment I felt stronger each day, until I completely recovered. The family still think that I entered dreamland. Take my word, Bernard, this was no dream. I was on the thresh-hold of Heaven."

I loved to hear the story.about Heaven above the bright blue sky,which reminded me of my Sunday School days. One thing I know for certain. Mary Howarth knew this was no figment of her imagination. It existed. It was as close as her living room ceiling. Mary has long since gone. I am sure she had no fear, as she walked through the valley of the shadow of death. Feeling no evil, she had passed that way before.

I left the house and ran frantically to catch the Hollingwood bus at the Tommyfield bus stop. I got on, just as it was about to leave. Arriving at school and listening to their latest adventures, I remained silent about mine, holding back on my ill-fated excursion, at least for the time being.

Mary Howarth's daughter Alice took some time to get over the death of her husband, never knowing why the man had taken his own life. She became the licensee of the pub in place of her husband, and was able to maintain the high standards he had put in place. When she occasionally suffered from bouts of depression, her friends came to help. Mary and I often visited the bar, when her health allowed it, we made sandwiches for customers. I was supposedly not allowed in the drinking area, but I often snuck into the lounge and talked to customers. They used to ask me about Guernsey and how I managed to escape from Jerry.

> Kenneth Crabtree, Agnes' son, and Marys only grandson was a pilot flying Lancaster bombers . He always came to visit her, when he was home on leave, and he was the apple of his grandmother's eye. He gave her special joy, when he announced that he would soon marry Dora, a sweet-natured girl. She was employed by the law firm of J.S. Smograss of Manchester. The wedding day was announced after a short engagement. Servicemen often married quickly, fearing they might never return from active service. Occasionally, babies were born just nine months after the wedding ,sadly, many fathers never saw their babies.

The wedding day arrived. Mary had remodelled Dora's mother's wedding dress and a going away outfit was supplied by the family. All the family's clothing coupons were pooled, though Mary insisted that the bridegroom's mother should have a new dress for the occasion. Dora looked radiant in her mother's wedding dress, which was pale blue with forget-me-nots in a deeper shade of blue. A reception at the Cotton Spinners Hall followed, and Mary considered the day to have been one of the highlights of her life. Waving goodbye to them on their forty-eight hour honeymoon, no one could foresee the tragedy that lay ahead. Kenneth safely ferried planes between Canada and England during the war, but when hostilities ceased, his plane crashed into a mountainside, killing all the crew and leaving his wife and Mary inconsolable. This happened after I left Oldham and school. Mary never recovered and went into a slow decline, which led to her death a few months later.

One late afternoon, Mary asked me to go to Briely's near Mumps Station to buy writing paper and envelopes. She loved letter writing to family and friends. The shop was a fair distance from Hargreaves Street and I ran all the way, just making it at closing time. Briely's was a well-established business run by a nephew of the founder who had departed long before. He left the business and a large part of his fortune to his sister-in-law's son by a previous marriage, causing a major division between the rest of the family.

Chapter 6 - A Lancashire Hot-Pot Mixed Stew

People hinted that there must have been an inordinate affection between old Briely and his nephew. Many dismissed the notion, others said - there's no smoke without fire.

I arrived out of breath and was greeted by the now middle-aged owner. He was a tall, slightly grey man with a sallow complexion and blue eyes, sporting a well groomed moustache. Though his uncle had financed his University education,he still retained a trace of the Lancashire dialect in his voice. "You made it just in time young man," he said, as he began to pull down the blind on his front door. "And what have you been up to today, young fellow?" he asked, edging closer to me, until his arm came in contact with my shoulder. "When is your birthday? How old are you?" he asked, looking at me closely, as I tried to get my breathing back to normal.

"My birthday is not till December and I am twelve, "I told him.

"I'll have to remember a birthday present," he went on, leading me back into the shop. I wondered what all this was leading to. "You're tall for your age, almost a man. I expect you're big all over. Do you play with girls and boys?" With the accent on boys. "What games do you play?, is kissing in the game? Whom do you prefer to play with, boys or girls? Aren't they lucky to be playing with you." He sat me down on a chair and continued - "At your age I loved playing with boys. Girls were too giggly. I still like boys," he said, placing his hand on my leg. Alarm bells had rung faintly in my head during this one-sided conversation. Though in a way I wanted to see how this charade would proceed, the alarm bells were much louder, when his hand began to move up to my shorts. I knew immediately that this spelt disaster, and my only thought was how to escape from this monster. I shoved his hand away, stood up and trod on his foot, as hard as I could, then ran to the door. Fortunately, the key was still in place. I ripped the door open and slammed it behind me, then ran like a bat out of hell, dodging cars and trams ,till I reached the safety of Hargreaves Street. With sweat running down my face and making an effort to regain my composure ,I explained to Mary, that, although I had run all the way, the shop was closed when I got there.

"Eh lad, you shouldn't run like you do," she said. "You'll be giving yourself a heart attack. You can go down to Briely's after school tomorrow. The owner is such a nice man, always polite to the ladies." Although she thought so well of him I never went back. I bought the stationery from Woolworth and never disclosed my encounter to anyone.This was a shadow in my life, which I did not dwell on I faced the light,while getting on with my life, not letting the experience festerer my journey.

Mary's sister Nellie lived at Failsworth, not far from Hollinwood, where our schools were. She was a foster aunt with the same warm disposition as her sister. I often travelled to her house with a garment, which needed altering; she had learnt her trade as a dressmaker. I loved to visit her neat and tidy home, which always smelt of home cooking, and I was always given a bag of sweets and goodies for my return journey.

Only one thing marred the journey to Nellie's home. A few doors away I had to pass the house of Pierpoint, England's number one hangman. The smoke-grimed house was a clone of the houses in the area, which had a spooky aura. I always hastened my steps as I passed his door, fully expecting this famed executioner to emerge, carrying a black bag containing the rope and all the paraphernalia required to end some poor wretch's life,as he hung from the gallows to descend into Hell "Because that where murders go unless they have asked for God's absolution " This I was told as a child."

During winter, as fog and smog blanketed the street, it became even more sinister, and, as darkness fell, an atmosphere of foreboding descended on his house creating awful fantasies in my fertile mind. Yet, this humble house was no different from scores of others in the street. His neighbours spoke highly of him and were proud to have such a distinguished gentleman in their street. On his retirement, Mr. Pierpoint acquired a pub aptly named 'Help the Poor Struggler'.

I never got a look at this man whose occupation sent a chill through my bones. His presence seemed to radiate through the smoke grimed bricks. I had no wish to come face to face with this infamous character and wondered, if when he drew a pint of beer, it felt to him like releasing the

Chapter 6 - A Lancashire Hot-Pot Mixed Stew

gallows lever and dropping some unfortunate creature to his or her doom. Did he suffer from nightmares in the due course of his work?

Life continued on from day to day, carrying with it the anxiety of not knowing whether or not some enemy German would release a lever and send a bomb into space, pouring death and destruction from the skies.

But the moral of English people showed that they were always ready to lend a hand, when the chips were down.

Meals were produced from very meagre rations ,while the government encouraged everyone to plant on a small allotment to 'Grow Food for Britain'. So people took up arms. Forks and spades became weapons, attacking the soil in the hope that the fruits of their labour would provide crops which were worthy of their time – and backaches.

For many this was a new experience. Numerous would-be gardeners continued to grow an assortment of vegetables and fruit for many years after the war.

Chapter 7

Christmas 1944

Turning back the clock, my mind again enters the world of memories, as we so often do when we are low in spirit. Back to Guernsey, that green isle. Oh, how I longed to smell the sea! To watch the waves gain momentum, as they beat against the rocks in a swirling of white foam. To catch the feeling of the spray against my checks, to be caressed by the wind, bringing with it the taste of salt, whenever the tongue wet the lips.

I remember the picnics on the beach, exploring rock pools, collecting sea shells, dislodging limpets from rocks as old as time. Winkles found on rocks and in pools, which made their way eventually in saucepans, to be boiled, and then finally removed from their shells with sharp pins, needles ,to be eaten with vinegar and chips. Not a Cordon Bleu recipe, but a feast for us kids.

I remember walking through green fields or meadows, with their carpets of shining golden buttercups and white daisies, fit to adorn the crown of a May Queen, as they mingled with the lushness of the grass.

There was always a jam jar, complete with string handle, ready to receive the gathered spawn from pools near streams. We would transfer the spawn into a glass jar and wait for their transformation to tadpole, and, finally to frog.

Or to walk through the market, smelling the fresh fruit arrayed on tables in stalls with the names of the stallholders appearing above them. They were usually of French extraction - Le Noury, Gaved, Jehan, Sarre and Madame Marie, who always dressed in black. Included in her ensemble was a large hat, firmly held in place by an ornate white pin. She was in mourning for a husband long since gone and assisted by her spinster daughter, who never spoke unless the matter concerned a purchase.

I remember wholesome vegetables, grown without chemicals, just natural horse or cow manure, yellow Guernsey butter nestled with white curds on cabbage leaves to keep it cool. Then wandering to another area with its delicate smell of the sea and all the creatures of the ocean. There were crabs, crayfish, chantres, ormers, mackerel, rays, conger eels, and longnose. And friends meeting for a chat at the stalls of Mrs. Cornu, the Petits, Langlois, Fergusions and Newtons. A host of people long since gone. Finally, progressing through the market, a different picture comes to mind. Hunks or whole sides of beef, lamb and pork suspended on S-shaped hooks over the butchers' stalls with their names clearly displayed ,names such as, R, Chillcott, E Best, T Elliston, Downs and Sibly. The smell of fresh meat and the faces of lopng ago remain alive in my mind to this day.

The reflection of the ever turning kaleidoscope reveals being embraced in my mother's arms, comforted in her love, when I took a tumble or when things went wrong. Sniffing the soap or perfume refreshing her body. And the clatter of Father's hobnailed boots; wondering what kind of mood he was in. I consider myself lucky to have grown up in a more leisurely time In a world where principles were ingrained into character. Today's planet seems to me to have had its resources raped and irreplaceable. Where recycling is a must, a world where the threat of violence or atomic fallout is endemic. Yet, there is still love to be received and given, and where there is love there is hope.We must no linger in the Shadows During the German occupation of Guernsey ,the islanders were determined to keep their peckers up. I have been, told that shows and concerts were produced by local talent. There were names like Dorothy Hurrel, Sid Gardner, Eddie Mann, the Brache

Chapter 7 - Christmas 1944

Sisters, Len Winterflood, Ken Langlois and Norman Langlois, to name but a few. Shows were staged, like No No Nanette and Sally, and First class productions staged at venues like Central Hall or Billy Bartlett's Regal Cinema. Unknown to me at that time, as a lad of eleven, was that the name of Langlois would play an important part in my later life.

I hold dear memories of Oldham, which was no tourist centre with its blackened buildings, snow, rain and icy cold winters. Two fine days, a thunderstorm and the summer is over say the locals. In spite of the bad weather the Pennine Ranges were a great place for hikers. There were venues, where refreshments were sold to ramblers. Time spent there at weekends were great fun, and I often accompanied Kathleen and her friends, as we climbed over the high terrain, returning as darkness fell upon us, sometimes cold and hungry, but all the better for having experienced the fresh invigorating air. The laughter and chatter took our minds off the war for the time being.Children only live for the present , disregarding what may happen in the future . I often wonder what happened to Kathleen Martin. Is she still with us? Did Phil Swallow return from the war to marry her or did Cupid's arrow shoot off in another direction? War changes the course.

Here in Australia, where food is plentiful, my mind goes back to the bleak times of wartime rationing. There were different types of ration books. The most common was buff coloured, issued to adults and schoolchildren. Green books were issued to expectant mothers and contained extra tokens, though there was a downside to them. The possession of such a book might give away a woman's secret. People were much more private about their circumstances in those days, and a pregnancy outside wedlock was considered scandalous.

The tokens had no monetary value; they were merely a means of ensuring that everybody got their fair share of what was available, trying to prevent stockpiling. In times of shortage the black market emerged.If you had the money, goods could find their way into your home. Unfortunately, this was and is the way of the world.

The tokens were for food, and later for clothing. Food rationing came into force four months after the war began, on January 8th 1940. To start with, the amounts allowed were 14 ounces of butter or lard, 4 grams of sugar, 12 ounces of bacon or ham and two eggs per week. As the war went on, bread supplies became very short. Queues would form very early in the morning, because, even if people had coupons, there was no guarantee that the shops would have enough for everyone.

Rumours would circulate that supplies of butter or meat were in stock, so people would shop immediately. Many shops opened only two or three times a week. Eventually, coupons became necessary for clothing. This seemed to affect women more than men. Silk stockings were impossible to buy, so many women came up with interesting solutions. They would stain their legs with tea, a mixture of sand and water or even a thin mixture of gravy colouring. Then they would make a line down the back of their legs with a eye liner to look like a stocking seam. Patches were sewn on elbows to repair damage on jumpers, cardigans or jacket sleeves. Sometimes this was done early to curtail the wear and tear, and thus ensure a longer life for the garment. These patches became quite popular, not a symbol of poverty. Special clothing, such as brides' or bridesmaids' dresses, were passed around by families to be worn again and to save on clothing coupons.

Bartering became a way of life, and this was where an illegal black market flourished. Children, aged from one to five years, were frequently included in their mother's green book. The mothers of those children sometimes had a few vegetables or a cracked egg slipped into their shopping baskets by kindly shopkeepers. Children over five had their own ration books. Rationing did not end with the war; it was years before the country was rebuilt and life returned to normal. Some things like sweets were still rationed till 1953. It was rather interesting to read the quote from a wartime schoolgirl.

"I remember my uncle fetching back some bananas, when he came home on leave. He gave me one and I took it to school. Everyone crowded around me and my teacher showed it to the whole class. It seemed like a priceless treasure. I was a very popular girl that day. Everyone wanted me to open it and eat it, but I wouldn't. I took it home with me, leaving it until it went

Chapter 7 - Christmas 1944

black. Oh, it still smelled so good. Even now I can't smell banana without evoking that memory."

Food was adequately good in quality, but did not include such pre-war luxuries as ice cream and ... so on. Each person got 24 points per week to spend on anything that was chosen, as long as the demands were not so big that they had to be refused by the shopkeepers. For example, rice was 4 points per pound, sultanas 8 points, prunes 6, tinned fruit about 8 points and luxuries like salmon, when available, 16 or 24 points per tin.

While clothing was also rationed, shirts would sometimes have a different pattern from the collar to the rest. If the rest of the shirt became unwearable, the collar would be saved and sewn on to another shirt whose collar had worn out. Children's clothes were of course recreated from discarded adult garments, and blankets were made into dressing gowns. Material that was either scorched or water marked could be bought, retrieved from bombed out warehouses or shops. The weekly markets sold collections of bombed goods, no coupons required. Newspapers were smaller, and paper was scarce. Anything that could be salvaged was saved. The dustmen collected salvaged goods once a week, including metal, rubber, bones or string.

People even removed metal railings or gates to help with the war effort. Every town had a book drive, where books were collected and used in various ways. Some went for scrap, but others, if they were in good order, were sent to libraries whose books had been destroyed in the bombing. The Forces also received any books that were considered suitable. These drives were often promoted by celebrities. I remember George Formby, star of stage and screen, encouraging the people of Oldham to part with their salvage.

Winston Churchill passed through the town, with his fingers giving the famous victory sign and receiving a tumultuous reception. His inspirational speeches, which were broadcast, gave hope and courage to the country, when victory seemed like a faded dream after Hitler's conquest of Europe. Whatever Churchill's misdemeanours may have been in the past, this was his finest hour. He was the right man in the right place and no other person could inspire the nation as he did. The Royal Family stayed at Buckingham Palace in spite of the heavy bombing on London. They often visited the bombed areas and showed compassion to families who had suffered damage to their homes, or who had lost relatives. During the war years, one of Churchhill's concerns was that the Germans submarines were taking a great toll of our boats bringing supplies to the country from far off places.

Christmas Eve, 1944, stays very clear in my mind. As I lay in my bed awake at 32 Oakfield Road in Stockport, I heard what I thought was a plane in distress. Some distance away I heard the engine splutter, then stop. Oh, I thought, some poor pilot is not going to make it back to base, when suddenly the sirens sounded. Before I could get out of bed, another plane seemed to be having trouble. But this time it got closer and closer. Then came an awful silence, followed by a terrible screeching, which got nearer every second. I lay on my bed as if I was frozen, as my mind took stock of the situation. I realized that this was no ordinary plane, but a V2, a doodle-bug, one 'of Adolf's 'secret' weapons programmed to reach its destination. As the noise cut off the bomb screamed to earth, destroying whatever lay below it. As I lay on the bed, frozen and unable to move, I suddenly became resigned to the fact that this could be my last minute on earth. As the ear-piercing sound filled my head, my only thought was - goodbye Guernsey. Then a deafening explosion shook the very foundations of the house, accompanied by the sounds of falling plaster and breaking glass. My nostrils became full of a mixture of dust and soot, causing an arid cough that tortured my lungs. Then the smell of burning really alarmed me. The thought of being burnt alive unfroze my fear and released me from the bed. Dust filled my eyes, as I fumbled my way to the stairs in darkness to find Aunt Alice crouched in her nightdress at the bottom of the stairwell, were she was clutching a touch , she being covered in soot and plaster. Poor Aunt Alice had been narrowly missed by a stiletto piece of glass, which could most certainly have stabbed her, probably severing an artery . I helped her to get up, and, still trembling ,we made our way to the cellar, which had become our air raid shelter.

For times of emergency, a survival base had been fitted out with candles in case the power failed, as well as chairs,-mattresses, a cupboard containing cups and saucers, plus food and drink to sustain us while prolonged raids lasted. Sometimes they went on for hours.

Chapter 7 - Christmas 1944

Poor Aunt was in a state of shock, as we all were, with chaos all around us. Mother rushed to the s cellar, while Uncle Bill surveyed the damage, with Aunt Alice calling out for him to leave the inspection till later, fearing that he might lose his life otherwise, if Jerry gave a repeat performance. As the night drew on, houses in the next street were hit, while others sustained severe damage.

In the middle of what seemed like an endless night, Uncle Bill ventured upstairs to boil water for a cup of tea. Lucky our gas was still on, to boil the water, and, while doing so, he inspected what had remained of number 32.

All the windows were blown out, the front door stained glass panels were in fragments, the rear door was detached from its hinges and ceiling plaster, mixed with soot and brick from the fireplace was scattered all over the carpets. In the hall and in the other rooms lay a sea of glass. When Aunt and my mother eventually examined the damage, they were reduced to tears, wondering where to start, but grateful that we were still alive, and longing for the night to end.

During the war everyone lived close to death, not sure whether or not the next bomb had your name on it.

Night, mercifully, gave way to dawn, with the four of us sitting in the shelter waiting for the all clear siren on that last fateful Christmas Eve of the war. People finally emerged from the bowels of the earth to face whatever lay before them. Though dejected in some way, there remained the determination to win this five year war, at whatever the cost in the slaughter of innocent people the world over.

Man has not progressed from the barbarism of Rome, though he has become more devious in disposing of those who stand in his way.

What a Christmas Present! At least we survived to tell the tale with no bones broken. A.R.P. wardens appeared as if from nowhere, assuring householders that help was on its way and asking if any person might still be residing in the premises that appeared unoccupied.. If so, the digging would begin to release those who were still trapped, alive or dead. Bodies had to be recovered to go to either hospital or sadly the mortuary. That Christmas for many a journey to Shadow--- land Gone was the message of Good will. Did tears blot out the message Good will to all men ----or has it!

On this birthday of Christ all hell had been let loose. All the houses in Oakfield Road had suffered damage, some worse than others. The full-blast of the bomb affected the whole length of Garners Lane. One Guernsey lady was killed and her husband was severely injured, bearing a facial scar for life. The irony of it was that, though they had escaped from the enemy in Guernsey, they had been killed by the Germans anyway. Mother phoned Mrs. Moss to let her know that we were alright, but would be late getting to work due to the rubble in the house, which needed to be cleared up.

Mrs. Moss offered her help, which Mother declined. Due to the petrol rationing, Mr. Moss's car had remained in their garage for most of the war, since he did not come into the category which received petrol - for special purposes. The only way Mother could travel to Greenbank was by bus and buses were in chaos due to the raid. Our usual breakfast was out, though we still had gas and water. There was no electricity. A cup of tea helped to sustain us, till help arrived in the form of the American G.I's. Once again, our overseas allies came to the rescue. Their generosity came in the form of a group of about a dozen men who appeared out of the blue. They were keen to clear the debris and to cover the roof with tarpaulin, so that the wind and rain would cause no further damage through the gaping holes. The G.I.'s introduced themselves, but their names, alas, have been lost in time. What remains in my memory is the spirit. Whatever odds were battled against, it was the approach that carried the allies to victory.

Mother and I made her way to the Moss's, uncertain as to whether or not the buses would be running. We had a ten minute walk along Garners Lane before the Cheadle Hume bus was due to arrive to take us to Greenbank. Proceeding along the road, mother glanced at the damage done during that fateful raid. Roofs were completely destroyed; window glass; was shattered into a thousand pieces; bricks and tiles were joined in what had been gardens with their flowers crushed; Trees were stripped of their foliage; a burst water main sent up a near icy volume of water; pavements were torn from their foundations; doors hung in space, their frames charred beyond use, and the cold misty air was filled with the aftermath of burning.

Chapter 7 - Christmas 1944

Shocked occupants bent low, as they searched for precious belongings, a look of total bewilderment on their faces. They would no longer sing out the joyous message of Christmas. This was war brought to the home front, as Churchill had predicted. 'We will fight on the land, sea and air'. This land is England, unscathed by foes for a thousand years. Blood, sweat and toil finally reached our shores.

"At least we are all alive," muttered a woman, as tears mingled with soot streamed down her face. A baby cried, perhaps oblivious of the chaos while its two young sisters, acting as nursemaids, cradle the child close to their young bodies. The mother was as yet unseen. Pray to God they are not orphans. The children made an effort to silence the wailing of the baby, which disturbed the stillness around them. Yet, this was no time for silence; grief must be released in the way that nature ordained, through tears that stem our very depths, regardless.

Suddenly and unexpectedly the eeriness of the place was broken. Jeeps and lorries appeared and once again it was the G.I.'s to the rescue. "Hi, Mam. Need help?" reached Mother's ears. She turned and shook her head. No words passed her lips in this desolate scene., Her innermost feelings choked, as she walked on. Greenbank was her only thought, with its ivy covered frontage, the vine creeping around the windows, the tall Araucaria reaching to the height and beyond the slate roof,. a sundial in the lower garden placed to catch shadows denoting the time, water lilies giving shelter to goldfish in the large granite stone pond, that seemed to offer tranquillity, as one gazed at the ever moving fish. Then therewas Tibbles, the Manx cat, lovable by nature and purring in satisfaction, when seated on its owner's lap. Yet also a hunter, as he waits patiently beside the pond, looking furtively around, as he dares to plunge a paw into the water. Claws grapple unsuccessfully, as he try's to obtain a tasty morsel. Perfumes of an icy winter's day freshen the air within this garden of peace. It is a semi Eden and hopefully will remain untouched by the violence of a screeching bomb.

Mr. and Mrs Moss wait anxiously for Mother's arrival. Yes, the Moss'es are good people, worried in case Mother had been injured during the night of terror. Catching her breath as she hurried along, her one desire was to erase the horror from her mind, a horror sent by a Nazi dictator on the edge of madness, whose insane dream included conquering the world and exterminating six million Jews in the process.

Deep dark shadows entered the world, as the light ceased to shine, Oh God, send the light was the prayer of those panting to breath

May the balm of Lebanon heal us, as promised of old was the cry of those stamped with J.[Jude]

In the beginning was darkness. God created light Why has the world turned its back on his light?.

Meanwhile, the American soldiers were working at top speed, making the houses watertight and habitable, before darkness and the blackout descended once more. It was no easy task, as they checked for gas leaks, fractured pipes and so on. Whatever stories have circulated to their detriment, we had nothing but praise for our allies. By the time twilight had fallen, most of the houses were liveable, and tea, coffee and biscuits were the order of the day. Auntie's Christmas cake was the highlight and much appreciated by those untiring workers. Where all the ingredients came from I can only guess. All I know is - it tasted tops! The lads handed out stockings, gum, cigarettes and chocolate; someone even produced a bottle of wine. They came back on Christmas Day, with a couple of ducks complete with feathers. No one asked how the birds were obtained, but my guess is, that some farmers were a few short that Christmas.

The house was temporarily watertight and liveable. Any further repairs would be carried out later by tradesmen. This took a while, owing to the labour shortage with most men in the forces.

Mother worked on Christmas Day, helping Mrs. Moss. Mrs. Woodland and her mother Mrs. Peaseland prepared our festive dinner. I say 'our,' because each year I was included in their family meal. Stuart came from Northampton with his mother and grandmother. He stayed for a week or so and we had great times together. There were visits to the cinema, where we saw such films as Gone with the Wind and For Whom the Bell Tolls, which were among our favourites. We also went to Manchester, viewing the bomb damage and visiting the shops. John Lewis was a must, when we visited the

Chapter 7 - Christmas 1944

city and a special restaurant for afternoon tea. Stuart found the best places for scrumptious cream cakes. The cost never seemed to bother him and I thought that it must be wonderful not to mind how much you spent.

My mother had to watch every penny, thinking that the Woodlands must be rich, but I found out much later that it was Mrs. Moss who supplied most of the cash. Stuart never went anywhere without his camera, having a great enthusiasm for trains. He knew the time tables, the departures and arrivals throughout England. We made countless short trips during the holidays, checking the schedules. This was great fun and sometimes the journeys were unpaid, as we slipped on to the platform without a ticket, and quietly boarded the coach. .

The Christmas dinners at Greenbank started around 12.30 with glasses of sherry for the adults, fruit juice or cider for the younger members, with plates of cheese with biscuits. Mrs. Peaseland's shortbread tasted out of this world and Mrs. Moss's table setting was a sight to behold. There were sparkling cut glass Waterford tumblers, wine and champagne glasses and place mats engraved with scenes of yesteryear on which the hot, Royal Doulton dinner plates, with their red, white and gold designs were placed. The service originally belonged to Mr. Moss's grandmother and was regarded as a very special heirloom. Mother dreaded washing up, when the Doulton service was in use, never forgiving herself if a breakage occurred luckly, this never happened. White linen napkins were enfolded in gold serviette rings, beside the silver cutlery. The centrepiece of the setting on the magnificent oak table, set for twelve, was a vase containing Christmas lilies, holly and mistletoe. Twelve high-backed chairs surrounded the table and on each one was tied a bow of green and red ribbon.

On a table, adjacent to Mr. Moss, stood a candle-heated hot plate which kept the poultry warm. This was usually a large chicken or a plump duck. Geese and turkeys were unobtainable in wartime, though some were sold on the black market. George Moss gave the blessing, and we diners prepared to enjoy the tasty soup prepared by Mrs. Peaseland from giblets and duck livers, when duck was on the menu. There were many contributors to the feast. Fresh, home-made bread came from Stuart's mother and a choice of home grown vegetables supplied by Barber from their well-stocked garden.

Waiting to be served in the warmed tureen was the duck in orange sauce, carved with love and tenderness by Mr. Moss. Each person received a generous portion of duck along with chestnut bread stuffing.

The taste still lingers in my mouth! And there was cranberry jelly and pickled walnuts. Grown in an area near the well-stocked orchard were luscious pears, apples, damsons and cherries and chestnuts, which matured in Greenbank's garden. To the complete meal, there was a rich, dark plum pudding, which was served with a brandy sauce, followed by tea or coffee. Fun time arrived. Upon our heads were coloured paper hats. Then came the time for pulling the crackers. Now that the meal was finished. A glass of port was on the menu, a bottle of vintage port being fetched from the cellar beneath the house. We would all read out the riddle enclose in the cracker, and display the trinkets, which seemed to fly everywhere after the tug of war between the people seated next to each other.

The highlight of Christmas Day was listening to the King's speech, bringing hope and comfort to his subjects. As 3pm approached, wine glasses were filled and as soon as the National Anthem began over the radio, everyone stood as we raised our glasses and uttered 'God save the King'. It was a very solemn moment with Mother and Mrs. Woodland shedding a silent tear, perhaps remembering past sadness and lost ones during the 1914-18 war.

Still impressed on my mind is the dining room with its long chiffoniere on which rested various silver bowls, plates and bric a brac. A chaise longue covered in red velvet, and, over part of the polished floor, a Wilton carpet in rather dull colours, but well preserved. Nearby, was a Lipp piano once played by Mr. Moss's long deceased sister, and several watercolour paintings by various artists hung on the wall near the entrance to the room. Over the fireplace were two oil paintings, one of an impressive gentleman in his forties. Benevolence shone from his kindly face. Indeed, this was a kindly man and his son George showed the same tendency; he never uttered an unkind word about anyone. Next to the portrait was another oil painting of George's mother, with her auburn hair and dressed in a long flowing cream dress. Diamonds and sapphires entwined a heart shaped locket, which sparkled around her delicate throat. A wistful smile caused one to surmise her innermost thoughts. Perhaps she was remembering a romantic encounter?

Chapter 7 - Christmas 1944

The artist had captured the gentle waving of a brightly decorated Japanese fan, perhaps a gift from an admirer; this gentle lady surely captured the hearts of many suitors. She held a red rose, which had perhaps been given to her by the artist, who, it was said, was in love with her. She was in her early twenties and a union with the artist did not take place.

The delicate smell of lavender polish permeated the house and my memories of the happy times spent at Greenbank will be imprinted on my mind forever.

Greenbank was sold by Mrs. Moss after the war when her husband passed away. The house became a private school and Mrs. Moss retired to Wales. A chapter was ended.

Does the warm atmosphere still prevail? Is the orchard, laden with fruit trees still there to provide the luscious pears that I sampled during school holidays? Is there hay in the stables? Has the smell of horse manure long since gone, to be replaced by the chalky odours of the classroom? Do the spirits of the past mingle with those of the children? Could they sense the warmth that was present in those who had lived, loved and worked behind those ivy covered walls? I hope so. Because those ghosts of yesteryear will remain with me ,till my last breath leaves my body.

At some moment, during that last Christmas day spent at Greenbank, my thoughts drifted to Guernsey. I wondered what sort of Christmas they were having. The Islanders would have had a very different experience under German rule. They would have had to make do with substitutes. Sugar beet would have been boiled and the juices pressed, collected and boiled again, until they formed a light treacle to be used as a sweetener in place of sugar which was virtually non-existent. I heard about dried blackberry leaves, green pea pods, camellia leaves, lime blossom, carrots and parsley shredded and baked for tea. Acorns, parsnips, lupin seeds, wheat, barley and beans roasted and ground for coffee. Potato- skins baked so that nothing was wasted, becoming the runners-up to today's wedges. Sea water was evaporated to obtain salt, and potato flour was mixed with ordinary flour for making bread and puddings. Carrageen Moss, an edible seaweed was dried and bleached to make jellies. But many articles could be bought on the black market at a price and the bartering of goods became popular. In spite of the shortages, the islanders banded together, helping each other. Parties had to finish before curfew to allow friends or relatives to get home.

Of course, there were a few who collaborated with the Germans. In the course of the occupation 800 babies were born. The girls earned the title of Jerry Bags, which was a rather sordid description, and it remained with them for many years after the hostilities had ceased. The occupation forces included many handsome German soldiers, and, nature being what it is, love knew no bounds. For those girls who fell in love, it was strong enough for them to leave the island to marry, when peace arrived. Some went to Germany, others stayed in England and a few went to Australia and New Zealand, leaving the horrors of war behind them, making a fresh start.

As for those who banded with the foe and informed on the islanders, they received their just reward. After the liberation the collaborators earned the full wrath of the loyal islanders. Before they could escape, they were made an example of with their hair shaved off for all to see.

When Mother received the 25-word message through the Red Cross some time after Christmas, it simply read – "A good Christmas spent with Jack and Doris. Health OK. Getting used to new menu. Our visitors feeling the pinch. Love to all, Charlie." Jack and Doris were Aunt Alice's son and daughter-in-law. Feeling the pinch referred to the food shortage under the Germans. When such messages were received, people exchanged notes, hoping to find hidden information which might have bypassed the censor's red pen. The war affected many relationships, both in England and on the Isles.

Some had no wish to return to the confined lifestyle of the islands after experiencing the wider spaces of the land that gave them refuge. Many young people found partners; married and set up home in their adopted country, while still retaining the pride of their island birth and returning to visit relatives over the years.

Others, on the Isles, whose freedom had been suppressed for five claustrophobic years, felt the need to leave the shores to widen their horizons. Changes in the education system gave students the chance to travel overseas to enter Universities or training colleges. Before the war

Chapter 7 - Christmas 1944

this opportunity was only granted to a privileged few. In due course, the Islands became a refuge as an off-shore investment location for the wealthy, bringing in new residents and thus reducing inter-marriage.

In the meantime there was a war to be won. There was no television to cover the world news. People relied on the wireless or newspapers to tell them what was going on. In cinemas, there were newsreels, which usually chose to show the horror of the bombing of enemy cities or the fighting actions of our soldiers on land or sea, or the capture of prisoners. On the other side of the coin were the 'stars' who went overseas to entertain the troops, or Winston Churchill touring our bombed cities, giving the V sign while assuring everyone that we would win. A new country would be built from the chaos of the ashes. And we saw the King and Queen visiting those who had lost everything and going to hospitals to give comfort to injured patients. They stayed in London in spite of Buckingham Place receiving bomb damage.

The only updated news of the Channel Isles came from a few brave men, who had managed to escape through the mines, as they made their dangerous way to England. Those men usually had a knowledge of the sea and its dangers, but some were recaptured and imprisoned. Because of the likelihood of fishermen escaping, none were allowed to go beyond one and a half miles from shore without a German escort. They had to leave one hour after sunrise and return an hour before sunset, and they were forbidden to leave in fog or rain. An uncle of my future wife, Edward Wilson, was shot at, while he was fishing. The Germans thought he was trying to escape. As a result of the shooting the boat capsized and he was drowned, leaving wife and children to greave . Another of the tragedies of war.

My future wife's family had decided to stay in Guernsey, and they lived at Thebes in the parish of St. Peter Port. They decided to face whatever might befall the islanders. Cecil Langlois' parents lived with them and had no wish to travel to set up a new home at their advanced age. Also, the Langlois' younger daughter Delma had just come out of hospital after a serious bout of scarlet fever, which nearly cost her her life. Like many others, Cecil became very alarmed, when, on the 28th of June, 1940, the German reconnaissance planes bombed and machine-gunned the town and harbour of St. Peter Port in Guernsey and St. Hellier, killing forty-four people. Unfortunately, the

British Government did not immediately inform the German Government that the islands had been demilitarised. Apparently, they were afraid that the withdrawal of the British army could provide them with the opportunity to invade the isles. That wrong thinking cost forty-four lives.

The Langlois, like many others, had had second thoughts about leaving, but since the last boat had gone, it became too late to depart. And so they were forced to spend five indelible years under the heels of their enemy.

The Langlois family group consisted of Mr. and Mrs. Henry and Bessie Langlois Senior, and also Mr. Mrs Cecil and Linda Langlois, along with their daughters Mildred and Delma. Granny Blestel, who was on holiday in Alderney at the time of the invasion left, with her daughter Alice and her family. They lived on a farm at Blunts Court outside Reading and stayed there until the end of the war.

A Channel Islands Refugee Committee was set up in London and within a few months twenty thousand pounds had been raised to assist those in need. The Channel Islands Monthly Review was published by the Stockport and District Channel Islands Society, which maintained a link between the refugees. Meetings were held in Stockport once a month, where people were able to enjoy each other's fellowship. Also, once a year, a big Channel Islands Rally was held at Belle Vue in Manchester, which brought everyone together to meet relatives and friends and to exchange news. The Stockport Branch was under the leadership of Messrs. Norman, Renier, Vidamour and Breslford, giving help to those in need of assistance, with the conjunction of the Red Cross. Donations of clothing were especially important and Mr. Norman was in charge of their distribution. Various fund raising groups sent money to support the Red Cross, which did such a tremendous job in both war and peace. So out of the Shadows the light shone for those in need,

Chapter 8

Sarnia Cherie

The house in Oakfield Road backed on to 23 Garners Lane, the home of a wizard who became my boyhood hero. In that enchanted house lived Mr. and Mrs. Norman Hazeldene, who, for professional reasons, became known as Mr. and Mrs. Norman. They came into my life, when I was twelve years old. I was sitting in the garden recovering from an illness which the doctors first diagnosed as being glandular fever, but which turned out to be nothing more than my having overgrown my strength, according to another doctor.

Suddenly a face appeared over the top of the back fence. It belonged to a man in his late fifties. His features resembled those of Sherlock Holmes, as portrayed by Basil Rathbone in the 1940's films, complete with pipe. He spoke in a gentle but manly voice. "My name is Norman," he stated. "I've seen you several times in the garden and I thought it was about time I introduced myself, so here I am. I gather your name is Bernard and you read quite a lot. You may like to visit my workshop?" He pointed a finger at an upstairs window of his typical brick house. "You might like to borrow some books?" Then, puffing his well-used pipe, which let out a wisp of not unpleasant smoke, he departed, saying - "Come and visit any time."

At that moment I did not know what exciting times lay ahead of me in that magical room at number 23 Garners Lane. I accepted the invitation the next day and made my way to the Normans, wondering what the lady of the house would be like. I had caught a brief glimpse of this grey-haired lady, as she gathered flowers in their garden, but no conversation had taken place. A stone pathway bordered by flowers led to a lightly grained front door into which were inserted a polished brass letter box, an ornate brass knocker and a brass bell push. When the bell was pressed, a welcome sound echoed to the visitor. I was about to ring the bell, when the door opened, and, as if by magic, the wizard appeared. Seeing the look of surprise on my face he smiled and said - "Welcome. Please come in. You caught me just as I was off to post a letter, hence the timely opening of the front door."

I entered the house in which a large hallway branched off with two doors, one leading to the dining room and the other to the sitting room in which Mrs. Norman sat on a blue velvet covered couch. She was cuddling a baby, which turned out to be a doll. With the introductions over Mrs. Norman spoke in a kindly voice.

"This is my little baby girl. She's very good and never cries. Come and say hello to Bernard." Then, she turned to me. "Would you like to hold her?" she asked. The doll was dressed in a long, white gown embroidered with pink and blue forget-me-nots. Speaking with a hint of sadness, Mrs. Norman went on – "Much to our disappointment we were unable to have children. We adopted this little mite, which brought us much happiness." Seeing a somewhat puzzled look on my face she asked - "Do you understand, Bernard, what adoption is?" Without waiting for an answer from me she continued - "It's taking an unwanted child and giving it the kind of love you would have given it, if you had given it birth yourself. This poor child had no one; goodness knows where she would have ended up. Adoption was the answer." She drew the 'child' closer to her breast. "I've become her real mother, loving her as much as if I had carried her in my womb. I give her the love that was denied her. That is what counts. We chose her and that is why she is special. Perhaps, you would like to nurse her? "Not waiting for my answer, she passed the doll to me. "See, Norman," she said, turning to her husband." At this first meeting," she said enthusiastically. "She is

Chapter 8 - Sarnia Cherie

smiling!" I wondered if Mrs. Norman, might not have been normal, but this thought left me as time went on.

Once again in my life the word adoption, which I had tried to wipe from my memory, came to my ears. But somehow, the way Mrs. Norman spoke about it made the dreaded word less painful. "Yes, it's love that counts," she said, and took the doll from my arms. "Time for a nappy change and Norman, Bernard might like a glass of homemade ginger beer." Norman departed and returned with three glasses of what turned out to be delicious ginger beer, and shortbread. "Enough chat from me. Take Bernard to your workroom, Norman," she said finally.

We left the warm comfort, of the sitting room and climbed the stairs. The door on the first floor opened to the room I had been longing to see. Norman stood aside, as I entered the medium-sized room which may once have been a bedroom. Once inside, my eyes spotted a work bench, paint spotted and gnarled over many years by chisels and saws. This was the bench on which Norman painted film posters, a job he had acquired after working as a sign writer. I soon found out that Norman was a man of many parts.

On the far end of the bench was a model railway, complete with engine and carriages just waiting for an enthusiast to throw the switch that would send it on its journey to Never Never Land. There were shelves on which were placed multicoloured articles of all shapes and sizes, made by Norman to be used or sold to illusionists or conjurers. Hanging halfway above the work bench was a silver screen, a part of Norman's film making. Poster paint and brushes neatly lined shelves on the walls, together with tools of all descriptions. The smell of oil paint lingered in the room. These were just a few of the things I observed, when I was first introduced to what to me was a boyhood wonderland. I spent many hours learning the tricks that magicians use on stage and helped to make some of the apparatus that Norman produced for illusionists and conjurors. In those far-off days I watched films he had made with his cine camera. These included animated train journeys, family outings, where the adopted doll daughter of Mrs. Norma, came to life on the screen. Walking, talking and crying with arms outstretched as if to be taken by its mother. To see the baby live on screen gave great joy to Mrs. Norman.

Norman taught me how to edit film on his home made machine, and talked to me about his wife's fantasy regarding the way in which the doll helped her to overcome her inability to have a child. She was perfectly normal in every other way. Playing the part of mother to her adopted daughter helped her to escape from the shadow of barrenness and focussed her to the light and life. Norman, through his love for his wife, willingly played the role of father.

I visited the Normans after the war, when they were in the autumn of their lives. The baby doll was still being loved by Mrs. Norman with the same loving care, and she was still the sweet, kind and warm person I remembered during the time I spent in their companyr. I was never told why they did not adopt a child and did not pursue the reasons.

Norman's books on all subjects were a joy to behold. H.G. Wells, Jules Verne and science fiction writers were added to my reading. I watched brush strokes   being yielded to form bold lettering heralding the sagas of Hollywood. Gone with the Wind, Now Voyager, Rebecca, My Sister Eileen, Intermezzo, Destry Rides Again. Sometimes there were caricatures of the stars, like Bette Davis, Clark Gable, Vivien Leigh, Errol Flynn and so on. They all succumbed to the curves of Norman's brush. The posters took up several hours of his time, so, when it was OK for me to visit, he devised a traffic sign on cardboard. A red circle and he was working, yellow, he would be free in one hour, and green meant that he was free.

As you may guess, I eagerly awaited the green circle, never quite knowing what lay in store. But you can bet your life that there would always be something interesting.There was never a dull moment. One day, Norman announced my enrolment into the Kaffra Club, a secret society for magicians. This was a great honour and enabled me to assist THE GREAT NORMAN ,as he was billed in stage shows. The golden rule of the club was never, and I say NEVER divulge secrets of the magicians to anyone. We would don colourful eastern garb, complete with turbans and an ornate jewel as the centrepiece of the head-dress. Oh, how I loved the smell of

Chapter 8 - Sarnia Cherie

the grease paint, as it was applied to give us an eastern appearance. With rings on our fingers, minus bells on our toes, magnificent ear rings and a nanny goat beard, we had the complete Ali Baba look. He would not have forbidden us to enter his Palace. The strains of eastern music herald our entrance from then on, for a short period, we were in the land of fantasy.

The Whoops, Ahs and applause sent the adrenalin tingling through my veins. Norman took it all in his stride. The more often we appeared on the stage the incentives grew stronger for me to devote myself to the stage full time, studying drama. But a change of events ordained otherwise, as we shall see later.

The model trains were set up to give me hours of fun. Norman would put a station master's hat on his head and a whistle on a piece of string around his neck. A 'travelling we will go!' Norman was very intent on his job, puffing away on his pipe. Those were the days before smokers were ostracised. The rail points diverted the trains to allow others to pass safely. My job in this pastime was to make sure that the signals were correct avoiding crashes. A simple pleasure but great fun. In those far-off days, children had to create their own games. The age of the computer was just a myth before becoming a must; a very costly must in nearly every home. Though parts of my childhood were spent in shadow, this was a time when shadows fell away.

When the war ended in 1945, our wireless sets were tuned to hear Churchill speaking to the nation. When we heard his wonderful words, we realised that our own dear Channel Islands would be liberated. Yes, this was true. Winston had said so, dispelling our disbelief that we would never return. In the sitting room at No.32 there were tears of joy. But the war with Japan was not yet over and Japanese were yet to suffer terribly through the bombings of Hiroshima and Nagasaki.

On VE Day crowds gathered outside all the Town Halls in the kingdom to sing and dance. Church bells that had remained silent only to be heard if the country was invaded, now rang out a joyous peal. Victory is ours!

Youngsters let off fire crackers and beacon fires were lit on the highest hills in the Realm or on the beaches. And there were street parties for everyone.

Bernard Blestel

The whole country was ablaze with light and excitement. The Rat –tat –tat of guns, the screech of bombs silent. There would be Blue Birds over the White Cliffs of Dover never to be scattered in war again. England held the key of peace to lock out the horrors of war. What has happened to that key?

But, in the midst of it all, were the memories of those who had lost loved ones, both on the battlefield and on the home front. Oh, what joy now that peace had come and tyranny had been subdued. No more wars, said the politicians. How wrong could they be.

We looked forward to returning to Guernsey. Till we received normal correspondence, we could only surmise what was happening on the Islands. Operation Nest Egg was the name given, under which Task Force 135 carried out the liberation of the Channel Islands. By the beginning of May 1945 the German army had been completely defeated in Europe. Brigadier Snow set sail aboard the destroyer HMS Bulldog from Plymouth, in company with HMS Beagle.

The war was over, all but the unconditional surrender of Vice Admiral Huffmeier in Guernsey and Major General Wolfe in Jersey. Without knowing what changes might be met, many parents, who had stayed under German rule, had to forge new relationships with their returning children, linking the new present with those five lost years. Some people found this very difficult. There were sad cases, when, after the liberation, parents knew for the first time that their child had died either through illness or accident - or bombing.

When the time came for me to return to Guernsey, I left the Normans and Mr. Mrs. Moss with a sense of sadness, not sure if I would ever see them again. Mr. and Mrs. Norman and Mr. and Mrs. Moss, I thank you for allowing me into your homes arid hearts. You gave me love and understanding at a time, when I needed understanding and security during a trying period in my life between childhood and puberty. Growing up when I did, certainly had its problems for me.

Children today undergo more pressure. Drugs and Sex, are bombarded at them through the media. Youngsters are approached at school, where they are offered drugs as a means of bringing an exciting lifestyle into lives

Chapter 8 - *Sarnia Cherie*

that are stressed out with pressures at home, school and university. These evil people acquire untold wealth, regardless of the misery caused to lives caught up in their web of deceit. As children, we created our own fun, enjoying games of a simple nature. The age of the computer or play stations was yet to dawn and TV was a dream of the future. John Logie Baird had not yet scanned any image on his workshop TV screen. Visits to the Moon or Mars were only carried out in stories inspired by H.G. Wells and such writers.

Time came for me to leave school, much to the relief of my Headmaster. So, at the age of fourteen I closed my desk for the last time, with a sense of gladness at all the knowledge I needed to equip me for life. Which just shows how wrong one can be.

So, bidding farewell to my school friends and Mary Howarth, I packed my humble belongings and went to live in Stockport. My great aim in life was to become an actor, though, of course, this does not happen overnight. In the meantime, before my name dazzled the public in lights, a job had to be found. Just how I came to work for Arundel Coulthards, a large textile engineering companyescapes me. The firm produced special machines for spinning cotton. I became an apprentice engineer and used my clothing coupons to equip me with a pair of overalls. With these on I felt that I was on the threshold of manhood! Once again - how wrong can you be?

Entering the workforce was certainly an eye opener for a somewhat naive fourteen-year-old. Every day, except for Sunday, at six in the morning, after a hurried breakfast I was alighting the bus at Davenport Station. My destination was Mersey Square. The journey to Arundel's took me under a viaduct over which noisy, rumbling steam trains commuted between the north and south of England. The area was built up with factories and with the streets half lit, due to the blackout I was presented with a lonely, gloomy and sinister journey. Travel became somewhat frightening, for I had heard that a razor slasher lurked under the viaduct. His victims bore scars for life, and, needless to say, I ran all the way to the factory. I arrived, breathless with fear that I would fall victim to this presumptuous murderer.

Bernard Blestel

On my first day I was introduced to the foreman of the drilling department, a Mr. Harry Docker. He was a quiet man but given to using swear words, if his instructions were ignored. The poor man walked with the aid of sticks. It was assumed that this was due to his arthritis, and, though lame, he never spoke of his affliction. One of the inmates of the room was Bow Leg Fred, whose language was foul. He always flourished the words fuck, cunt and Jesus Christ. I could not believe my ears at first, because these little jewels of speech had been banned from my childhood vocabulary with severe punishment from my parents, if any were used. Here I was, hearing these words used in everyday conversation by adults..

Then there was Arnold, a sandy-haired apprentice, called a fucking cunt by Fred for no apparent reason. Poor Arnold was not one of the brightest. The senior fitter in our room was Herbert, who had been exempted from the services because of his essential work at Arundel's. Though he was married, he was given the term Rake in the workplace; known to be ready to fuck anyone, which he did with expertise or so they !? Randy women in the factory, whose husbands were away fighting for King and Country, were only too pleased to accommodate what Herbert had to offer. All's fair in love and war?

Another apprentice, Eric, was a sixteen-year-old being cannily taught the ways of life and women by Herbert, beginning to turn him into a clone, a second Herbert. My special friend Leslie Phipps worked in the fitters and turners department. We became real pals and met each morning in Mersey Square. We started walking under the viaduct, but, whenever our nerve left us, we broke into a trot. Early one morning we spotted someone crouched behind half a brick wall. He wore a duffle coat and the hood covered most of his head. The only part that was visible was wispy hair, which lay over a blood-shot eye as he watched us. Leslie nudged me, which was a signal to scarper, no time to linger. I immediately imagined feeling my warm blood escaping from a wound that was so deep, that even my mother would find it difficult to recognise me as her mutilated son. Yes, I thought. This must be the Razor Slasher, ready to strike his victim whose destination could only be the undertaker's cold slab. A barber's cut-throat razor sharpened for the occasion would be secreted in the folds of his shabby, torn black coat!

Chapter 8 - Sarnia Cherie

Gathering momentum we turned to see if he was following us. Then, Leslie's fear turned to laughter. "He's having a piss," he said, grinning from ear to ear. But he had certainly put the fear of God into us. Thankfully, we never did encounter the slasher, but we remained vigilant, always wondering when he would loom before us.

The new apprentices were subjected to initiation into factory life. This was generally accepted, even though it was sometimes foolish. On his first day he might be sent to the main store on many occasions to fetch glass nails, a rubber or glass hammer, a pennyworth of steam in a jug, a noiseless bell. Or he might be sent to the Fitters and Turners section to ask Nellie - who was known for her liberal sexual favours -:"Please Nellie, Bert has sent me for a long screw."

To which Nellie would reply - "Get out you dirty little bugger or I'll clip your ear hole and kick Bert's arse if he sends you down here again!"

The poor lad would keep well out of Nellie's way just in case she carried out her threat. Another form of initiation was being Greased. A thick grease was applied to various parts of the newcomer's body with the onlookers yelling 'grease his balls!,' which sent fear into the victim, as he expected he would be ruined for life. On another occasion he would be sent to a local chemist to ask the female assistant for a stamp to put on a French letter. Or the poor lad would be petrified, when he was placed inside a large wooden box with the lid closed. "Fetch the petrol!" was yelled by one of the perpetrators, after which water was poured over the box. By this time the poor boy inside the box was shaking in fear. An acetylene torch produced a flame and rolled-up cellophane paper, ruffled in the hand, simulated the sound of burning timber. "Okay," shouted the ringleader of this foolish 'prank'. "I reckon he's baked by now."

After his release the apprentice was shaken, but he was still able to laugh. They parted as friends and it was all taken as good fun. No boy complained to his parents, for this was the way of things in the factories and other workplaces, when I started my trade. Nowadays, the perpetrators would go before a court on an assault charge. Such is progress.

In some ways I was sorry to leave Coulthards and Leslie, but the excitement of returning to Guernsey compensated for the farewells. Yet, at the back of my mind I still wondered whether my father had learnt to control his temper. Unfortunately, No.

In August 1945 our belongings were packed up to leave and Aunt returned the key of 32 Oakfield Road. Mrs. Moss extracted a promise from my mother, that, if she were not happy in Guernsey, she would be more than welcome at Greenbank. After five long years we said goodbye to neighbours and friends, and, as the taxi passed Garners Lane, I fancied that I saw my magical friend in his doorway. Tears welled in my eyes. Shall we ever meet again?

The hustle and bustle at Stockport Station caused my Aunt to worry that seats might not be available, that we would be stranded with no home to return to. A kindly porter, seeing her distress, came to the rescue. He informed her that there was no need to worry. That there were plenty of seats available in the end compartment. Once seated Aunt relaxed and began to enjoy the journey to Weymouth; it was quite unlike that of 1940. There were no diversions or stopping to be handed refreshments by generous folk and no wondering which country would accept us. Like the Hebrews of old, we were returning to our Promised Land.

On and on we went, the clatter of the wheels creating an abstract rhapsody, the song heard only by those ears attuned to their rhythm. Singing, without pausing for breath - here I come, here I come, here I come, clickety click, interspersed with short blasts of the whistle. The hissing of steam added to the fantasy of the music.

Glancing through the not too clean windows ,we caught sight of the homes bought with hard-earned savings, and so often destroyed by one who thought he could destroy the English spirit, thus claiming their land. He should have heeded Shakespeare's words, when he said - 'This land will never lie under the foot of a conqueror'.

At last, the smell of the sea air brought a rush of eager people clambering to the windows. Five long years had passed before they had caught a glimpse of the sea, the English Channel, housing their homeland. Excitement,

Chapter 8 - Sarnia Cherie

mixed with tears, portrayed the emotions on that day in August, 1945. Some were returning with uncertain feelings, leaving friends made over the years and secure jobs, which had provided the necessities of life for their families during the exile. The fear of unemployment on a war-torn island lingered in the mind; no one had received a guarantee that work would be found. The Islands had changed over those five years and information regarding the situation had not been forthcoming.

No luxury liner awaited us. Instead it was the Hazelmere, a cargo ship that had joined forces with the hundreds of little ships at the miracle of Dunkirk--- - snatching the remains of a brave army, whose spirit was never daunted. They were ready to fight again to liberate those, who had failed in their battles to suppress the war lord.

Once past the officials, we were allowed to board, pushing our way up the gangway with cases holding precious belongings, clutched tightly, taking no chance that they might be lost. The islanders did not want a repetition of 1940, when they had to leave all their worldly possessions behind, only to be claimed by alien hands.

There was anticipation combined with uncertainty. Many had left husbands to endure the rigors of occupation. Could five years of oblivion in marriage be rescued? Or would the partner say that he had found someone else? 'Sorry, those five years were just too long to be apart, I never knew if you would return, or, perhaps ,you too would find somebody.' In many cases that is what happened. Some women came back to confronted their husband with a new baby or a young child. Some were welcomed by their husbands, Others ended in divorce.

The men, who stayed, also confronted wives, regarding relationships. Five years is a long time without the companionship of a loving wife or husband. So who can judge,unless you have experienced the situation?.

The day we left Weymouth was dull and dismal. The ship's rails were occupied by those wishing to catch a final glimpse of their adoptive land. My own feelings, as the gallant little ship sailed into the English Channel, coincided with the rolling of the ship. One minute I wanted to stay, at the next swaying I thought that we had made the right decision in returning to Guernsey. To come back held a certain thrill for me. Would there still be German prisoners on the island?---thus giving me the chance to see the enemy, who had changed the whole course of our lives. Are they the cruel race as portrayed by the media? Will they look any different from our own soldiers? Or will they be just like our servicemen with their one thought being able to return home to their loved ones? Unfortunately, the bombing did not only kill the armed services but also civilians on both sides, each enduring pain and grief.

On we sailed through the turbulent sea, and many on board were sick. It's a well-known fact that the English Channel can at times upset the strongest of stomachs.

As we passed the Casquets, we knew that our exodus was nearly over. Tears of joy welled in our eyes at the sight of Castle Cornet and a ripple of song echoed around the ship. Our National Anthem Sarnia Cherie was not rendered so passionately as on that return journey. It will remain in my heart forever.

> "Sarnia dear Homeland, gem of the sea
> Island of beauty, my heart longs for thee
> Thy voice calls me ever
> In waking or sleep
> Till my soul cries with anguish
> My eyes ache to weep
> In fancy to see thee again as of yore
> The verdant clad hills
> And thy wave beaten shore
> Thy rock sheltered bays
> Ah, of all thou art best
> I'm returning to greet thee
> Dear island of rest
> Sarnia Cherie, gem of the sea
> Home of my childhood, my heart longs for thee
> Thy voice calls me ever
> Forget thee I'll never
> Island of beauty, Sarnia Cherie

Chapter 8 - Sarnia Cherie

>I left thee in anger, I knew not your worth
>Journeyed afar to the ends of the earth
>Was told of far countries, the heav'n of the bold
>Where the soil gave up diamonds, silver and gold
>The sun always shone
>And the race took no part
>But thy cry always reached me
>The pain wrenched my heart
>So I'm coming home
>Thou of all art the best
>Returning to greet thee, dear island of rest
>Sarnia Cherie, gem of the sea
>Home of my childhood
>My heart longs for thee
>Thy voice calls me ever
>Forget thee I'll never
>Island of beauty, Sarnia Cherie

As the Hazelmere sailed through the Pier Heads, crowds gathered on the jetty to welcome us back. They waved and cheered as the words reached their ears. "I'm coming home; thou of all art the best!" Oh, how the waiting people cheered. The rain did not cloud the sunshine in our hearts. No shadows today, as we embraced our loved ones, on that cold wet jetty on that day in August, 1945. Home once again to the island I remembered as home in childhood.

My eye glanced over the crowd to the background, way up to the left of Castle Cornet. The Guernsey cliffs were always a paradise of wild flowers at certain times of the year. Fragrant primroses and the bluest of bluebells. As the season progressed there were foxgloves, sweet honeysuckle and a mixture of wild flowers along the borders of the paths which brought a sense of calm, while the perfume drifting to your nostrils intoxicated you with the beauty of this land. Catching a glimpse of a sunset, I beheld the blue sky and white clouds intermingling reds, pinks and yellows into pure gold rays---- from a creation before time----placed in the universe by the Creator, who made man in His own image. Changing the blue of the sea to a deep amethyst, the foam of the seashore was touched by gold, as it gently beats against the shore.

It was so firmly planted in my memory from a childhood raped by war and superimposed by a picture of smoke bellowing from factory chimneys. No sea, no cliffs. The barrenness of windblown moors, their harshness only mellowed by the kindhearted folk with strange accents. Sheep and cows were so different in colour from the golden breed of the Isles. Munching or chewing the coarse grass to produce milk or beef, seeking shelter from inclement weather beneath low walls, built by those who first claimed the land. Huddled together for survival, till the sun shone again to warm chilled bodies. No human contact, only hearing the farmer's voice at milking time or when they were transported to a place which would end their bleak existence.

I was returning to recapture a long lost mirage. Yes, a mirage. That is what it had become over five long years. Years when you came to hate your enemy and to despise him. Only to find, when the guns and bombs had ceased to pour out death, that they too were human, sharing the same emotions and programmed to hate the opposing side. Will the peace I had known return? I left as a child, returning as a teenager. Will the gap be too wide to cement relationships?

Lost in time, as I was looking at the mass of people below, my thoughts were broken, for there, in the throng of faces, was my father. Cousin Jack stood next to his friend Bill Garland (cousin of the famous actor Roy Dotrice), who acted as chauffeur, transporting us to 14 Burnt Lane. Memories of another return years ago from our father's temper. Had he learnt control or will he be just the same?

It did not take long before we found that nothing had changed. Doris prepared a much needed breakfast. Meeting her for the first time one is reminded that there are some people we like at first introduction, and Doris was such a person. Doris and Jack enjoyed a good marriage. Later, after finding a house near my Aunt they were blessed with a daughter, Maureen.

The house looked as spic and span as when I had last visited Burnt Lane. Aunt Alice was fortunate to have had Doris and Jack living there during

Chapter 8 - Sarnia Cherie

the occupation. So many islanders lost all their furniture. A thousand and one thoughts went through my mind as I travelled to Aunt's house. Will I adjust once again to island life? The roads were so narrow after England and even the houses were Lilliputian. People I knew would have changed; will they accept me? These proved to be negative shadows. The islanders were only too eager to hear of our exploits, such as the bombing etc and then there was the uncertainty of finding employment, which later proved to be unfounded. The biggest factor of all was my father's temperament, his sudden outbursts. As a child I had remained silent. Now that I was older would I be able to cope and to hold my tongue, avoiding his aggravation? Voicing an opinion could lead to an unholy row. Could we forge a relationship that would bring companionship and love? Did I want harmony with a man who I thought was unworthy of my mother's love? Which of us is at fault, was it him or me? That gap between us was never bridged.

On the jetty he embraced me, but my arms folded around him, lacked the warmth a son should have for his father. So sad. We had had a short reunion in Reading soon after the end of the war, when he was still allowed to travel to see his elderly mother and sister Alice. Mother and I travelled down to Blount's Court to save his coming up to Stockport. He greeted his wife as if she had been away for a day shoppings, when we returned after five long years. He was incapable of showing or offering love to those nearest to him. Oh, the sadness of missing so much! Yet, underneath it all, I believe that he did care, and never understood why he was unable to show it. I loved him half heartedly, or so I thought. You give full love, and, if that's not there, then it's not love. There are no half measures. Perhaps I deluded myself that that was the reason we were never close. Yet, he took me in, fed, clothed and educated me, still I rejected him. Was it my fault, or his? It is too late to know the answer. In the background there was always the anticipation of trouble. One could see when his mood would change. What I did not foresee was meeting a young girl, who would alter the course of my life.

Guernsey saw many changes during those five years. A railway had been put down from the harbour to St. Sampson, which, in the process of being demolished, was scattered along the coast. Vast fortifications were erected by slave workers from all over the world. They were treated harshly by the Germans; given little food, footwear or clothing. Many died as they built those fortifications, and were buried in the concrete or in unmarked graves with no committal prayers.

The Germans who were left were still the enemy. When I first set eyes on them, how could it be any different? I had experienced the raining down of bombs on the towns and cities, bringing death to innocent people. But one day my attitude changed. One of the prisoners, who was helping to cut down barbed wire, glanced at me and gave me a sad smile, saying in broken English - "War is a terrible thing, a waste of life. It is the leaders who cause war. Both sides are to blame for the death and destruction, not the man in the street."

Yes, he was right. Oh, how we cheered, when the media gave an account of our victories in battle, how we destroyed German towns. We were no better. Then came the horrific atom bombs, causing life-long suffering to those who had not been killed and left to suffer the effects of radiation. . This was the price of glory, to obtain peace in our time. Where is the peace? Cannot man live in harmony? A sad smiling prisoner's family suffered the same nightmares. The foe and the victor were bonded by a smile and death. Prisoners, guarded by British soldiers, helped to clear the land mines on the beaches and cliffs. Some of the gun emplacements and towers remain to this day as grim reminders of that part of our history.

Near the end of the war, those islanders who had stayed were saved from starvation ,when Switzerland, a neutral country, sent the Vega, a ship under the flag of the Red Cross, which brought in food parcels. Imagine the feelings of those hungry people, when they received those cardboard boxes, which contained provisions enabling them to create various meals, at last. The gratitude they must have felt towards their saviours was overwhelming.

There was much chatter during that reunion breakfast. Our main questions concerned the islanders' survival during the occupation. Were they ill-treated? What made Cousin Jack join the island police? Was he forced to do this by the Jerries? A thousand and one questions passed between the little group around the table.

Chapter 8 - Sarnia Cherie

Time came for the three of us to leave Burnt Lane, and, thanking Doris for her hospitality, we departed for Mount Durand. The house was very much the same, but Mother said, out of Father's hearing, that it needed a good polish, reckoning that it had not seen a duster for five years. (A bit over the top I thought). If I had expected to find any of my books or toys, I was disappointed. I had also had a sailing ship in full sail, which I had sailed in the model yacht pond at Castle Cornet, a dream of a place for any youngster. The model boat alas, gone,. Father had sold them during the occupation, as toys were hard to get in the shops. I trust that the new owners had had as much joy in playing with them as I had. I searched for the precious book that Stan had given me so long ago in Southampton. It too had disappeared. Losing toys did not worry me as much as losing that book. You see, it was a link with Stan and the respite he had brought to Mother.

A few weeks later, Granny Blestel rejoined us. Everything seemed so different and quiet. There were new neighbours in houses that had been left empty by our old neighbours, who had fled in fear or others not yet returned. The Vernons found another house. We never renewed relationships as in the past. Time and space alter a lot of things. My schoolmate John Mallet, and I remained the best of pals for many years. He worked at the States Electricity Department with me after I found employment there. Schoolmates, Terry MacLean, Jim Taylor, Frank Robbilliard and Courtney Selous who married Molly Doyle, remained very dear friends to this day.

One of the features the islanders painted on walls everywhere were large V's for Victory for the Allies. The Germans countered this by inserting laurel wreaths beneath the V's to signify German victory.

Miss Steadman lost no time in calling to ask if I would return to Trinity Church to join the youth club, which was being reformed. And the Rev. Roy Jeremiah accepted the call to take on the appointment as vicar. He became a friend of the family, a few years later marrying me to the girl of my life, and when our daughter arrived, he gave us the honour of becoming her godfather.

In many ways it was good to be back. Though I missed the expanse of England, I slowly became accustomed to the island and living with my parents again, though I had no wish to become insular in thought or deed. One morning, as she wiped away the perspiration, which came from the hot steam issuing from the wash tub, which held the weekly wash, my mother asked me what work I wanted to do. As I told her that I wanted to go on the stage, she threw up her hands in horror. She informed me that the stage was only for 'common' people. I had no idea why she would say that - we were only working class. To please her, as we had not lived together as a family for five years, I turned to the next job which held my interest.

I would become an electrician. Fortunately, an interview with Mr. Fosebrook, one of the heads of the States Electricity Dept., secured me the job. And so I started a three-year apprenticeship. In my wildest dreams I could not have imagined the part I would play at the end of Mr. Fosebrook's life, some twenty years later.

I enjoyed working at the States Electricity Department, learning a trade, but my heart was still yearning to go on the stage. I fulfilled these desires by doing amateur productions at the Holy Trinity Drama Club. Miss Steadman asked me if I would become a Sunday School teacher. And so, with fear and trepidation I began teaching the Lord's work to a class of nine boys.

What some of them got up to in class was an education in itself. One of the boys brought two pet mice, which he hid under his shirt in the class. He released them in front of the girls, causing mayhem. Another brought in a hamster, which he insisted I should hold during the lesson. So, for the sake of peace and quiet, and because he might otherwise have sent the wretched animal over to the girls, I agreed and nursed it during the class. It was a special privilege to teach those children and I must have passed on something over the years, because some of my pupils went into the ministry and others became missionaries. One such boy was John Blanchard who became an international Christian author. John Elliston, who was not the best in class, became Dean of the island churches, a high honour. I must say that the boys were real tricks but lovable

Chapter 8 - Sarnia Cherie

Under the very able guidance of the Rev. Roy Jeremiah and his wife Lucy, the church congregation grew. Islanders, exiled during the war years, found their way back to their Parish Church. This was a time of thanksgiving for returning peace to the island. As I joined the activities of the church, I was destined to meet Mildred Bessie Langlois, the daughter of Cecil, who was the Verger at Holy Trinity. His wife, dear Linda, played an active part in the running of the church. She wielded a duster, and, complete with Mansion Polish, she attacked the dust of this Georgian church. Due to her efforts, on worship days a sparkling church greeted the congregation. At times, their daughter Delma who was five years younger than Mildred assisted with the chores.

Those post war years were happy times in my social life. The church played an important part then, and lasted all my life. But there were shadows yet to come. We moved from Mount Durand and my parents bought Exeleigh, a house in Gibauderie. Unfortunately, it was a half hour's walk from the church and Mildred's house, Thebes. (Love was in the air!) My mode of transport was a bicycle, which I purchased when I started work. This got me to the church and my place of work, and, more importantly, to Mildred's house.

Things were looking up. Father installed a bathroom, then, through my efforts in the trade, Exeleigh was converted from gas to electricity. At long last we now had all the modern conveniences, complete with telephone. Mother found employment with a Mrs. Chambers as a daily help and she, like Mrs. Moss thought the world of her.

The quarries did not reopen for some time after the war; then they closed again. Father found work in the building trade and never returned to the quarry, much to Mother's relief, as he often came home with some injury. He was no stranger to the building trade. In the middle of the 1930's the quarry was shut due to a slump in the stone trade. Record was the name of the firm for which he worked and they acquired the contract to build the Regal Cinema, which became the Odeon after the war. The Odeon was demolished a few years later, to become a car park. Such is progress.

Record also built a house at Jerbourge with Father's help. The house was built for a Mrs. Longhurst. In the lounge, through a large window there was a panoramic view of the sea, and another feature of this room was the blue ceiling, encrusted with seagulls in flight. Miniature lights twinkled as stars of heaven at night. It was a sight to behold and shows what money can do. There was also an oversized sideboard made from oak, which contained a drawer inside which contained a large assortment of toys for her much loved dog to amuse itself with, when, for example, she went shopping. The little darling gained a new object to chew or cherish every time it was left alone. Lucky dog. Canine life has its pleasures.

Life at the Electricity Department consisted mainly of rewiring houses to the British standard, as the Germans had converted the system to that which was used on the Continent.

New houses and other buildings replaced those that had been destroyed. Replacement greenhouses were put up, so that the growers could start to cultivate and export the famous Guernsey produce, like tomatoes, grapes and flowers. In competition with Holland and fearing that the Dutch would control the market, the States looked towards tourism to boost the island's economy. Hence, the State's Tourist Board which successfully encouraged visitors to come to the sunny Isles. Subsequently, the influx of tourists became Guernsey's main industry, a wise decision. As an off-shore island Guernsey also attracted the rich to overseas investment, turning the island into a tax haven. It also became a place where death duties could be avoided.

Even though revenue came to the island, there was a downside. The price of property rose and forced the States to bring in laws to protect the overflow of people wishing to live on Guernsey. There were two categories in the Open Market Law system. Outsiders could only purchase land iand houses,i f they intended to live there. These were listed up to a certain value, by a points system. If Islanders had lived overseas for more than seven years, they had to receive permission to reside once again in the land of their birth. They were unable to buy a Market house, unless they had a permit.Further to this,the States introduced a local Market law to ensure that the locals could purchase houses at a realistic price.

Chapter 8 - Sarnia Cherie

Trade Unions became more prominent in industries, helping to create a better living wage and standards for the working population. The winds of change were blowing in the direction of a once peaceful island, which for a thousand years had seen little change in its laws or government. Integration of the younger generation produced a mixed strain of islanders. Norman blood became mixed with inter-marriage to non islanders. The island patois was only spoken in the country parishes, and slowly the pre-war identity of Guernsey lurked in the background .

The island, as I knew it, slowly became conditioned to the overseas winds of change.

The Holy Trinity League of Youth reformed after the war and attracted some pre-war members to rejoin. I must say that some had passed the bloom of youth. Many young ones joined and among them was fifteen-year-old Mildred or Mill, a lovely girl with a beautiful smile and a great sense of humour. God had given her a sweet singing voice and so she joined the St. John,s church choir at an early age. Her voice never failed to stir emotions within me. Mildred had lessons from one of Guernsey's music directors and entertainers, Muriel Luckie, and further voice training with Miriam Blondel. She often sang solos at Trinity Church, which the family attended after the war, also in various choirs in Guernsey. Later, in Australia, she was invited to sing at weddings and joined the Eastbourne singers after which both Mildred and Delma became founder members of the Peninsula Singers.

Mildred always invited me to any parties at the Langlois. In those far off days, if one went out with any boy or girl, it was known as 'keeping company'. I wanted to keep company with Mill, so at the age of 15 teen I had fallen in love, and she was the only girl I ever wished to marry. To my great disappointment she turned me down, saying that she did not want a commitment at that stage of her life. She later admitted that she had wanted to say yes. When I later asked her why she had refused, she shook her head and said she didn't know. (Girls are funny.) True love finds a way, and, after a short period, when I showed some interest in other girls, Mill changed her mind and we started keeping company. How old-fashioned this sounds in these so-called enlightened times. So, at the grand old age of sixteen Cupid shot his arrow into my heart. It was love, it was love, so say the words of the song.

When you are in love at that age, you bask in the light that shines in and out of you. Can we ever recapture that moment when the arrow strikes, filling a desire to be in love with a partner in whom, at the time, you can see no wrong? Blinded by passion, or so the romantic novels say, I shall always remember the joy of our first kiss. On the way up Victoria Road, when passing the Methodist church,I saw lanten hanging from the arch of a wrought iron entrance gate . From its globe shone a light, which shone brighter than the sun and stars in Heaven. Oh wonderful love!

Turning the pages of yesteryear, I see a picture of that beaming rustic lantern in my mind's eye. I treasure the memory of that ever glowing light. It was the symbol of the reassurance of our love at that time. I am a romantic at heart.

Returning many years later, I found that the church had been sold and the purchaser had turned it into a furniture store. But the rustic lantern still hung there with pieces missing and no bulb to shine as it once did, neglected and unwanted. Standing and looking at this sad lantern I thought - there is a lesson to be learnt here. So many, like the lantern, shone out their love. Then, on the way, it dimmed and was neglected, simply because we did not take care of the precious love we had received. And, un-nurtured it died.

Luckily, we were blessed, because both of our parents approved of our relationship. A party was arranged for the engagement at the Trinity schoolroom. So, at the exciting age of eighteen Mildred received a diamond ring, sporting three small stones. They sparkled, like her eyes, when she opened the little box and saw the ring seated on its cushion. It cost me all my savings ,but was worth every penny, as I saw the look of joy on her face.

We celebrated the occasion by going to England and staying with friends Ivy and Fred Jenner, who lived at Greenford in Middlesex. This holiday put us to the test; whether or not to go the whole hog in love making. We resisted the temptation. I think it was more out of fear than moral obligation, for, in those days, having a baby before marriage was regarded as sinful, immoral. Only 'common' girls let themselves become pregnant. Of

Chapter 8 - Sarnia Cherie

course, the male did not share any of the blame. People spoke in whispers if a girl fell by the wayside. In most cases the child was adopted out. With my warped sense of humour I often passed on this fact to the young lads, who were in unmarried partnerships. Remember the muscle you have in the centre of your body, whether it be large or small, be careful where you put it, I would tell them. It could bring you a lifetime of happiness or sorrow. It always brought a smile to their faces and they assured me that they would remember my advice. I wonder whether they did, or if the pull of sex was too strong? Perhaps they thought me a crank?

Adoption. The word kept cropping up. Prior to our engagement my mother informed me that my natural mother had died just after I was born and that Lena and Charlie were my adoptive parents. Tears rolled down her cheeks, as she sobbed out the words.

"We both love you as if I had given birth to you myself," she said, hugging me tightly as if afraid to let me go. My tears mingled with hers, as she uttered the words. I remembered Mrs Norman speaking the same words, as she hugged her baby doll I was no doll this was for real.

"I love you both as a son. You are my real parents," I told them, stretching out my arms to include my father. In that embrace I detected tears in my father's eyes, and I cannot remember any other occasion when I saw them. Perhaps he cried in private.

The shadow that had engulfed me since birth was now behind me, as I fixed my eyes to the light. That word 'adopted' was now relegated to the memory box. Mother never knew the anguish I had experienced during my childhood, particularly whenever people made remarks like - 'Lena and Charles are not his real patents. He is adopted, because she is unable to have children. I suppose to adopt is better than not having a baby'.

All this was said as if 'adoption' was a dirty word, etching in my mind the painful question - to whom do I belong? Did the truth come too late now that I was on the threshold of marriage. Would I have to tell my future wife? The question was not fully answered, and meant that I had to pass through a few more shadows before knowing the answer.

My father reached into a sideboard and withdrew a beige coloured envelope, saying as he did so - "You'd better keep this in a safe place. You may need it, if you inherit any money from your real family." He handed me three A4 sheets of thick paper, neatly stapled together. My thoughts at that moment turned to my natural family, to the man who occasionally gave me sixpence and who became Uncle Charlie by respect, whose breath always smelt of alcohol and who patted my head with the remark -"He's tall far his age."

This was the person who signed me over in a lawyer's office, waving all claims on me---- a father whose blood ran in my veins and thought it fit to change the course of my life, paying the lawyer's fee and thus making the transition complete. I now belonged to someone else, or did I? Did the document I held in my hand have the power to bond me to a family, to be accepted as their child? Can I truly believe that the word 'adoption' as described in a dictionary - 'to receive the child of another and treat it as one's own, to select and adopt as one's own.' Is the exodus of that fearful word gone out of my life forever? Or will it raise its ugly head whenever my parentage is discussed. The words my father had spoken - 'your REAL family'. Real, real. The word stuck in my throat. Am I not his REAL son?

I never disclosed to my mother that I knew their secret from an early age. I held back in fear that it would upset her, giving her cause to think that she had failed by not conceiving, plus the fact that she had enough in coping with Father. On reflection, did I act stupidly in not disclosing my knowledge? It made no difference, I loved them, I had no other parents but them. In my child's mind I could only see unhappiness for them, if their secret was divulged, and this caused me to remain in the shadows. Could I now turn to the light, get on with my life and let the shadows fall behind? Was the stigma now finally laid to rest and could I truly believe that my mother is alive and that the person I call Dad is my real father? Do I belong to them and they to me, or have those unguarded remarks, uttered in my ignored presence long ago, forfeited my acceptance of being a member of their family? Will those childhood wounds heal? Only time will tell. This I did know, I had no wish to accept the man introduced to me as Uncle Charlie as my father, In a state of denial I had no wish to accept this man, who drank, often appearing in a state of inebriation, when ever we met,

Chapter 8 - Sarnia Cherie

whose blood shut eyes and slurred speech somewhat frightened me at an early age, whose only benefit I received was the occasional sixpence he put in my hands With the words You and Lena have done a fine job. He's a fine boy. Was it pride that I rejected him as my father? If so, I had a lot to learn, Years later, when he was in the Paupers' Accommodation Hospital, I occasionally visited him taking him chocolate and tobacco I went as a visitor to some one, who needed help not as his son. I still kept him in a shadow ,It was not till I attended his funeral, that i acknowledge him as a relation. Charles and Lena Blestel were the only parent's I ever had'

We arrived home after the holiday ,and began to save hard to buy our furniture. One rainy day in 1950 we chose our bits and pieces at I.C. Fuzzey, a renowned furniture department store. The next thing was to find a house or flat, which in those days were hard to find, due to people returning and the number of houses damaged by the Occupation Forces. It was almost like waiting for someone to die, not a very nice thought but unfortunately true. Knocking on the doors of owners or tenants who had passed away was not a sympathetic act.

The call for me to tread the boards on the stage still burned within me. I needed advice to fulfil my ambition. During my father's time in the army, he was posted as batman to Barry Jones, a well-respected stage and film actor both in England and America. He was born and bred in Guernsey and lived with his friend Maurice Colbourn at Le Cathoric , in a delightful hilltop house overlooking Perelle Bay. During the German occupation they requisitioned it and built an observation tower. When Barry returned after the war, he refurbished the structure as a part of the house.

It was to him that I turned for advice. He very kindly sent me a letter suggesting that I should apply for entry to the Royal Academy for Dramatic Art, and, included in the letter, he wished me luck. He suggested that one should always follow ones heart when undecided. In due course, my application to join RADA arrived in London. Great news! I would be able to fulfil my life's passion and train to be an actor. Unfortunately, fate stepped in.

Mildred's cousin Norman got married to Dorothy Hurrell, and a flat at her mother's house in Saumarez Street became vacant. Perhaps it was the thought of sex. Anyway, the flat won and RADA lost a potential star pupil. All was not lost, because years later in Australia, I was able to do film work - but I'm jumping the gun.

With a flat and furniture we were all set to get married. The flat needed decorating, including a partition dividing the lounge from the dining room, which I put up. Complete with hammer, nails, wood, paintbrushes and wallpaper, and so on, I set to work to make our first haven liveable. Delma, armed with a paintbrush, gave the place a new look. I must say, without boasting, the finished rooms looked great. A previous wall had been demolished to make room for Dorothy's Dance Studio, but after sixty years I have discovered that the wall I put back is still standing.

Meanwhile, Mildred decided to become a good housewife and enrolled in a dressmaking class. She chose to make a green sheared nightdress, every stitch a labour of love, doing a first class job. Unfortunately, on our honeymoon night, the stitches came away, which left it looking like a sack. I really thought I had rolled over and squashed her. The wage of a night of passion.

Funny things happen on a honeymoon. Oh, how shall I tell her, father?

In between decorating the flat I attended a woodworking class. I made a table lamp and a stepladder. Both of us felt that we could approach marriage with these new skills, with no fear of the future. How little we knew, there was still a lot to learn. What we did not take into consideration were the ingredients of marriage, consisting of love, disputes, hard work at times and the possible loss of your individuality. Little money to spend on yourself, mood changes, grief, loss of sexual desire and so on. All these at times testing happiness you hoped for and expected on the day you said, 'I will'. Weathering the storms together, you may be able to make the marriage survive and work.

The flat consisted of a lounge with a glorious panoramic view of Castle Cornet and the neighbouring islands of Sark and Herm. It was the very view I had enjoyed as a youngster from the Audoire's windows. The dining

Chapter 8 - Sarnia Cherie

room, kitchen and downstairs bedroom overlooked Ebenezer Church, the home of the turkey dinners I had enjoyed as a boy. After three years engagement a wedding was arranged.

My cousin John Pomeroy and friend Courtney Selous were the ushers, Delma and Molly were bridesmaids, looking very pretty. The flower girls were Doris and Jack's daughter Maureen and Wendy Hohle, Mildred's boss's daughter. The page boy was Dorothy and Norman's son Alistair, and the best man was a workmate called Raymond Mayer.

Mildred and I were so happy to have found each other. This was an emotional time, when friends and relatives packed the church and I was proud to walk down the aisle, arm and arm with the only girl I ever loved. God bless her. I never ceased to love her, though our personalities were sometimes miles apart. Yet, bonded in love, a love that never wavered, I felt very blessed that she had become my wife, even though we were both strong characters who liked our own way. We never, let the sun go down on our wrath, always making up before we went to sleep if we argued, though I must admit that I prayed for the sun to come up again in the morning. Did these things come up in our lifetime, or was I dreaming? Oh, how those ghosts of long ago live again in my mind, and it only seems like yesterday when those ghosts were living flesh. The real shadows and darkness were yet to descend. When you are in love, you live in the warmth of the sunshine and believe that you have a lifetime ahead of you to accomplish your desires. Ah, how long is a lifetime? For some it ended so young, but Mildred and I were blessed in having many years before the shadow cast before us became truly testing.

Mildred's parents contributed a lovely reception at the Masonic Hall. Though certain things were still rationed, Muriel Parsons, who owned a tea shop next to Mildred's workplace made us a beautiful three-tiered wedding cake; how she got the ingredients remains a mystery.

We saved one layer for our daughter Kay's christening two years later.

Leaving the guests to enjoy a party that evening; we flew to Jersey for our honeymoon, staying at the Portland Hotel. At the tender age of twenty-one we married and with God's help we survived together for 53 years, through

Sunshine and Shadow. I guess we must have done something right on the way through life's journey. One thing is certain. We both shared a faith knowing that Jesus played an important part in our lives, even though we might have failed Him at times. The wonderful thing was that He lifted the shadows to let the sunshine filter through to us in times of need. A great sadness is that today's parents do not attend church, or see their children go to Sunday School. I am grateful that my parents saw fit to send me, because it equipped me to deal with the dark shadows that would fall later.

I ponder sometimes on what I may have lost of the family unit, when I left my parents in June 1940. That gap between leaving and returning was never bridged. In many ways, I learnt to cope with situations that would never have a risen if it had not been for the war. As a result, I matured at an early age. Mildred often said that in some ways she would have liked being evacuated with the school. On the other hand, she would have missed the experience of being occupied by a foreign power.

The years after returning to Guernsey were a carefree time to grow, while adjusting to a changed environment, with the horror of war behind us. Let there be peace in our time. Too many lives had been lost or shattered in the useless pursuit of war. During the first half of the twentieth century politicians vowed that the mistakes made during the first half would not be repeated. Alas, the plans of mice and men go oft astray.

Meanwhile, life continued with parties, picnics, trips to Jersey and my apprenticeship work friends. We saw famous motor racing drivers battling to gain first place on St. Heliers racing circuit. In Guernsey we sported the Hill Climb up the Val des Terres where racing cars fought the hazardous twists and turns to reach the top in record time. There was also sand racing on Vazon Bay. Unfortunately, during one of the races at Vazon, David Bourgourd, a cousin of Mildred's, was fatally injured.

On a brighter side, there were summer trips to Sark or Herm with Trinity Youth. The boat was often captained by the infamous Bonny Newton. Speeding across the blue sea, the salt spray hit your face, and a rush of wind invigorated the colour in our cheeks, while the sun always seemed to be shining in those far-off days. Landing at Creux Harbour, we enjoyed the

Chapter 8 - Sarnia Cherie

scenery that Sark had to offer and respite from the hustle and bustle of the modern world.

Life was before us to enjoy. Youth is not concerned with what lies ahead. The moment is for living, or so we thought in those halcyon days. The winter of war had passed so let's live to the full. I cannot help feeling that those days, when I grew up, were easier than they are now, even though the pitfalls were there. Or is this a myth?

The young of today face terrible trials and temptations --- the glorification of drugs, which give false illusions, leading to changes of personality, either seeing the world as a bowl of roses or a pit of degradation---- sex abuse, the uncertainty of a job, the hope for sanity of marriage or de facto relationships. The majority are not taught moral or Christian principles, promiscuity too often leading to unwanted pregnancies, the transfer of sexual diseases etc. etc. In spite of all this, Youth still carries the torch for the future.

This story is about the past and present. Let's leave the future to be written, when it is the past.

Chapter 9

Family Matters

In my work, I rode all over the island by cycle, often carrying long lengths of conduits strapped to the cross bars. At first this was a hazard, as it caused a lack of balance, but as time and practice prevailed, I got the hang of it in spite of a couple of tumbles. In those days one was lucky, if one owned a car in the late teens. My friend, John's father, owned a Ford. At times he allowed John to use it after work hours, but he still had to use his bicycle to and from work.

Our group enjoyed bathing at Les Vallett, which was one of a number of open air pools, filled by sea water each day at the turn of the tide which guaranteed that the water was always fresh. Before the war Mr. and Mrs. Thompson (or was it Johnson?) were the superintendents making sure that no one got into difficulties. Near the entrance to the pool a Miss Audoire ran a tuck shop, which was destroyed by the Germans during the occupation. When peace returned, the Thompsons retired and Roy Langlois, a champion island swimmer, supervised the pool.

During those post war years a mixed bunch of work mates and friends would cycle our way along shaded lanes, intertwined with hedgerows. Bluebells and primroses added colour to the pathways and nearer the cliffs yellow gorse flourished, giving out a fragrance all of its own. Finally, we would reach our favourite beaches like Fermain or Saints. We would dive off the rocks or clamber down the steep cliffs to sandy Jannaires Bay to swim, or sunbathe on the large flat rocks. The gentle lapping of the sea created music to our ears. Many composers were inspired by the sea as a basis for their music. John Ireland and John Longmire were among those who found beauty as an incentive to work on the island's Writers were motivated to locate romantic stories and intrigues here

Pearl of Pearl Island by John Oxenhope, Claret of Sark, Appointment with Venus, and Sarnia,were other novels set on the islands, not forgetting Toilers of the sea by Victor Hugo. Artist were inspired by the beauty of this jewel set amongst the sea with its rocks that claimed many unwary ships, Renoir was one of the famous who painted here .

How time and thinking have changed. In those days the sun did not seem to attract skin cancer, so we lazed there and enjoyed the rays that warmed and bronzed our bodies. On odd occasions, we might call into a pub for a beer or cider. Cigarettes were no cause for alarm either. They were an initiation to manhood and to inhale was simply a way to enjoy it. The possibility of acquiring cancer was unknown at the time. At a later date, my mother succumbed to cancer of the lungs, even though she was not a heavy smoker. My father never put a cigarette in his mouth.

After the drab scenario of Oldham, Guernsey with its old-world charm, was a sheer delight. The island has always remained dear in my heart, even though I now live thousands of miles away and have travelled to many parts of the world. I still remember the words of Sarnia Cherie. 'Thy voice calls me ever'-- - but I have no desire to live there permanently. It is a chapter in my life for which I am grateful. Each chapter in the book of life has its highs and lows. As I write this, Australia is my home. It is a country that has wrought many changes in my life. A times it is a country where the Sun rose and set in the shadows

Still on Guernsey, Mildred continued working as a hairdresser after we were married. Willy Hohl was the owner of the salon and we remained friends after he sold the business in the Grange. He and his wife, Olive, with their

Chapter 9 - Family Matters

two children ,Wendy and Ulrick immigrated to New Zealand. Mildred was very happy working for them before they left. We enjoyed their company at Christmas and Birthday parties at Thebes. When Olive writes she always remembers those parties and the fun days, when we played such games as Spin the Plate, Postman's Knock, Hunt the Slipper or Film Stars, where the star you chose, would be a girl or boy you fancied, so that she or he would give you a kiss, and so on. All these are now replaced by the computer.

Lost are the family gatherings, the get-togethers at meal times. Lost is the art of conversation, not like when we sat around the table talked, and enjoyed the food that Mother had slaved over the stove to prepare. No, she had not slaved. To her it was a labour of love. She preferred to stay at home amidst the chores of daily living, while the husband was the bread winner and she the home maker----the mother caring for her children and choosing to care for them herself. Very often, the purse was empty, but something was achieved that money could not buy. Establishing the family background, caring less about making both ends meet, but always there when I arrived home from school. Have we lost something by the 'liberation' of women? Can we merge a career with the role of mother and housewife to equip our children to manage the traumas that lay ahead? Have we bartered the stability of the family for material chattels that too often leave us empty and unfulfilled? And those within the walls without a sense of direction?

In those far-off early days after the war, Mildred and I filled our spare time helping out with church activities. Sundays were dedicated to teaching, and the choir for Mildred and Delma, both with lovely soprano voices; I never made the angel chorus. And there were outings with the youth groups, picnics on golden sands with our close-knit family and friends. In those days, in retrospect, it seemed that the sun always shone, although that was of course unlikely. We like to remember the good times, enjoying the company of those we hold dear, though some have passed on to greener pastures.

The island was going through political changes within the States. The basic system of government remained the same as it had been since Norman times, but people's Deputies were introduced ,which gave the islanders a chance to air their views in the running of the islands' affairs. Slowly, remnants of the occupation were cleared away, leaving only the largest fortifications which were too large and solid to remove or destroy. But they remain to this day as reminders of another era. Over the course of years, museums have portrayed those grim years, when Guernsey lost its freedom. And while tourism and investors replaced the tomatoes and grapes as the main sources of revenue, changes were also taking place in the Blestel family, changes that would alter all our lives. But before this, occurred, Mildred and I experienced the greatest event of our lives. Kay Susan was born on the 15th of February. As she gained her entrance into the world, it was fraught with drama, throwing the family into a state of alarm and worry.

Once again, the plans of mice and men went astray. Mildred had decided to have the baby at home. Dr. Strickland assured us that the pregnancy was straightforward and that he had no objection to a home birth so long as someone was there to look after Mildred. Mrs. Hurrel, our kindly neighbour, offered her services to assist the nurse. I had taken a holiday to help after the event and also to enjoy the first few weeks of our baby, whether it be a boy or a girl.

In those far off days, parents did not seek to know the sex of the unknown. If it happened to me today, I would have no wish to know the wonderment is gone, and, with it, the element of surprise. Que sera - whatever will be will be.

Mildred began her labour early on Saturday morning. The District Nurse arrived,and, announcing that the baby was not yet due, departed to attend another call. Poor Mildred started on her walkabout around the dining room, which had been temporarily turned into a bedroom. This went on for forty-eight hours, until the doctor and nurse gave up any hope that the baby would be born at home. By this time, Mildred was exhausted and her fear of hospitals was gone. All she could say was - "Get me there!" The ambulance arrived and transported us to the Princess Elizabeth Maternity Ward, where we were greeted by Dr. Strickland and Sister Walters. Dr. Strickland informed us that Mildred would need a caesarean operation.

This was a very worrying time for me, as I thought about what had happened when I was born. Although Mildred still had a fear of hospitals, she coped

Chapter 9 - Family Matters

well. Little did she know that, years later, hospitals would become part of her life when we had to face yet another hurdle in life's journey.

If, having a caesarean was necessary then, then that was the way to go. At the time we did think that the doctor should have diagnosed her condition during her monthly check-ups, and this did give me a little loss of faith in the medical profession, but none of us are perfect. So, without further ado, into the theatre went Mildred, to produce our lovely daughter. She was brought into this world by Dr. Bisson who had attended Mildred's own birth. As soon as she saw him, she knew she was in good hands. And then came another surprise. The nurse who assisted in the delivery was Jean Elliston, one of our friends at Trinity. Mildred was delighted.

I cannot describe the feeling I had ,when I gazed at the little pink one, lying in the cradle, complete with all her pieces. Unbelievable! Incredible that this was my very own daughter! Mildred was overjoyed at having a daughter,because, deep in her heart, she had wanted a girl, a daughter that has brought us a wealth of happiness . God Bless her!.

Today, that sense of unknowing anticipation as to the sex of the baby is taken away. Now we want to know the answers to life's mysteries, which is not always a good thing. Science does not know the complete answer, only what God chooses to reveal. If we knew everything, we would become the Supreme Power and the world would be in a worse mess than it is now.

Mildred had her wish that the baby would be a daughter – next time a son? We hoped that four pairs of tiny feet would be running over the floor of our domain. Yet, we had to wait quite a few years before Kay presented us with two grandsons, Matthew and Benjamin, who, like Ka,y brought us heaps of joy and love, all very precious .

During our 53 years of marriage, we have received blessings from above, while our lives consisted of sunshine and shadow. We always knew that our faith saw us through. Though we failed Him many times, He never gave up on us in sickness or in health. Christ was always at our side.

Mildred was a wonderful mother and Kay grew into a lovely child. She became very popular with her friends and our house welcomed them from an early age, so that she was never without playmates. We encouraged her to discuss any problems she might have, even down to the birds and bees. I became very close to her in those early years. She was Daddy's girl.

As I write now, it seems like only yesterday, when we were all together in our little flat in Saumarez Street. All too often we did not cherish the years together; like a puff of wind they are swept away only to be retrieved in memory.

When Kay was a few months old, the sun became overcast, leaving us chilled. It took a long time before the sun warmed us again. My mother, who had felt out of sorts over a period of weeks, chose to ignore the problem, till I insisted that she saw a doctor. She was diagnosed with lung cancer.

Shadows crept into our lives. How would we cope? We took life a day at a time. Here was my mother, a hard working, loving lady with a darling granddaughter. Would she be restore to good health?

Cancer is a word that would come to our minds and lips in the future, concerning another loved one in the family. The news concerning my mother came as a shock as we pondered anxiously about its seriousness, what were her chances of a cure, and, if there had to be an operation, what further treatment would be required. None of those questions could be answered. Only time would tell. Guernsey Hospital did not have the facilities to perform such a major operation. Dr. Razzak was a locum from the London Hospital in Whitechapel who was standing in for Dr. Strickland in absentia, and he made arrangements for Mother to be transferred to the London Hospital as soon as possible. He was a very caring man who asked his wife, nursing at the same hospital, to visit my mother, knowing that she was far from home. Strangely, I worked with Dr. Razzak many years later when I became a nurse and started a dialysis department.

Father accompanied his wife to the hospital and waited with her till after the removal of the lung. When she was on the road to recovery after a month, she returned to Guernsey. Even though she suffered a lot of pain, she remained cheerful.

She came to live with us, until she was well enough to return to her own home in the Kings Road. Mildred did a wonderful job in looking after

Chapter 9 - Family Matters

her. As she grew stronger there were trips to the beach, and, of course, Mother had the joy of seeing Kay grow. In the few weeks when she lived with us, she remarked that even if she only had another year to live, the time with us had been a happy time. Mildred played a large part in helping my mother to enjoy life, in spite of her pain and discomfort for which I was grateful. The two women always got on well together, as I did with Mildred's mother Linda.

Sadly, the storm was not yet over. The poor soul developed cancer of the brain. As you can imagine, this was a worrying time for us all. The prognosis spelt doom and the doctor advised us that 'it was only a matter of time'. The poor dear soul firstly lost her memory, not even knowing who we were. She then became paralysed down her left side and finally blindness overtook her. The end came after three months.

Again there were questions. Why, we so often ask. Why? Why did this dear, hard working, good mother have to endure the pain and suffering which she did not deserve?

On my journey along life's highway I have since tried to avoid the why's'. To those families, who have to face such traumas, I offer this advice, for what it's worth. Look beyond the shadows ,for they will always be prevalent. Look towards the light, when shadows fall across our path. Look towards the light, and the shadows will fall behind us. Suffering in this world can only be beneficial, if we gain enrichment to carry us through our journey. To remain in the shadows, however small or big, does not allow us to use the potential we have to offer in life, for without light nothing grows., The Rev.Geary Stevens spoke from the pulpit during my mother's funeral service.

"You may ask yourselves why this good woman was allowed to suffer. I shall not attempt to answer why. What Lena said to me during a visit I made to the hospital was that God was more real to her now."

Can it be that we are given the chance at certain times to accept and feel the warmth of the light - or to reject it and remain in the shadows?

During the time of Mother's illness the chance came up for us to buy a house near Thebes. It needed some tender loving care, but I knew that

I was capable of restoring it to a liveable condition. But Father stepped in, telling us that there was no need for us to buy a house, as King's Road would one day be ours anyway. In return he suggested that he should live with us at King's Road.

"You will not have to pay rent. Treat the house as if you already own it," he said. It seemed good to us at the time, so, stupidly, we agreed. I should have known the whims of my father. What could have turned out well became a disaster. The accent was on the capital D - for disaster.

Even today I find it difficult to write about the three to four years of my father's stay with us at King's Road, so I will make it short. My father's moods took him from one kindly extreme to the other, which was often devious and unpleasant. We really did not know from moment to moment how he would behave and this kept us on edge, when we should have been relaxed and happy with our lovely daughter and the life which offered us so much joy. I have never forgotten the goodwill he showed, me when I first came to live with him and with Lena as a baby, which was probably the reason why I chose to tolerate his whims for so long, as did Mildred, whose patience knew no bounds.

Our move to King's Road was undertaken by the Ogier Brothers who were professional removalists. They were very humorous characters and we never knew what would come out of their mouths next. They lived three doors down from the Langlois.

Apart from the difficulties created by Father, this was truly the beginning of a new era for us, with a lovely garden for Kay to enjoy in her early childhood. She always maintains that she had a very stable environment, as she grew up, and this served her well when she had to deal with marriage problems during her adult life. Thank God, that she had faith to weather those dilemmas. Again I repeat' we are blessed to have such a loving and caring daughter, who returned our love'.

As the years rolled on, I became restless with my job at the States Electricity Department and a chance came up for me to join the Hoover Company as a representative. I applied and was accepted. This meant going to England to train, after which exams had to be passed. Luckily, I passed the exams

Chapter 9 - *Family Matters*

and got the job. Kay who was a sweetie, went through a stage of sleeplessness keeping me up half the night, as I paced the bedroom floor and sang to her, as I tried to induce her to sleep. Morning was nigh before I managed to creep to bed beside Mildred, who was usually enjoying the sleep of the gods.

And so, I started with Hoover Ltd. There were plusses to the job. A good salary, a car allowance and trips to England. I had to service Alderney, Sark and Herm; a bonus on your sales meant that things were looking up for the Blestels. On the minus side, there were late nights and Mildred did not care for my absence, though she accepted the situation, if that is what I wanted.

It was not so much what I wanted. I felt that the job would give us a better living standard. Unfortunately, money brought other costs with it. In life one has to find a balance, which is not always possible and can lead to breakdowns in a relationship. Thank God that did not happen in our case. Our love managed to weather the occasional storms that blew through the household.

And then, unfortunately, Hoover began to get high pressured, expecting more and more sales. Though the product was good ,the pressure began to have an effect. Though I enjoyed the service part of the job, I became unhappy with the way things were working out, and, so after three years, I decided to go into business on my own, which became a disaster of a different kind. I bought a small general store, which had been established for many years, but, in order to buy it, we had to sell the house at King's Road.

During the first year or so we managed to make a living. Our customers were a mixed bag. Some people would come in and ask for credit. Of course we trusted them, but they continued to run up their accounts, leaving us to pay their debts, though most customers did pay cash. And then, to top it all, Woolworths opened a super market a few doors away, which did not improve our financial position. In the end, we had to close the shop with a debt of four thousand pounds. This was certainly a time when we saw how the other half lived. If anyone was in trouble they would arrive on our doorstep and Mildred, like me, never turned anyone away. We listened to some fantastic tales, helping when we could.

One such tale concerns Gerald, who, at 48 years of age, was not quite right in the top storey and not too clean either. Nevertheless, as a customer he always paid cash and never asked for credit. He had no faith in banks and kept his money under the bedroom floor, saying - "Those buggers, will never find it!" Those buggers, being his sister and nephew, who shared the same house. He arrived early one morning, saying that his mother was unwell, and what should he do? I had never met the lady, let alone her doctor, but after much debate I phoned another doctor, who kindly went to visit her. We thought that we would hear no more, but he arrived on the following evening in a state of agitation with the news that the doctor had called again and given his mother an injection, muttering that it would help her. It certainly did. The doctor never spoke a truer word. Ten minutes after his departure she went to God, or maybe the other place. We received an invitation to inspect the corpse and were informed that her face was as black as coal. Apparently, she had been sleeping in a chai, since she had wet the bed after rotting the mattress. We declined his invitation, so away he went again, only returning an hour later with the news that he and his sister had laid her under the kitchen table, so that his niece would not be upset when she arrived home. She also lived in that house of horrors. During this act of mercy, his sister apparently suggested that they should keep her there till the following Tuesday, so that they could draw her pension. Thank goodness this did not come to pass. When I asked him if they had informed the doctor of his mother's passing, I was told that he had not, because he had lost the bloody number! So, of course, I was left to make the arrangements, to have her transferred to the mortuary, as well as organising the funeral, which I learned later, proved to be something of a comedy show.

Poor Gerald. I shall never forget the time he arrived to show me his body, which was covered in red spots. "What's bloody wrong with me?" he asked. I knew that they were flea bites, thinking that the doctor would probably diagnose the cause of the bites on his return. When I later asked what the doctor had said, he replied - "Bloody lousy. The verdict was - use this cream and wash!" So, I bathed him and I suspect that this was the only time the whole of his body had seen soapy water!

Chapter 10

Trials and Tribulations

We had nowhere to live; our furniture was in store and our daughter was still at school. If I had lived by my faith at any time in my life, then this was it. We found furnished accommodation at Cambridge Park in a house that projected bad vibes. A sense of foreboding chilled the house and the owner did not improve the atmosphere. She was an elderly spinster ,who relied on a walking stick to combat her lameness. Her wispy grey hair partly hid a face that was devoid of colour. She was dressed in a black skirt and grey blouse, and an off-white shawl draped her shoulders, knotted in the front of her thin body. Her voice was cracked with age and fitted her appearance. When we were in her presence, we felt a strangeness, almost a fear. Her eyes seemed to penetrate one's soul. Kay, in her childish fantasy, vowed that this was the first witch she had ever seen. Perhaps we were unkind in making this assumption. In Guernsey folk lore witches did exist in years gone by. They suffered burning at the stake, set alight with faggots and yellow gorse gathered from the cliffs. Possibly this lady was a witch. Who knows? Witches have a way of disguising themselves.

Luckily, a kindly lady called Mrs. Bennet lived in the flat above ours. She made sure that Kay was safe and sound after school, if, on rare occasions,

Mildred was shopping. But we always made sure that one of us was home if possible. Oddly enough, after we left that house, another tenant committed suicide. I felt that evil lurked in that house. We were glad to move to the Alma house, to a lovely flat overlooking the sea at the Saleire. The only sad part was that Kim, our dog, was not allowed in the house. We smuggled him in for a few days, hoping that the owners, Mr. and Mrs. Adams did not discover the stowaway. The tension created by this state of affairs proved to be too much for Mildred, and I could not take the chance of giving notice to quit. We would never find another flat, as rents went sky high, particularly during the tourist season. The heartbreak came when we found that no one would take Kim. He had to be put down. My heart was very heavy, as I left the vet, knowing that Kay was so upset at losing her beloved Kim.

In the meantime, I found work in my original trade once again. I became employed by Lakers, a well-known electrical firm. Trevor, one of the Lakers sons' was in Oldham with me and so the Lakers knew me and were willing to give me, employment. In charge of the Service Department I found the work interesting, though deep down I felt that God wanted me to do more with my life, but at the time I did not know what journey lay in store for me on life's highway,and was fulfilled in my working life.

At the time the big question was - how was I going to repay the debt to the bank and creditors. There was only one answer - work, with a capital W. When you are in this predicament, the mind is never still, as you wonder how you are going to get out of the mire. Sleep does not come easily through the long hours of the night, worrying where the next meal is coming from. How will you pay for the necessities of life or pay off your debt? Only those who have lived through such trouble know that hell is very near. Overcoming what seemed to be impossible was only achieved with God's help. A lot of help!

I set about finding ways to earn the extra money we needed, and came up with the notion that cleaning offices, shops and houses and so on might be the answer. There had to be places to which I could go after working hours, day or night. I managed to come up with eight jobs, starting at 4am till midnight, doing my electrical work between times. I managed to do this

Chapter 10 - Trials and Tribulations

for about three years. Though it was pretty tough, I received strength with God's help once again.

I am a firm believer that if you can only achieve 10% then He will contribute 90%, or vice versa. It is true that God will help, you if you do your part. There are, of course ,circumstances where you cannot achieve anything, and then He will contribute 100%.

I cleaned a variety of places, offices, schools, shops, the homes of business people and the most famous of all – the Victor Hugo house in Hauteville. It was a study of light and dark, a house of sunshine and shadow which depicted the moods of one of France's greatest writers. As I walked through the rooms, in a strange way I felt his personality in the furnishings and decor of this unusual residence. After his exile from France in 1855 he settled in Guernsey having previously lived in Jersey. He was asked to leave Jersey ,as his son Charles wrote an article attacking the British Crown, which his father endorsed. Unable to live in his homeland, Victor Hugo set sail for Guernsey, where he lived for seventeen years. After his death the house became a museum, kept exactly as he had left it.

The house was reputed to be haunted by the spirit of a young woman, who had hanged herself there, having been jilted by her lover. I believed this,as I used to enter at 4am with an uncanny feeling. I switched my little radio on to its maximum volume in the hope that the music would scare away the creepy crawlies, as I unlocked the front door and stepped into the claustrophobic darkness that seemed to stifle my very existence. I would reach for the light switch quickly and turn on the light. It was only then that breath returned to my body. The dim light bulb mellowed the shadows with its meagre rays.

As I write, the ghosts of yesteryear keep me company. Sweet smelling lavender of the Mansion Polish, spread evenly over the brown linoleum floors, to wipe away the foot marks ingrained during the last 24 hours by tourists, paying homage to one of France's greatest literary geniuses. And there was the chill of despondency regarding the poor girl who took her own life within those walls, as well as the laughter of the poor children and orphans of St. Peter Port, gathered in the house to be given a meal their parents could not provide. Given to them by a man, who himself knew tragic's suffering, and that is why his writings vividly portray the hardship of others. In my mind's eye I could see Victor seated at his desk writing his masterpiece Les Miserables. The window of his study overlooked the very scene that I focused on as a child, from the Audoire's window. His affinity with the sea appeared in his writings.

My eyes wandered everywhere in that interesting house. I remember baroque furniture, rich tapestries and richer drapes, rugs imported from Turkey and North Africa. Expensive paintings lined the walls, gold and silver plate, blue and white Delft china also dinner and tea sets made by the finest craftsmen are still exhibited in various places, and bric-a-brac overflows in every room.

This is what I faced and cleaned in the early hours of the morning, keenly observed by the oil painting of Hugo and his family. You may ask if the house was truly haunted and the answer would be - yes. Not by the poor girl who found and lost love, but by Hugo himself, whose very presence lives on in sunshine and shadow. Take the time to go and visit this residence ,if and when you holiday in Guernsey, and perhaps you too will feel his presence.

Life, at that time, was not easy, but the work helped us to pay our debts and I felt humbled as I dusted those heirlooms from the past.

Mildred (Mill) began employment at the Guernsey Press in their stationery department, before going on to work for Roy Sarre at the Bedding Centre. As the summer drew near, it became time for yet another house move. I was tramping the streets to no avail only two days before we had to vacate the flat. Mildred was in tears by this time. I tried to reassure her that all would be well, even; though my heart felt that a miracle was required, which did not happen. One must not question God's timing. On the streets again, I knew that I had covered all the likely places, so where would I go from here?

As I walked on aimlessly, unsure which direction to take and feeling hopelessly inadequate, a strange thing happened. I found myself in Queen's Road, where the houses were occupied by wealthy people. This was not a street for one who did not know when the next; penny would find a way

Chapter 10 - *Trials and Tribulations*

into my purse. The Governor was housed in this street at Government House. So what hope did I have of finding a flat here? I underestimated God. Never be surprised at what He can do.

I walked along the road, while surveying the Georgian and Victorian fronted houses and wondering what on earth I was doing here. These places were well above our means, and, anyway, there was nothing empty. Or was there? I stopped in front of a three storey white-fronted building - Maison Blanche. The name stirred something in my memory. Yes! I remembered Mother working there before I was born. Casting my eyes to a first floor window I saw a grey-haired lady sitting and smiling warmly at me. I learnt later that this was Mrs. Cook, a friend and companion to Mrs. Marion Simpson, who owned the building. What attracted me were two tall uncurtained windows on the ground floor. A ladder rested against one of the shutters with a paint pot hanging from it. This 18th century building was being restored.

I gathered up all my courage and walked up a pathway, lined with flowers and I arrived at an ornate porch. Before me was a beautiful and elaborately carved front door, complete with a shiny brass knocker, and, inserted into the lintel, was a round brass bell push connected to chimes. I stood on the steps, waiting to ring the bell, yet afraid that I would receive a negative answer. Was the flat available for rent?

Nothing ventured, nothing gained - so the saying goes. So, I rang the bell and the door was opened by a lady in her late seventies. Her hair was a sandy grey and her eyes twinkled as she spoke, with a warm Yorkshire accent. Her face was lined through the passage of time and gave me the feeling that the person standing before me had known trouble in her life. A feeling of empathy came over to me, and, though no words had been exchanged between us, I instinctively knew that this would be our new home. The clouds were lifting.

"Good evening. Will you come in?" she asked. Those were the first words Marion Simpson uttered. I learnt that Mrs Cook had injured her arm in the washing machine and that both ladies had been expecting the Vicar to visit them. We shared much laughter about that first visit of mine, when we became good friends.

The house became a haven for us and the road to recovery from our troubles began. Mrs. Simpson was a gem of a landlady, who shared the upstairs flat with the wounded Mrs. Cook. She quickly understood our financial position and I am sure that she could have charged a higher rent than she did. She even had central heating installed, so that, when Kay came home from school, the flat was always warm during the winter, at no extra charge to the monthly rent, think what you may!

After what Mildred and I had been through, we knew that God had ordained that we should live in this house. So, on gift day at the Holy Trinity Church I decided to give five pounds as a gift in thankfulness for all the blessings we had received. You must understand that at this point in our lives our budget forced us to rob Peter to pay Paul. In other words, if the gas account was more pressing than the electricity account it got priority. It was a pure case of juggling our pennies. On many occasions there was nothing left in the kitty at the end of the month.

When I dropped the bombshell to Mildred that we were giving five pounds, her look suggested that I was mad, then she promptly asked me where the money was coming from? I foolishly replied that Mrs. Simpson was away for a month's holiday, so I could take the fiver from the rent, which we would of course repay later. Well, to say the least, Mildred was not impressed, even though she wanted to give something in gratitude. "But, and it is a big but, not five pounds!"

In my heart I felt l had done the right thing. If anything was given to the Lord in thankfulness, then that was it. Never have I given a gift with such sincerity. When Kay saw the fiver in the plate, she thought I had won the lottery!

As the weeks went by, it became time for Mrs. Simpson to return. Yes, you guessed it. No five pounds had been replaced. In fact, things got worse. I could not pay Paul, because there was no money in Peter's bank, only the rent with five pounds short. All Mildred could say - and think - was that we would be out of a home again because of my foolishness. I tried to reassure

Chapter 10 - Trials and Tribulations

her that all would be well, but this fell on deaf, ears so up the stairs I went to face the music.

By this time my courage began to fail, knowing that Mrs. Simpson might require the money now and in full, or she might give us notice to quit. Either way we were in trouble. Ascending the stairs to her flat and holding my breath, I gently knocked on her door, hoping that she might be out, thus delaying the confrontation. No such luck. She opened the door with a sweet smile and welcomed me in. I felt like a lamb going to the slaughter. Oh, ye of little faith!

"Are you all well and happy?" she asked. "I trust that things are working out for you. I am so pleased that you are here. It is a comfort to know that someone trustworthy is here, while we are away on holiday. Both Mrs. Cook and I feel at ease knowing that you are looking after the place. I see that you have cleaned down the back steps and I thank you for that," she concluded.

My mind was a blank. How to delay the awful truth? And so I mumbled how was the holiday, did they enjoy themselves, was the weather kind, how about the food and did she have enough time to shop ....and so on. "Have you got bread, butter, eggs and milk? Can I get you anything?" I asked finally. She said that she did have enough food in the house and that Mrs. Cook would be shopping next day.

"It is very kind of you to ask," she said. "And yes, we did have a lovely time. The weather was mostly fine, mostly with sunshine."

The time had arrived. I could not delay my mission any longer. Mildred must be having fifty fits, as she wondered what was happening. "About the rent," I began tentatively. Before I could conclude my statement Mrs. Simpson interrupted.

"Ah yes, the rent," she said, smiling again. "I've already told you how much we appreciate your being here, so please take thirty pounds out of the rent."

I am sure that God had a hand in this. 'Cast your bread upon the waters and before many days you will receive it'- a true saying. God is no man's debtor.

As I returned to the flat, Mildred was waiting to hear the outcome, expecting the worst. Needless to say she was much relieved to hear that the investment of five pounds had given us such a good recompense.

Meanwhile, Kay, at the Ladies College, was happy and made many friends and enjoyed her studies. There was always a string of children at Maison Blanche, and, in return, she was invited to many birthday parties. The childrens' mothers breathed sighs of relief whenever Kay attended, because she organised the games and therefore kept their children out of trouble, and fully occupied. It was good training, because Kay hoped to become a teacher, if she passed the requirements needed to enter the Teacher's Training College. She subsequently passed and studied in Salisbury.

Through the Trinity church, Kay joined the National Young Life campaign, a Christian youth club. There she met Val, a good-looking 19 year old Australian. He was four years older than Kay. The purpose of Val's visit to Guernsey was to renew his, British visa. He had been told that this was possible in the Channel Isles, but this was not so. Renewals could only be affected in Australia, if the visa was overstayed. Which is what happened in Val's case. This oversight changed our lives in, at the time, unseen directions.

Originally Val's destination was 'Jersey, Guernsey's sister isle, but, during the flight over, Val found himself seated next to a young Guernsey man who encouraged him to disembark on our isle. He had learnt of Val's reason and believed that Guernsey would be better suited to his requirements. He went on to suggest, that, if Val did not find Suitable accommodation, he could stay with his new-found friend. Val quickly accepted the offer, as he knew no one else.

After staying with his friend whose name has long since been forgotten, Val found a more permanent lodging with a Mrs. Bichard and, through the good offices of this Christian lady he became interested in the Church. We had misgivings at first about the age difference and the fact that he was otherwise unknown to us. Most people on the island knew just about everything about everybody. They could check whether or not a person was suspect in any way. Our fears were unfounded. It was the usual case of parents being too protective. Val proved to be a great help to Kay regarding

Chapter 10 - Trials and Tribulations

her studies and we grew to love him as a son. We knew that we could trust him in their relationship and never feared that Kay would become pregnant. He respected her and both found love.

Another chapter began to evolve in our lives. Mrs. Simpson felt that it was time for her to return to England, as her friend Mrs. Cook had decided to go back to Canada to live with her family. This came as a great shock of course. If she sold the house, what would become of us? We did not need to fear, because the dear lady had, arranged with the buyer to loan us the money to purchase another property and then to pay them back in rent over a period of time.

If the prospective buyer was not agreeable then there would be no sale. To allow for this to occur Mrs. Simpson had lowered the sale price for Maison Blanche. The people who were interested in buying agreed to Mrs Simpsons terms. They were overjoyed as one could imagine.

We were overwhelmed that Mrs. Simpson should look after us in this way. It made her indeed a very special lady. Yet again the Lord had his hand in our welfare, amid great things that were yet to come. After the Reddys bought the house, Val presented Kay with a golden Labrador bitch puppy called Georgy, who exuberantly chewed a hole through the bathroom wall. So now we had another family member.

Our search for a house ended quickly, when we found a four bedroom Georgian house in, believe it or not, Mount Durand! This was where, as a child, I had said farewell to my parents to escape the onslaughts of war. Oddly enough the house was named Tasmania. Could this have been an omen to further adventures? The removal entailed a certain amount of sadness, particularly in leaving Mrs. Simpson of whom we had become very fond. She also shed a few tears as we departed. It seems that life has to change. Mine was certainly about to take a turn, which would alter my working life..

So once again we settled into another house with the help of those characters the Ogier brothers, Stan, Les and Charlie. As had already been mentioned, they ran their business in Victoria Terrace and were neighbours of Mildred and Delmla's parents. One never knew what would come out of their mouths - a cheeky word or a naughty joke. I often wonder if they are still being cheeky in the Great Beyond; let us hope that the Chief Vicar up there has a sense of humour. He will need it with those three.

It was 1968 and we stayed in the house called Tasmania for some three years. Just prior to moving in, another adventure flew into our lives. (Adventures certainly had a way of attaching themselves to us!)

Mrs. Bichard, Val's landlady, fell ill and he had to find somewhere else to live. Mrs. Simpson suggested that he could move into the spare basement room, if he could make space for himself in what had been used as the store room. It was full of things she never used but never got rid of. So, after shuffling things around, this became Val's bedroom, and he became an unofficial member of our family.

Certain members of the Church had misgivings about this arrangement, thinking that Kay was entering into an unsavoury relationship with this man who was four years older. We knew that our daughter could be trusted, but unfortunately some nasty things were said by people who should have known better. By today's moral standards the questions would not have arisen. How the world changes. And, of course we also trusted Val, or Valentyne, to give him his full name.

When we moved, Val came with us. He left the bakery, where he had been working and joined the Guernsey Press. His fertile mind was always coming up with new projects, which he hoped to develop. His future adventures will be recounted as the story progresses.

In the meantime, I received a phone call from Dr. Wade, a geriatrician at the St. Peter Port Hospital, asking me if I would be interested in becoming a member of his team. This came as a complete surprise. The question in my mind was - why me? He must have read my thoughts.

"You do a lot of voluntary social work," he said. "We need someone who cares and your name came up as just the person we need. If you are interested, come and see me as soon as possible."

I went to see him and learnt that I would assist in the physio department. I would undertake training in this field under the guidance of a dour

Chapter 10 - Trials and Tribulations

Scotsman called William Bruce. I learnt a lot from him. He was a hard taskmaster but we forged a good relationship over the time that we worked together. He did not have an easy life. His wife Winifred suffered advanced arthritis, which left him to care for her after his work hours. I helped them in my spare time to ease their burden. Life is sometimes unfair. Here was a man who spent a lifetime in hospital service and naturally looked forward to his retirement. He would count the pay days before, as he jokingly called this release from bondage. As the time grew near with only nine more pay days to go, the bomb dropped. He complained of pains in his neck and cancer was diagnosed, with only a few months to live. William was never able to retire as he had wished. He received some treatment in London, returned to Guernsey and passed away.

His wife Winifred vowed that the wrong person had died. It should have been her. We never know what is before us. 'Have no regrets for the past as that cannot be changed. Cherish each hour of today, as thje sun may not come up tomorrow' How true in this day and age.

On life's journey certain milestones stand out. My time at St. Peter Port Hospital began a phase I never thought or dreamed of - entry into full-time nursing. I truly feel that God led me into this service to others to bring me fulfilment, a job that could bring comfort to others in my care.

One sunny day I received a telephone call from the administrator of Princess Elizabeth Hospital asking, if, because of my electrical experience, I would be interested in starting the new Dialysis Department. Yes, of course, but I knew nothing of what this entailed. My fears were set aside, when I was told that if I accepted, then a full nursing training would take place in Guernsey, at Charing Cross Hospital in London and at St. Mary's in Portsmouth.

I talked all this over with Mildred and we decided that, if this was what I wanted, then I should accept the position. Her only concern was my having to go to the mainland. Mildred, bless her, was content in having me by her side 24 hours a day and doing nothing else. Jokingly, I suspect that this was her way of making sure that I behaved myself. This was in many ways a compliment, because, as much as I loved her, which was very much, as a Capricorn I'm like the goat that hates being restricted or tethered to one place. In other words, I was a roamer. Although she did not always agree with me, Mildred accepted me as I was, and though I did not always agree with her, I understood her. We must have been on the right path, because we survived 53 years of marriage.

I left Guernsey to train at Charing Cross, later at St. Marys and at the Princess Elizabeth and St. Peter Port hospitals, and finally began my new career. It has given me much satisfaction as well as helping those under my care. As the years flew by, Kay did well at the Ladies College, passing her exams well enough to get into teacher training in Salisbury. In the interim she looked for various jobs. Peter Giraud, the headmaster at the Catel school, gave Kay a position as a pupil teacher which gave her a real taste for the teaching profession. The time came for her to continue her training in England.

Mildred dreaded her leaving, but she came to terms with the situation after she saw the training college for herself, and also the pupils. It was the kind of anxiety that every mother experiences.

Chapter 11

Time Well Spent

In the meantime, another drama loomed in our lives. Immigration informed us that Val had overstayed his visa. They threatened to deport him back to Australia or send him to prison, if he did not obey their orders. You can just imagine the turmoil this caused Kay and the family. He had no wish to return to the land of his birth, plus the fact that his parent's marriage was floundering. Once again we were in God's hands.

An orphanage in Morlais in France, badly needed unpaid staff, and if he was accepted, his meals would be provided free of charge. We were told that, if he resided in France, he would be entitled to apply for his visa- or so the story went! Yes, you've guessed it. Yet another red herring. The bureaucratic hierarchy informed us that this was untrue and insisted that he would have to go back to Australia.

Poor Val did not have the money to pay for his fare. Another alternative was that if he became a student he might be able to stay in England, provided a place was available at a training college. In the meantime, he started work at the French orphanage.

We had faced problems before, but they seemed minute compared with this latest saga. Over the course of time Val decided that his life was going nowhere and felt that God had called him to the ministry. (Many are called, but few are chosen.) During his stay in Guernsey he had become involved with the Baptist Church and often assisted with Youth services, occasionally preaching the sermons. So, this was great news for Mildred and for me. Val, unlike Kay, had not been brought up to attend church. As Christians, Mildred and I had always hoped and prayed that Kay would meet the right person to share her life. Val, at this time, seemed to fit what we had hoped for.

The orphanage where Val worked was supported by the French Baptist Circuit, under the direction of the Rev. Edward Somerville and his wife Janine. Both had served in the Congo as missionaries to the Morfo, a tribe living deep in the jungle and known to very few Europeans. This group at the home were boys and girls of all ages, who had been plucked from extremely bad environments. Many had been ill-treated or neglected by their parents. Others had seen their fathers or mothers murdered. Some left to roam the streets and ended up in prostitution. Two brothers, of small stature, were taken in by a Fagan type of man, who taught them to climb through skylights or windows and to open doors, which allowed the thieves to enter. A few were there because their, parents were unemployed with no money in the kitty. Rather than let their children starve to death they put them in the care of this home, which functioned quite well and maintained a happy atmosphere.

A while after Val began to work in France at the home; a plan was devised whereby I would look for homes in Guernsey, where families would take one or two children for six weeks. They would treat them as their own with love and discipline if needed, for some were unruly at times. Finding the right homes incurred many hours of asking people to open their hearts and homes to show love to those who had never received it .

The main reason for this operation was to introduce the children into a home atmosphere, so that, when the time came for them to leave the orphanage, they would have some idea of home life. The plan worked well. The children loved coming each year to meet with and stay with their foster

Chapter 11 - Time Well Spent

parents. As many as thirty or forty arrived, full of the energy that only the young know. As the Condor sailed in through the Pier Heads of the harbour, we could sense the excitement of the youngsters, cramming the ship's rails in anticipation of what lay ahead for them.

As the new foster parents awaited them on the jetty, they wondered if they had made the right decision. Would language be a problem? In fact we had very little trouble during the years that they came to the island. Each year, as the numbers increased, I spent many an hour finding the right homes, but the effort and perseverance were well worthwhile.

Michel and Remie were our two adopted sons for the holiday. They were a couple of live wires and kept us on our toes, but they were very lovable. The word 'adopted', which had caused me so much anguish during my young years, seemed to lose its significance, when it was applied to others. I often wondered if they too asked - to whom do I belong - or did they just accept their destinies without hang-ups?

Because the children arrived during the holiday period, some homes could only accept them for about three weeks, so, that they could take their own vacations away from the Island. I would never refuse a child the experience of the comfort and love of a family. Finding interim accommodation was not easy. There were people who declined having a child, saying that they supported the scheme with prayers and donations. Sometimes, in desperation to find a place for a child, Tasmania entered my mind. Poor Mildred never knew how many would grace our table till the last moment. After a few words in my ear, which were not always, complimentary, she forgave me and enjoyed their stay. All of a sudden, we had six children! I often wonder where they are now. I expect that many have families or even grandchildren of their own.

I like to think that we made a difference in their lives all those years ago. It's a pity that we lost contact, when we came to Australia. While they were staying with us, we took Michel and Remie camping, together with Val, Kay and Delma, either to Sark Alderney or France . It was great fun and I was the chief cook and bottle washer. Val would play his guitar, while we sat around the camp fire, singing the songs of the day. Our two

Labradors Georgie and her daughter Star always accompanied us on those trips, enjoying the free and easy life on the islands, sniffing out new smells and chasing each other in the fields.

All of us hired bikes on one of our Sark visits. Remie, who was always a daredevil, cycled down a hill with his hands everywhere but on the handlebars, took a curve in the road too quickly and lost control. He sailed through the air and landed in a nearby duck pond, whose murky water received him with a gigantic splash. The ducks took fright and fled. Mildred, as always on these occasions, burst into fits of laughter as the poor boy emerged, covered in mud but unhurt. He laughed and uttered words in his broken English that I could not repeat here. Michel added his comment - "Ha, Remie has fallen into the shit!" - and taking great delight in repeating the story many times to his friends in Guernsey.

One clear night, during this trip, I awoke to see the stars twinkling far above me. As I looked, I suddenly realised that the tent had been blown away during the night. Here we all lay in the open for everyone to see. So, at about three o'clock in the morning it was a case of all hands on deck to re-erect the tent. Most of us said later that nobody talked. I wonder why?

How we enjoyed those years, with the war behind us. Terrorism had not yet raised its ugly head, casting a shadow of fear that a simple plane journey could end up with all on board being blown to bits!

Those six weeks came to an end only too soon, as the hosts came together to say their goodbyes. A few tears were shed as a part of the extended family left for another year. I often accompanied them to St. Malo in Brittany, where the Director of the home would take charge and see them safely back to Morlais. For a time the shadows had lifted for those children as they glimpsed, at the light I sincerely hope they managed to stay. So, many children today are caught up in child abuse or have Dysfunctional parents, whose only goal in life is alcohol, drugs, perverse living and a exit from moral and Christian teaching, What hope have these children got in emerging from the Deep dark Shadows that has encircled them from the cradle. In many case they become clones of the parents, To those who are less fortunate than ourselves let us spare Love .

Chapter 11 - Time Well Spent

On odd occasions I stayed in St.Malo overnight to catch the hydrofoil back to Guernsey next morning. St. Malo is a very picturesque town, walled and very French in its design. A leisurely atmosphere prevailed with tables set outside cafes, Locals and visitors enjoyed the balmy evenings with conversation interspersed with laughter, while eating food and drinking wine most satisfying to the most critical appetites. And while you ate and drank, music would drift through the air. It was played on the accordion, as only the French can do.

The player would be dressed like an old-fashioned gigolo and accompanied a singer, whose sad love songs and ever changing demeanour portrayed a look reminiscent of Edith Piaf, the Little Sparrow, as she was called. The singer was dressed in black in a 1930's dress, and her music entered our very soul, leaving us bereft of love and loss in the cold human jungle.

As I wandered along the cobbled streets, listening to the sensual tunes that followed me till they were out of hearing, I trusted that I would find a hotel for the night. Hopefully,one where the owner could understand my poor French. By chance I spied the Victoria Hotel which sounded English enough. A window displayed photos of scantily clad dancers performing the Can Can or some such dance. The contents of the windows were highlighted by an ever-hanging kaleidoscope of lights, which, in my innocent mind, were inviting to the tired traveller.

As I searched for the entrance, I came across a door without a handle. I did not pay much attention to this, because I thought it might be a French custom, and knocked on this rather stout, dark-coloured, ornate door. A rather handsome man came to the door. He was about forty years old and dressed in a black suit and pink shirt, finished off with a bow tie. With a nod of his head and a smile (that spelt disaster) he ushered me into a large reception area. The walls were lined in off-pink wallpaper that, in my opinion, matched his tie and, in the centre of this garish room was a chaise lounge on which lay a tall Jamaican, puffing Turkish tobacco out of his lungs. The smell was overwhelming and came from a cigarette injected into a long, flamboyant gold holder. He smiled, showing very white teeth through the smoke and gestured towards a bottle-less bar behind which sat a dark-skinned woman, resting her rather large boobs on the counter.

Above her head were two speakers blaring forth music with a rather sensuous flavour.

As I entered, her look of boredom changed to one of smiles. In my best uneducated French I asked - "Au chamber pour nuite silvou place."

"Certainly, monsieur," she replied, and then asked me a question which I found rather odd. "Will you take your shower now?" I nodded my head, thinking that this must be the custom in France. The 'garcon' was summoned with instructions to show Monsieur to his room. As I mounted the stairs behind the man in the pink shirt, my thoughts went to Mildred. I knew that she would be glad that I had found a hotel, and decided that I would telephone her after the shower to put her mind at ease.

When we reached the top floor, he ushered me into a garret room built in a semicircle. A bed took up the central position, covered in a patchwork quilt and stuffed tiger pyjama case lay on the pillow. A multicoloured shade on a lamp sat on a bedside table and a chamber pot sat under the bed. The pot was useful as the bathroom was three floors down. A pull down blind completed the furnishings of this sparse, but clean, night abode. The Garcon held his hand out in anticipation of a reward for services rendered. I was uncertain of the tipping rate and dug into my pocket, giving him a coin of some denomination, having no idea of its value. The look on his face told me that I had not paid too little or too much.

I found the bathroom, which catered for six unisex showers. Resting on a dish was a bar of highly flavoured soap, though the smell of carbolic also came through. Needless to say, this was not for me. At least the water could be adjusted without scalding or freezing, as so often happens in the cheaper hotels. Mission accomplished, I made my way down to the basement in which there was a highly priced and well stocked bar. The room led off to private cubicles and I saw that several girls sat at tables with one or two in the company of well dressed men. As I entered, a twosome made their way to the private quarters.

Suddenly, the truth dawned. This was no ordinary hotel. I retired to my room poste haste, grabbed my night bag and descended out into the night. As the Garcon unlocked the door, he asked if I would be late returning,

Chapter 11 - Time Well Spent

and trusted that I would enjoy my walk. Little did he know, as he closed the door behind me that I had no intention of returning. Who knows, if I did, I might end up with one of the Can Can dancers? If Mildred heard the slightest whisper of my night escapade in a brothel, she would never let me out of her sight again. Or maybe she would! I booked into another hotel, where the entertainment did not challenge your blood pressure. The receptionist asked me if I had stayed in St. Malo before. I told her about my adventure.

"Mon Dieu," she cried. "You go out with more than you go in. It is a terrible place!" I thanked God that though the flesh was weak, the mind was strong.

The years when we hosted the children were truly great times. There were times when Val was forced to camp in Sark, as the orphanage closed for long periods. He was not allowed to stay in Guernsey or England till his study visa arrived. I will never forget the day the telephone rang. It was a call from Val, supposedly on his way to the Baptist College in Bournemouth. Due to a blunder by the Immigration Department, which is a dab hand at these kinds of mistakes, his visa did not permit him to start college for a month or so. You can imagine how we all felt, especially when he informed me that he was being held in a detention camp to stay there, till arrangements were made to deport him back to Australia. Kay was naturally upset when she heard this, as they were to become engaged.

I pleaded with Immigration to hold fire till I came up with a solution. I had no idea that the solution could be, but, being an optimist or pessimist or whatever, I played for time, as I put the pros and cons of Val's plight to them. Eventually they advised me that no action would be taken for 48 hours so that he could be settled, God knows where. The picture of his being incarcerated in a prison cell jump-started my brain. I hit on the notion that the sister college in Paris might accept him. After much prayer, many telephone calls and letters, as they asked for references about his good behaviours and honesty, the clock was ticking with so much still to accomplish.

I spoke to the Director of the college in Paris and he agreed by some miracle to enrol Val who never had an entrance exam. Because Val had no money we wired the cash for his expense and flight, and so, he was released and on his way to gay Paree, arriving there little the worse for wear. Kay breathed a sigh of relief as we all did, and, when he finally settled in at the college, we thought that at last this was the end of our troubles Ha' Ha' How wrong can you get?

Technicians arrived in Guernsey from England to install the dialysis machine in a cabin at the Princess Elizabeth Hospital, ready for the first patient. And what a patient! Mr. Atherston Ridgeway was 55 years old and was married to Nicole, a French girl who was only 25. He was a professional writer plus running a correspondence school for budding writers. A bohemian bordering on the eccentric and quite a character. How he came to be chosen to go on the machine, God only knows.

In those days, meetings were held in London by a selection board about who was to live or who would die. Patients were given the opportunity to go onto dialysis through a sort of points system. If you scored a ten, it might prolong your life. For those on a low score they had no chance ,unless they had enough money to buy a machine. Even then, there was a waiting list. Many people died before they could receive treatment. The irony of it all was that money could always be found when a country went to war killing people. But it was always difficult to find the money which might save lives.

Because this treatment was new in Guernsey, the Press sent a photographer to record the historic moment. This became more than a historic moment for him and one he was unlikely to forget. Atherston was thrilled with the idea of appearing in the local paper.

Let me explain as simply as possible what dialysis is all about. Because the kidneys are no longer functioning as they should, the blood is taken from the body and passed through an artificial kidney to cleanse it, and this takes several hours.

And so, the scene is set Atherston is on the machine and the photographer knocks on the door of the cabin and asks if it is alright for him to come in. I

Chapter 11 - Time Well Spent

tell him yes, and ask him if he is affected by the sight of blood. No he replies. He enters, takes his pictures and thanks us. He departs suddenly and we hear a terrific crash outside. On inspection, I find his body prostrate on the ground. Yes, the sight of blood did affect him and as a consequence of falling, he spent three days in hospital for observation. Now if that was not dedication to the job, then what was, Mr. Atherston Ridgeway thought. The whole episode was hilarious.

On one occasion, during a thunderstorm Atherston asked me if he could make love to Nicole while he was on the machine. How he would do this I could only hazard a guess. No, I told him, it would upset the system. "You see, Bernard, I don't like storms and if I made love I would not be frightened;" he suggested. What a way to take away your fright, I thought.

When he died a few years later, I attended his funeral. What a fiasco! In the middle of the committal prayers his brother stood in the pew, hands waving up towards heaven and shouting "Send him back! Send him back!" Then he burst into weeping and wailing. Needless to say, Atherston did not return. One should not laugh at these sad occasions, but I'm afraid I did, and I was not alone. I think Atherston would have enjoyed that theatrical moment.

The cabin bordered on to the land of Le Vauquedor House ,which was owned by Atherston, and it is interesting to note that the previous owner was E. Phillips Opperheim, the acclaimed author.

When I worked for the States as an electrician, I carried out repairs and met the author and his wife and family, the Noel Downs and his grandson John. They were all characters, prone to consuming quantities of gin and tonic. One was always sure of a generous tip, when one worked for them. They were very nice people. When Atherston heard that I had known the family, he plagued me with questions, wanting to know all the nitty gritty of their lives.

At about this time Oliver Reed, the actor, came into my life and we became friends. In fact, I am one of the names which appear in the dedication of his book - Read all about me! He was a bit of a hell raiser, when he was in touch with the spirits, and I do not mean those who have preceded us. He was a lovely guy when he was sober and a giver to his friends. Before he hit the big time he promised a workmate, Bill Dobson, his wife Jenny and son Ian that he would send for them and give them employment. And so, Bill, or Dobbo, which was his nickname, became Oliver's gardener and Jan was his housekeeper. They were delighted with their positions and stayed with Oliver until the end of his life. Olly adored his two children, Mark and Sarah who both loved their unusual father. Jacquie, his partner never quite knew what antics he would engage in, some of which attracted police attention when drink got the better of him. But she always stood by him and was a lovely person.

Sometime after I left Guernsey I heard that they had split up. He married a girl who was young enough to be his daughter, which, true to Oliver, caused a bit of a scandal. They remained together for the rest of his life. He died suddenly while on location, filming Gladiator and dying at a place he would wish to be. Yes, you have guessed it----In a pub, which was one of his favourite haunts. He once told me that he had left ten thousand pounds in his will for his wake.

OIly, I am glad I met you and Peggy and all your friends. God bless you and may you find peace. Oliver was an art collector and once asked me if I had ever come across a painting of clowns during my visit to auctions, which were a hobby of mine. Sure enough, in due course, I bought The Melancholy Clown by a painter called Mendelssohn. It was a water-colour painting of a clown with his arm in a sling. The artist had caught a look of sadness in his face. The poor clown sold for 36 pounds, which, was a bargain price. Unfortunately, OIly was out of the country filming, so the painting remained in our house for several months.

Mildred began to think she was going to be left with two clowns, me and the painting. Oh, you of little faith! In due course Olly returned. Would he like the painting or would I be left to find a place for it on my wall? To quote an Australian saying - no worries mate. "Hm," he said. "I like it." Then, we had to haggle over the price. Where does one begin to haggle, I wondered. Seeing my reaction, he said, "OK. Let's start at a hundred pounds." There was no need to haggle further. I immediately agreed that it was sold. Oliver enjoyed a challenge and was disappointed that we had

Chapter 11 - Time Well Spent

not haggled further. I was satisfied, though I expect he would have gone a lot higher, but he was a friend.

During my stay in Guernsey I met some other very interesting people. Government House often asked me to carry out repairs and I remember one particularly amusing occasion.

The phone rang on a bright sunny morning. Capt. Mellish, the A.D.C. to the Governor, requested my presence to repair a light over the bed in the Royal suite. The room was to be used that day by the Duke of Gloucester, who was expected to arrive in the next hour. So there I was, all fingers and thumbs, working at top speed and getting nowhere. At last I found the cause of the failure just as the Duke arrived. I gathered up my tools and rushed along the passage to escape the Royals, when I discovered that I had, left my pliers lying on the pillow where the Royal head would rest. Racing back I retrieved the offending weapon. By this time, much to my embarrassment he was mounting the stairs, leaving no room for my escape.

Oh, my God, I thought. Will I be shipped off to the Tower of London? Absolutely still, I, became part of the decor, standing against a wall next to a huge and ornate bowl of fragrant flowers. I held my breath, as their scent began to irritate my nose. I did my best to avoid sneezing. I stood adjacent to an oil painting of a Governor long since departed. His wrinkled face bore a look of disapproval, which seemed fitting in the circumstances. The Duke arrived and glanced at the Queen's representative, adorned in an overbearing gilt frame. Then he smiled and blew his nose in a large handkerchief emblazoned with a coat of arms and proceeded to the bedroom, oblivious of me. To tell you the truth, I did not know whether I should bow or curtsy, but what I did know was that I had to scarper. Luckily, my cell in the Tower remained empty. The A.D.C. laughed when I told, him later.

I still support the Royals. The incident did not bar me from being invited to a cocktail party hosted by Sir Thomas and Lady Elmhurst for all the tradesmen, in appreciation for the work that had been carried out at Government House. It was a very nice gesture on their part.

Wedding photo of the happy couple.

Wedding group from left to right, back row; Delma Langlois, Bernard and Mildred Blestel, Raymond Mayer and Mollie Selous. Front row; Maureen Salmon, Alistair Langlois and Wendy Hohle.

Mildred and Bernard, engagement photo at the age of 18 years.

Wartime photo of Lena Blestel, my mother, with Eleanor Moss and Dorothy Woodland in the garden of Greenbank.

My father, Charles Blestel.

Cecil and Linda Lanlgois, Mildred and Delma's parents with baby Matthew.

My dear mother-in-law, Linda - God bless her.

Yours truly and Mildred, Matthew and Ben. A happy Christmas party.

Matt as Santa Claus with his father Val.

Young Ben taking a bow or is he about to fly?

Our darling daughter, Kay Susan, in her Ladies college uniform. We are so blessed to have the love of such a daughter.

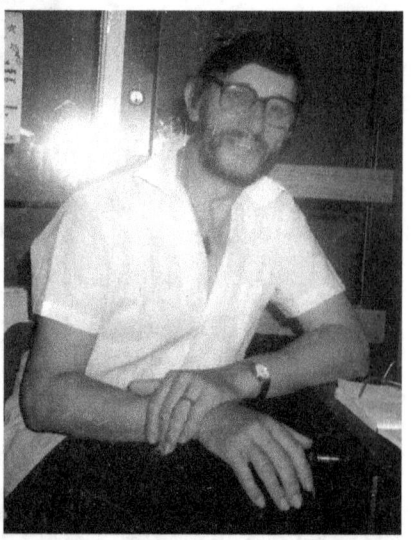

Your truly - during my nursing days.

Family group of Kay's wedding to Russ - a joyous day. Mildred in remission of cancer, seventh from the left, still smiling as the shadows had lifted for a while. Praise the Lord.

Florence McCormack, my aunt and godmother who arranged by adoption. Left to right, Ruth Ozanne (showing the signs of the occupation), Lady Ozanne and Florence McCormack, unknown lady in background.

Ruth Ozanne's house at 40 Hauteville St Peter, Port Guernsey, where Florence, Tom, Ruth and Lady Ozanne lived (situated next to Victor Hugo's house when exiled, he lived there for 17 years).

A wartime photo of our class in Oldham (some boys are not longer with us). I'm sitting fifth from the left.

Aged 5 years with my Aunt Alice in her garden.

Aged 3 years, looking miserable with cousin Elsie. In the background is the greenhouse where my Aunt produced luscious grapes.

Uncle Bill and Aunt Alice Golden Wedding. I loved Aunt Alice and uncle Bill how never mentioned by adoption. God bless them - I spent so many happy hours with them.

Guernsey Police Force during the Occupation.

My father with his second wife. An unhappy marriage sadly ending in separation.

Billie and me on holiday in Norway. Happy Days.

*Billie and me in an ice bar in Stockholm
- the only things not frozen was us!*

My Grandson, Matthew, on the threshold of cooking. An occupation he enjoys.

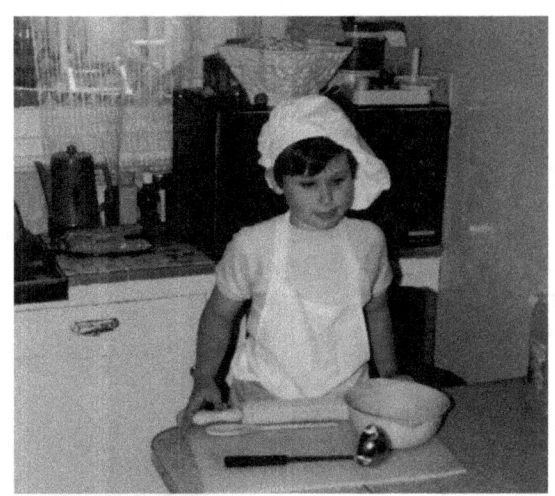

Playtime Ben as Robin Hood.

Ben & Val, his father, with Kay and Mildred in the background with Matthew.

Matthew with his cousins, Jodie and Rebecca.

Aunt Alice and Uncle Bill - a visit to the photographers.

May Queen Time - Mildred in back row second from right.

Mary at the Transplant Games.

My school photo at age 9. How we change!

Billie and me in New Zealand.

My Aunt Florence, second right. Ruth Ozanne fourth from right. Their story is in the book, Life in Occupied Guernsey.

Marian South, on her wedding day.

Marian with her mother, Mary. After Marion's death, Mary succumbed to cancer.

Marian with husband, Matthew, and their two children. Granny Heyfield (left) - nursing home.

Marian with her boy, Stephen.

Newspaper article photo taken when raising money to pay for treatment Avasten at the time not covered by government funding.

Marian - brief 6 week remission period.

Part 2

New Horizons

Chapter 12

The Journey

Tick toe, tick toe. The swing of the pendulum banishes the present and reduces hours to minutes. Time is a fast-flowing river racing on its journey to the sea to be consumed forever by the ocean. There is so much I still wish to do and tell. All of us are caught up in the river's flow. We have yet to learn that every second of our journey is precious, as we move on to oblivion or eternity.

And so we return to our story. Kay and Val were engaged in 1972, when Val was still with us in the house called Tasmania. It gave us great joy when Kay told us that she and Val would tie the knot the following year. With this announcement, nostalgia crept in. Have we heard this right? Surely this cannot be our daughter already getting married! Why, Mildred and I were not old enough to have a child ready for marriage! Where has the time gone, since we pledged our vows in Trinity Church all those years ago?

Here was our only child embarking on one of the most important steps in her life. We wondered if we, as parents, had equipped her for the rigors of life which would enable her to branch out to become a wife, and, hopefully a mother, sharing the highs and lows with her husband. As parents, we could only hope that the standard we had tried to instil would guide her through the sunshine and shadows. This I do know - whatever we said or did was said and done with love.

Invitations were sent, and the list grew from day to day. There were Kay and Val's student friends from England and France, plus our overseas friends. They amounted to eighteen and we had to find accommodation for them. Tasmania would be packed tight. Then, two days before the wedding Georgie gave birth to six pups, much to the delight of Remie and Michel, the two young French orphans. A delightful addition to the general chaos.

Kay had chosen to hold the reception in a neighbours lovely garden for well over 150 guests, so the house became a hive of industry. Daphne, one of the bridesmaids, will be unlikely to forget shredding a never-ending supply of cabbage for coleslaw, but Delma, as usual, had all the arrangements under control. A dab hand and a born organiser, bless her.

The garden at Summerland made a delightful setting for the reception. All we needed was good weather, but, alas, clouds appeared on the day, threatening a downpour. And so, at the last moment the reception was transferred to the Grange Hotel. Oh, the plans of mice and men!

Finally the hour arrived for father and daughter to leave for the church. Mildred looked wonderful as the bride's mother, dressed in a fuchsia coloured dress with matching hat and coat, giving great pride to her daughter. And Kay wore a white bridal gown with a lace veil. As I looked at her, as we entered the taxi, tears came to my eyes. Could this lovely young bride be our daughter? As we drove away to the church, the neighbours waved with shouts of "Good luck!"

So this was it. Kay had now left the family home, never to return in the same capacity - but I underestimated. She has always remained with us in love, as she built her life. She has always been a caring, loving and generous daughter, always there when she was needed. No, she was not leaving, but forging a link with her new-found happiness. A link that remains to this day.

What excitement there was as we arrived at the church. The entrance was filled with well-wishers calling out - "You look lovely, Kay," and "God bless

Chapter 12 - The Journey

you!" The bridesmaids joined us and applied their final touches to Kay's dress and veil. She squeezed my arm, as we made our way down the aisle past the crowded pews and smiling guests.

Val was supported by his best man and groomsman, but none of his family could travel all the way from Australia, which, to me was a great pity. I handed Kay over to Val which meant that my part in the ceremony was finished, and went to stand beside Mildred who had a wispy look in her eyes. Smiling at me, she mouthed - "She looks beautiful," to which I replied "Just like you on our wedding day and still today."

My dear mother would have loved being with us on that day, but cancer had claimed her life, while Kay was just a few months old, as has been recorded earlier. And so, after hymns, solo prayers and communion we all departed for the reception. The cake was cut, the telegrams and cards were read, speeches made and the happy couple left for their honeymoon in a private speed boat to enjoy the beauty of Sark and each other.

May God keep them in His love and the love they had for each other, I thought. Over the years that followed they still loved each other, though life wrought changes, as you will see. But on that day love blossomed with the intensity of youth. Some times youth makes excuses for each other faults   Failures could happen to each of us, when put to the test. It is not a bed of roses; thorns are ever present.

Four years later, Kay gave us the happy news that we were to become grandparents. You can imagine the joy we felt. This was indeed sunshine!

Then came the sound of clicking needles, as Mildred and Delma produced baby clothes and a shawl in the finest wool – only the best would do for our grandchild. There were, of course discussions as to whether it would be a boy or a girl, but we had to wait for the birth before we got an answer. Those of us who are grandparents know that this is a milestone in our lives, bringing great happiness.

Kay remained well during the nine months, visiting the doctor every four weeks. Then, when the time came, it was decided, that, like her mother, a

Caesarean would be required. Matthew James came into the world on the 2nd of October 1977.

While Kay was still pregnant, she and Val dropped a bombshell. They had decided to fly back to Melbourne, Australia, to Val's home town. Poor Mildred was in a state of shock, sure that we would never see them again. But then, in her own positive way, through tears she said - "We must not say anything to put them off." As it turned out, we did not have to say anything.

"Mum, we want you and Dad to come and live with us," they said. So once again we were in shock, as we contemplated an entirely new lifestyle. Our minds were working overtime. Here we were, approaching fifty and about to become grandparents, when out of the blue came the request for us to uproot and depart to the other end of the world. It would be a place where we knew no one, where the only contact had been letters or cards to Val's parents. They were naturally overjoyed that he would return and assured us of a warm welcome, if we took the plunge and left the island, a step which was not unknown to me.

For both Mildred and Delma it would be a change they might not easily accept. And there was the matter of Mildred's aged parents. Her father was not in the best of health and eighty years old, and her mother, though nine years younger, would not be able to cope if he passed on.

Would it be selfish to leave them? Could we live with ourselves, if we moved so far away? Would Delma, who was living with us, be willing to give up employment as a senior operator at the Guernsey Telephone Department, on the chance that she might secure a similar position in Australia? And, importantly for myself, would I be able to continue nursing?

The thought of a different mode of work did not appeal to me. Meanwhile, my father had remarried, but the relationship was going through traumas. It had not taken his new wife long to find out that his mood swings made their union very uncomfortable. After some time, they separated, and she went to live with her daughter in Alderney.

Chapter 12 - The Journey

We asked my father, against our better judgement, if he would care to come to Australia with us. In spite of what had happened when Mum died, we felt that we had to give him the option. He was, after all, my father and had brought me up to the best of his ability, for which I will always be grateful. I feel sad that he was incapable of forging ongoing relationships. He missed so much in his marriages. He was always the bread winner without ever understanding my mother's need to be loved. When I asked her, after one of his tempers ,why Mother had married him, I remember that she looked down at me, and, with a sad, faraway smile, she shrugged her shoulders and told me that she didn't know. .

Oh, what sadness to recall those words today. Though the words were insignificant to me as a child, I now realise that one can enter, into a relationship through circumstances which are incompatible with one's nature,and, therefore, spending the rest of one's life in shadows, instead of the joy which should have been there.

Eventually, Father settled into a retirement home, old age mellowed his temper and he adjusted to his environment. He died aged 93 years. After we settled in Australia we keep up correspondence.

The mists of indecision finally lifted and rays of hope appeared, when Mildred's parents decided to emigrate.

Australia - here we come!

But there was a prologue before we could start a new life. The Residential Visa, which allowed us to remain in Australia, became one of our first headaches. Due to bureaucratic inefficiencies in the processing of our application, they never gave us a positive or negative answer, till the week before we were going to leave.

By this time, the two dogs had flown to Australia ,our houses had been sold and our furniture was on its way tour destination. And then it was completely lost. The insurance company never paid us a cent, because they could not establish when or where it had vanished! Much later, when Billie and I visited England once again, we discovered that there had been a series of container robberies at the time of our furniture despatch. And you can imagine how we felt, in shock Our two dogs had travelled ahead of us to be quarantined for three months, while we hated being parted from them for so long. If all that wasn't enough to try the patience of a saint, then I am no saint. The Immigration Department decided to delay our visas for twelve months, due; we were told, to the upheaval of the Whitlam Government.

So, here we were still in Guernsey with no home and no furniture! This was indeed a time of shadow lands. Val and I flew to London, which cost us even more money when every penny counted. But we needed to put our case to Immigration, while throwing ourselves at their mercy. We found our way to the Australian Embassy and then to the Immigration Department. After we had stated our plight, they considered reviewing our application.

They eventually agreed to issue visas, if I was prepared to work in a country district, which of course I agreed to. After a delay of a further two weeks the visas finally arrived, much to the relief of all concerned. The shadows lifted and rays of sunshine dispersed our despondency. We were ready to embark on a journey to a land which was over twelve thousand miles away, leaving the country of our birth and the security of the Isles to settle in a place I had only read about. D.H.Lawrence described Australia as a 'weird land,' when he visited in 1923.

I remember thinking deeply about our decision. Had I examined the situation thoroughly? What prospects would be offered to me in my late forties? Had I left it too late? Had I been selfish in bringing my aged in-laws with us and expecting them to settle in a new way of life?

Val's parents, our one and only contact, wrote to assure us that we were making the right move. Things seemed to be alright – on paper, though reality is a different kettle of fish. A thousand thoughts crossed my mind, as the shadows loomed in the fading light.

What would we do if we did not settle? Yes, we could return, but that would cost money which we could ill afford. Was it too late to avoid disaster?

For those who look toward the light, the shadows will fall behind and my eyes were out of focus. I should have looked to the future positively, so that the shadows would fall behind me.

Chapter 12 - The Journey

Just as we were about to leave, a heavy shower of rain delayed the case's being loaded into the taxi, but it stopped almost as soon as it started and we were on our way. We had said farewell to friends and relatives at the O.G.H. Hotel, which had been our home for the previous three weeks. The staff had gathered at the hotel with our good friend Peggy Collin. What a character she was. Both Peggy and the hotel manager Carlos had made our stay most enjoyable, hosting our silver wedding and farewell party. What a night that was! A wonderful evening for everyone.

It seemed unbelievable but true, that we were on our way to the airport. At last the taxi drove us from Ann's Place where the hotel was, into St. Julian's Avenue, past the front gates of Elizabeth College, just as a snakelike trail of boys emerged carrying small suitcases. The taxi slowed down, then stopped to let them across the busy road. As I watched, a chill went through me and time stood still. I found myself returning to that fateful day in 1940, when I too walked in a procession to an unknown destination. The only difference was that those boys were holiday bound. As my 1940's exodus had taken me to the unknown, our departure was once again a similar event, not knowing how it would end.

As the taxi started on its way again, I glanced at Saumarez Street on my left. It was hard to believe that 25 years had passed, for it was here that we had started our married life. I wondered what the next 25 years would hold. Familiar buildings came in sight; some, perhaps I will never see again. But it was no use being sad or negative I should leave the shadows behind me and look forward to the Australian sunshine.

The taxi sped on its way to the airport and arrived just in time for us to check in our luggage. Which was found to be, grossly overweight. Later, in London we had to pay 500 pounds in cash before we were allowed to continue our journey. The rain had ceased again as we boarded, with a tinge of sadness in our hearts. No one mentioned their feelings ,as the plane soared high up into the cotton wool clouds. The sky had never looked bluer while the rays of the sun cast yellow lights, intermingled with a warm orange glow. To the emotional beholder it was a fairyland painted by the Master of Creation. Oh, what a magical environment it was! Then, through a brief break in the clouds came one last look at Sarnia Cherie, gem of the sea, the land of my birth. I shall never forget you.

Of course, we will return - for a holiday. A serious promise that was given to those left behind. In the words of Vera Lynn - we'll meet again some sunny day. Unfortunately ,that day never dawned for two members of our family. We were due to land at Bahrein, Singapore, Sydney and finally Melbourne.

Poor Kay was kept busy during the flight, as Matthew was only three months old and required breast feeding, and nappy changing was not easy when travelling. Kay, like Mildred, took to motherhood like a duck to water. Fortunately Matthew, like his brother Ben later, were good babies.

When you board those international planes, you sometimes wonder how they could ever reach the sky. Having never travelled on such a large aircraft I was filled with awe, as I witnessed some 480 people trusting their lives (and mine) to a juggernaut controlled by unknown pilots. Their responsibility was for the welfare of the passengers and crew, and their unspoken promise was that they would safely land us all at the agreed destination. Trusting that their judgement would not succumb to human error was truly an act of faith.

Our first stop was Bahrain, and the excitement of landing in the Middle East sent our pulses racing. Then, as we disembarked, we were assaulted by a surge of heat with the temperature over 40°. Not being experienced travellers ,we had to acclimatise quickly and the air-conditioned building was truly a life saver. The comings and goings of people dressed in their traditional garb was a far cry from the old Guernsey costumes, which had been used only on special occasions.

The heat which radiated through our clothing made us aware that what we wore was quite unsuitable in this fast growing land of commerce. As oil gushed from their wells, which was their prime economic advantage, money also flowed quicker than quicksand. Western influence was obvious, but culture remained, a fusion between east and west. As we observed everything around us, it was a heady mixture.

Chapter 12 - The Journey

Father-in-law decided to exchange currency at the airport. In front of him at the bank counter, was an Arab conducting business, almost in silence. He was dressed in flowing white robes, and pinned to the head cloth of this eminent man was a crescent moon with rubies set in gold, emeralds and diamonds fringing his heirloom brooch. There were rings on his fingers, bedecked with jewels of various shapes and sizes, and they sparkled as his hands moved under the lights.

Once the business was complete, the sheik bowed, and, with a look of satisfaction on his face, placed his hand on his chest and departed. The bank representative smiled and shrugged his shoulders with his arms extended, as if giving a blessing. Then he said in heavily accented English - "No more business. That very important man has just bought the Bank."

He picked up a broom and proceeded to usher us back out into the oppressive heat. We found our way to the refreshment bar and ordered long, cool drinks while, thankfully the announcement to board our plane again did not come until we had already been served.

Our next stop was Singapore, where we stopped for only a couple of hours at Changi Airport. I found the humidity distressing and hoped that Australia's climate would be bearable. As it turned out, I need not have worried, because there are many times when Melbourne has four seasons in a single day.

Much to our relief, Father-in-law now seemed to be enjoying the journey. The teething troubles, which he had experienced on leaving Guernsey, were behind us. To be fair to him, emigrating at the age of eighty years and over was truly a gigantic step to take, but due to his ill health we could not leave either him or his wife behind. My mother-in-law went with the flow. Her only, concern was that they would remain with us wherever we went. They had lived insular lives, only leaving Guernsey to go for holidays. It is to be expected that shadows will be cast during the winter of our lives. The inability to cope with issues sometimes find us resisting change, often much to our detriment and frustrating to those nearest and dearest to us. Occasionally, we draw the blinds on decisions we have to encounter regarding the travel pathway on our journey through life, happy living in the shadows, which give us a false sense of security. Looking towards the light seems to accentuate the possible pitfalls as we do not quite know how to face them. So we stay in the safety zone.

Sleep does not come easily on the long haul, as people move in front of you on their way to the toilets, unless you have an end seat or are already standing or exercising to prevent blood clots in the legs.

Announcements from the pilot come to us over the sound system, keeping those of us, who are still awake, informed about the height of the plane or of what country may lie beneath us. One such piece of information came to us, as he informed us that a beautiful view of India could be seen through the rear window.

I was feeling restless and turned to Mildred, who was on the edge of dozing off and not very receptive. I told her that I was going to the back to see what I could on the land of the Taj Mahal. To which she replied - "Don't be all night." I thought this was a pretty silly statement and told her that I was only looking, not visiting. The expression on her face said a lot. "Knowing you, Bernard, anything can happen," she stated. And, of course, it did.

When I got to the back of the plane, I was surprised to find only one person at the window. It was a man I supposed to be in his late twenties, fair headed, dressed in sports clothes and looking just like your average traveller. I had no reason to suspect anything suspicious about him, except for the fact that his right hand was clutching the handle that controlled the opening of the emergency escape door. And there was nothing strange in that, until I engaged him in conversation. "Are you Australian, or perhaps returning from a holiday?" I asked him.

Still clutching the handle, he hissed - "No! I'm being deported!" Then his left hand went to his head and he moaned – "Oh, the pain in my head, oh, the pain. What am I going to do?" As he said this, I found myself staring at the handle which might send us all into eternity, if he gave it a sudden pull, and at that moment the film Goldfinger came into my mind. I remembered the villain being sucked conveniently through a large hole in a plane, James Bond being the star.   I think that Bond managed to avoid the same end by getting to the safety catch handle - just in time. It would

Chapter 12 - The Journey

require very quick action on my part, if the man suddenly gave the handle a forceful pull.

"Have you seen a doctor?" I asked him, moving anxiously closer.

"No doctor can help me," he answered angrily. "I'm being deported I told you. Don't you understand? Deported, and I don't know why!"

"Have you asked the police?" I enquired, perhaps unwisely. This question made him even more irritable and irrational.

"They can't do anything, not the bloody police," he shouted, still gripping the handle tightly. "Help me," he cried then, staring at me for the first time. "I can't go on!" After suggesting that an aspirin might help and hearing his refusal, I became desperate to find an answer to his problem. There seemed to be only one other solution.

"Have you tried prayer?" I asked him gently. After all, here we were thousands of feet up in the sky, so, if heaven were somewhere up there then, as the, hymn says - nearer my God to Thee.

"No, mate, I haven't," he said quietly.

"Give it a go," I advised him and so we both prayed.

I have never said a more sincere prayer than I did on that plane. It was quite obvious to me that our future was not in the hands of the pilot, but in one, who, to all intents and purposes, wished to send us all crashing down to India's teeming millions. God did answer our prayers.

"Thanks, mate," he said after a long moment. "I feel better and here's a packet of Camels for your trouble," he concluded with a slight smile.

As he passed me the cigarettes, his hand was released from the handle of loom. He never told me why he had been deported or from where. What God thought of my reward for services rendered, I shall never know. He shook my hand and returned to his seat.

Apprehension still lurked in my mind, and, for the rest of the flight, I kept a close watch on him, having no wish to be sucked out of the plane.

I remained an unsung hero and returned to my beloved who asked, in no uncertain tones - "Where the hell have you been? Looking at India does not take an hour and twenty minutes. What have you been doing?" I was quite aware that I was not the flavour of the month ,and, so I retold the episode with a touch of drama, intimating that I had saved the plane, and, of course, Mildred and the rest of the family. Somehow I sensed that my effort was not appreciated ,as she said - "This plane holds over 400 people, and, out of all of them, trust you to get involved. We are not even in Australia yet, and God only knows what will happen there."

God did know, but he wasn't telling me. As a former Australian Prime Minister once said - life wasn't meant to be easy. But to quote yours truly - but it can be exciting.

Chapter 13

Australian Transformation

Clouds were not encircling the plane as if there would be a storm, but they were white fluffy clouds, as white as snow with a tint of yellow, and formed a carpet beneath us. My eyes looked up to an azure blue sky. It seemed as if we were in a world of our own with the glistening sunrays dazzling the window panes. Outside was a world of silence, only broken by the voice of the jet, as it carried us along this ethereal passage, which in its own time would terminate in the real world, in this case, Sydney. Commands came from the front for us to fasten our seatbelts. The plane gradually lost height, as we approached the runway and I caught my first glimpse of Australia. Lower and lower we came till the wheels of this trusty steed touched down on the concrete. We were now on Australian soil and our journey of over 120,000 miles was almost complete.

The sun welcomed us on that day in the seventies. Far behind us was the patter of the rain that had farewelled us at the onset of our journey. My adrenalin worked overtime, as we waited for the Melbourne flight and the final leg of our emigration. Unbelievably, I was actually in Australia.

As we crossed the tarmac from the plane, two white-suited officials, carrying what appeared to be fish nets, made their way to the plane we had just left.

They carried goggles and gloves and my thoughts immediately returned to my Goldfinger friend. Did he have a bomb secreted in the folds of his anatomy? Perhaps I had not saved the plane and all those who travelled in her after all. My impulsive nature tempted me to ask what the two white clad aliens were about. Much to my relief, I later learnt that two rats had hitched a ride at Singapore, hence the nets. Mildred offered a piece of advice in my direction. "Don't go and help!" she said firmly. As if I would.

All the family were glad that we were on the last lap of our journey. As we came closer and closer to Tullamarine Airport, I once again asked myself many questions. Have we done the right thing in giving up our home to come to a land about which I knew so little? What sort of people are Val's family? Perhaps they dislike Poms. Val's Mum Betty had written nice letters assuring us of a warm welcome, but sometimes what is written does not match reality in certain situations. Here I am, in a strange country at 48 years of age and with no promise of work - or furniture. And finally, were we selfish in uprooting my in-laws at an age, when many are already in nursing homes. With such thoughts in my mind, the lure of Australia dimmed. Having left Sydney we were on the last lap. Once again the jet forged its way to the airport. Soon my feet will touch the earth, setting me on the path to incredible adventures, unforseen in my wildest dreams. Sunshine and shadow will cross my path during this time of learning. One important factor came with the realisation, that people are more important than the things we spend a lifetime gathering - elusive wealth and bric-a-brac. Yet to come in our lives, was a hospital or nursing-home room with a bed and a table, on which sits a cherished vase and a family photo that belonged to mother that once hung in the dining room, to gather with a delicate water coloured picture painted by a friend that in the past was admired by many, as they enjoyed our hospitality. Also included, was a silver framed wedding photograph, these items being the only precious things that we owned all nestled, in-a crammed space that would become the very centre of our existence. We would await our departure from the shadows that increased daily due to the inevitability of adversity. It will be people who will sustain us during those times of overcast shadows. Family and friends and loved ones we have endeavoured to help and nurture during our own journey.

Chapter 13 - Australian Transformation

The stewardesses checked to make sure that our seat belts were securely fastened, as we descended. I gazed at the surroundings through the window, hoping to see what Melbourne had to offer and to catch a view of Val's family, not that I would have recognised them. We had seen photos of his parents, but people have a way of looking different in the flesh. As we touched down, I offered up a silent prayer of thankfulness that we had arrived all in one piece. I must admit that there were times, when the turbulence gave us a bit of a scare as our stomachs seemed to shift while the rest of our bodies shifted elsewhere.

We were eager to disembark, and, after going through all the preliminaries ,we eventually caught sight of the welcoming party waving frantically. Val's family rushed to greet us with hugs and kisses and I sensed that they were genuine in their welcome. The journey was over at last.

We arrived at Val's parent's house in Dandenong on Christmas Eve, and stayed with them for three months. It was rather nice that we spent our first Christmas in our new land with Val's family, which consisted of mother Betty and father Jim, plus Betty's mother Nan and Val's younger sister Kathy, who was born after he left Australia. Alan, an unmarried brother, also lived with his parents at Hilton Street. Siblings Beverly and Steve were both married and lived elsewhere. Young Kathy had a passion for dressing up her cat, pretending it was a baby, complete with pram. The cat took it all in good part and never murmured. The dog Buff became part of the game, but was not so accommodating, when it came to dressing up. At the first opportunity it scampered under Nan's chair – for safety. Nan had some interesting tales to tell about the 'stars' she had met, while she worked as a dresser at the Tivoli Theatre.

While we waited for the return of our furniture (which never came), the Taylors' hospitality was always first class. I shall never forget the love Betty showed us during a difficult transformation.

Our furniture was lost forever, never to be found. The insurance company refused our claim, because they said they could not decide how or when it had disappeared. So here we were, in a strange land with no furniture; the bulk of our belongings lost, so it became a case of starting all over again.

Poor father-in-law could never understand the why's or wherefore's of this loss and why there was no reimbursement from the insurance. We learnt later that a number of containers had been stolen and assumed that ours was among them. This was indeed a time of dark shadows. The pantechnicon contained, not only Mildreds and my home, but also Kays and my in-laws homes. Imagine how we all felt. Losing the furniture was bad enough, though that could be replaced in time, but photos of childhood, weddings and special occasions were gone forever. Our greatest sorrow.

Yet, in those shadows there was a glimmer of light. After all, we had lost material things - not people. We could have lost a life, or limb or had a terrible accident, leaving one of us an invalid for the rest of our days. Once the initial shock subsides, the shadows will begin to lift. Focus your eyes towards the light. I have learnt that, when the cards are down, take a pen and paper and jot down your positives and negatives, and you will be surprised at how many positives you have accumulated in doing so. You will move into the light and only then will you be able to tackle the problem. Remember - a problem is only a problem ,if you make it so.

So our first move into the light was to find rental accommodation in the hope that our goods and chattels' would eventually arrive. At our first house in Cranbourne the agent informed us that we could stay as long as we liked, because the house was not going to be sold. As it turned out, we had only been there for a week, when we were told to vacate the premises within a month, because the house was sold! Yet another shadow.

We decided to move to Frankston, a suburb of Melbourne. 8 Cliff Road became our next abode. It was a lovely cliff-top house overlooking beautiful Port Phillip Bay. We looked out at magnificent miles of blue sea that changed with every mood of the weather. Sunsets were reminiscent of the paintings of Michael Angelo. As I surveyed the wonders of nature, I saw the work of a Supreme Being.

Travelling through life and the world, I receive the assurance that God created the universe. Genesis Chapter One, verse one states That there was darkness inthe world and that God created light so that all can see, thus enabling each one of us to seek out a path from the shadows into the

Chapter 13 - Australian Transformation

light, which represents Life. Forward we must go whatever the adversities, leaving the darkness of trouble behind us.

On my journey I have learnt this truth. If there is another way, I have yet to find it. In nature, the darkness of the soil prepares the plants to emerge into the light, progressing its growth to achieve its full potential, so it is with us. The shadows or dark periods in our lives will hopefully give us the incentive to seek out the light, which is life. To reach this status is left to the individual, whatever creed or colour. No one should be denied the freedom of choice to bask in the sunshine.

Our stay in Dandenong came to an end, when our two dogs came out of quarantine, prior to our move to Cranbourne. I found employment at Hedley Sutton in Canterbury, a first class private hospital and nursing home, an hour's drive from Cranbourne. I spent five happy years there and it was where, I met William Lowe, Billie, to his friends. He was to play an important part in my life. Our loving relationship as brothers and soul mates has progressed over thirty years.

The wonderful thing about love is that you can love your mother, wife, husband, brother, sister, house, dog, friend and so on, all in a different way. Yet it's still love.

Someone asked me at my farewell party, when I left the Hedley Sutton Hospital, how I came to take up employment there. Firstly, there was a broken journey - if Val had not broken his journey in Guernsey and gone on to Jersey, he would not have met and married Kay. Secondly, the nurse whose position I filled, left to go into the ministry and prayed that a caring person would take his place. (Perhaps God had got the wrong message?) Thirdly, I scanned the yellow pages, taking a chance that the hospital needed someone. I went for an interview with Lola Henderson, whose care for patients and staff made her a very able Director of Nursing. She took the chance that I would be the right person for the job.

You may ask whether or not it was a coincidence that I came to be there, or did the direction come from a Higher Authority? In retrospect ,I realised that it was no coincidence. Working at the hospital became one of the many sunshine periods of my life. I considered it a privilege to help those who were in the autumn of their lives. Unfortunately old age, is sometimes not pretty, and it is at this time that we need support and tender loving care, which helps us to cross the bar. Many people came to me to seek comfort and I found this both humbling and a privilege, to be taken into their confidence or to be with them as they passed away.

Dying is as natural as being born. If we could remember how it was when we were in our mother's womb, experiencing the fear of coming out into an unknown world, we would not know that in most cases we would be received into loving arms. The same may apply to death. Dark shadows encircle us before we breathe our final breath, and it is then that the shadows disappear into the light, to extinguish the fear that had lain before us. If we have lived a life of faith, then this will be our ultimate gain---- finding the peace that passes all understanding.

The reality of this understanding opened up new chains of thought for me. While nursing at Hedley Sutton a patient of mine, a dear Christian lady, who was the mother of Sister Mary Evans, OBE, Sister Mary Evans was the matron of the District Nursing Association between 1963 - 1978 and was included in the first Victorian Womens' Honour Roll of 250 women, who helped to shape the Australian nation. She was widely known as the mother of modern district nursing in Australia. Her vision produced a reconstruction of the program, which brought nursing up to the standard that it is today.

In appreciation of my caring for her elderly mother, who was a fun person, Mary and her sister Lorna presented me with a copy of the book Daily Light, which consisted of helpful daily readings. It took over twenty years, when dark shadows clouded my life, to discover the ultimate reason for their giving the book to me. I will say more of this later.

In the meantime, let us be on our way. Each one of us has landscapes within us---- secret gardens, where feelings and impressions grow like a little garden, waiting for us to arrange them into our lives. How do we use the potential that has been working away? We may discuss these issues with others, write letters or poems or paint, or maybe take a walk and reflect on our life. But what is common to all of us is strong emotional feelings, which

Chapter 13 - Australian Transformation

are a pattern to our nature, essential strength from our hearts, which give us the impetus to achieve our aims.

Over the years, the desire to direct a part of me to the stage eventually became a reality, soon after I arrived in my adopted country. There goes that word again! The word that caused me so much distress as a child. The search to discover to whom do I belong has taken me a long time to come up with an answer. Perhaps, at the end of my journey the question will be answered. Who knows?

The chance to do TV and film work came through New Faces, which was a TV show hosted at that stage by Bert Newton, a performer, who had brought much laughter to audiences over the years. The judging panel consisted of Bobby Limb, Geoff Cox and Rod MacLean. The concept of the show was to discover new talent. In the course of a conversation with someone whose name I have forgotten, he mentioned that the name of the show's producer was John Proper. He was now living in Australia, but had come from the Channel Islands and he might be interested in talking with a fellow islander. I did speak with him, but, at that time, I had no idea that I would be a contestant on his show. Anyway, I decided to try my luck as a stand-up comedian, writing my own material.

It was a brave step. Here I was, in a new country, and I had never appeared on TV before. A thousand, and one thoughts entered my mind against performing. Perhaps, on the day the show goes to air, nerves will take over and I will make a public spectacle of myself in the eyes of the thousands of people, who nightly glued their eyes to the box? Plus Mildred and Delma, who would be in the audience, would be embarrassed if I made a fool of myself. In cases like this, I suggest that you think positively, and, with a bit of luck, everything will be alright. As it turned out, the judges enjoyed my performance and gave me the high mark of 78 - the winner was a singer who was marked at 82.

I will pass on this saying to others- today's worries can be tomorrow's joys. How often have you worried yourself sick about a situation when, in fact ,it has turned out to be enjoyable?

The panel invited me to reappear at a later date, working a double act. Unfortunately I never appeared again, as the proposed partner, Harriet Hicks, in the act which I had penned to bring the house down - ha, ha - had to travel to England on business prior to our performance.

The Athenaeum Theatre, whose directors Jeff and Russel had seen my act, phoned and asked me if I would like to audition for a part in The Cactus Flower as Signor Sanchez. I got the part as well as an agent called Jill's Casting. They have looked after my entertainment interests for many years, casting me in films, on TV and cinema.

So life has a funny way of sorting things out. I am doing, at the other end of my life, what I desired when I was younger. Over the years I have produced plays for various repertory companies. Mildred and Delma became choristers for the Eastbourne Singers ,after which they became founder members of the Peninsula Singers of which I became President, producing and writing many successful shows over the years.

Mildred and Delma found temporary work at the Heinz International Food Company situated in Dandenong. Part of their job was in the processing department. What one would do to earn a crust! Still, the money was good. Mildred would inspect the conveyor belt as it travelled past her, making sure that the debris or stalks were not included in the new batch of tomatoes, as they made their way to be cleansed.

Delma, in another department ,overlooked the loose, cooked baked beans, as they reached their final destination to be tinned. These were feats requiring constant vigilance. If the lever which controlled the machines was not pushed at the right time, disaster and all hell would break loose.

One fateful day, which I am sure will live in her memory for years, due to the heat in the workroom, poor Delma failed to reach the lever in time and guess what! The bloody beans, as she called them, came off the conveyor, pouring thousands of beans straight onto the floor! Oh, the poor girl nearly had a fit. All those little monsters around her threatened to bring down all her efforts to achieve the best beans in the market. Doing the light fantastic through the massacre of sticky pulses united with tomatoes or whatever goes to make Heinz Baked Beans a number one product,

Chapter 13 - Australian Transformation

slipping and sliding, she managed to reach the lever before the next deluge arrived. Somehow, I think that, she may have lost her taste for one of Heinz 57 Varieties. The foreman fortunately had a sense of humour. 'No worries' - so often used in Australia, came forth from his mouth. Nevertheless, he transferred her to a less stressful department with no more runaway beans.

Another of my patients was Margery Lyall, a sister of Ian Lyall. He set up the cardiac care unit at Geelong Hospital and also worked for twelve months in what is now called Bangladesh, playing a key role in planning a hospital there.

He was proud of his Scottish heritage, living by the clan Sinclair motto - Commit thy work to God. Another brother was the headmaster at Strathcona.

Margery, in her forties, suffering from multiple sclerosis bore her infirmity with fortitude and courage. She was an example to us all, if we grumbled when things did not go our way. When she was diagnosed, she turned her back on the shadows, to her they no longer existed. In her mind's eye she faced the light, oblivious of the paralysed state of her body and speech. The light that guided her out of the shadows radiated in her face. Yes, she did have her highs and lows, she was only human, but the rays were never extinguished. All too often, patients who were restricted in their movements would comment – 'I am useless now that I can't get about and am just sitting still'. To which I would reply that nothing is useless, in life. Remember spring cleaning time? Clearing out all the bits and pieces you considered were taking up too much cupboard space, while you had no more room for them? Your loss was the O P shop's gain. Those little discarded items became treasures to the buyers.

Have you thought about stillness? There is a verse in the psalms that says - Be still and know that I am God. When a child's mother said - for goodness sake be still - in no way would our childish exuberance be quelled but, when work, marriage and family enter our curriculum, stillness takes a back seat. In the winter of our lives there is a forced stillness. It is then, if we have gained wisdom on our journey, that we can pass on helpful words in the course of conversation. Very often, ,people will say that the conversation has changed the way they were thinking, and that they had been given a different slant to the subject at hand. At this time of forced stillness, we reflect on the past to allay our fears for the future. It is a time to advance closer to the light and to the essence of life, or to recline back into the shadows.

The working relationships at Hedley Sutton were first class. Lola trusted me to nurse her father, which showed me that I was doing something right on the job. Job is the wrong word. I should have said vocation. When you enter into nursing, it's the caring for others that counts, and going that extra mile.---- creating in patients a desire to emerge from the shadows of ill health to the path of recovery. Some people choose to stay in the shadows, having no wish to continue, and others feel that their family has rejected them by putting them in a nursing home. In many cases this was not true, because circumstances forced the families to seek help.

There is an intermezzo that bridges life and death. I enjoy listening to Jules Massenet's Meditation from the opera Thais. Music is a universal language. I encouraged my patients to listen to recorded music as therapy. The soothing and healing power of music assists in the patient's recovery.

Typing away on the computer with headphones plugged into my portable CD player, I listen to the Masters, changing to tunes and songs of the twenties up to the present day.

The staff at the hospital consisted of nurses and cleaners from different parts of the globe. Too often we class people who are not of our nationality as 'foreigners'. A lovely Phillipino woman, a nurse married to a trainee minister, asked me to show her a photo of my six month old grandson, Matthew. On looking at this chubby babe, she passed a remark that changed my way of thinking.

"Oh, what a lovely baby! How old?" she asked. When I told her that it was a boy of six months she remarked that he was big for his age,-----saying foreign babies are big for their age not like ours. . 'Her remark made me think how often we use the word foreign towards other cultures, as if they are not up to our standards .When, in fact, we are in the same category.

Chapter 13 - Australian Transformation

I felt that it was time for another move. Lola retired after her father passed away. She had trusted me to nurse him while he was still alive, and I had been privileged to be with him during his final moments. But the next Director did not have the same qualities as her predecessor. The politics of the administration changed, and not for the best. Even though I was sad to leave, it was time for a change.

During the time that I was still at Hedley Sutton I had an experience, which made me think that I had entered a dream world. Or, I was on my way to the funny farm. I was asked to direct a pantomime for the Frankston Theatre Company. All went well till a fortnight before the show was due to go on. Then the stage manager decided to go on a holiday, from which she would not return until a couple of days before the performance. So, before she departed for Queensland, I called to see if she had everything under control. As I made my way to her house I chose a different way than the one I usually took. Oh boy, did I regret that decision! I arrived at the entrance to Gould Street where she lived and found a broken down car barring the way to her house. I stopped the car and a lady constable drove up in a police car. She stopped beside me, got out and asked me what I was doing there. I was at a loss to understand the reason for her question – you can imagine how I felt. Was this really happening?

"Stand away from the car and empty your pockets" she ordered. Her face was devoid of any emotion with only a look that matched her commands.

"Please tell me what this is about. Do you think that I have committed a crime?" I asked.

She looked me straight in the eye and said in a flat voice - "That's what we're here to find out. So tell me your movements since you left work," she went on. By this time, I began to feel hot and bothered. Here I was in a new country and knowing very little. The people who could vouch for me were not with me. I explained the way I had come, only stopping at the traffic lights, to which she said that she was not satisfied, and then, 'pocketing' my keys she told me to get back into my car. As she did so, she summoned another police car which turned out to be a van, the type in which prisoners are transported to jail. It arrived with two more policemen, in case I gave them trouble or resisted arrest.

Well, this seemed to be the end. My blood ran cold with the thought that I must have had a brainstorm, leading me to have committed some dastardly crime - of which I had no knowledge. (The shadows were fast overshadowing the sunshine.) There were still no answers. 'Tell us what you did' seemed to be the only answer I was likely to receive. I made one last effort and asked again - "How can you suspect me of anything, unless you tell me what you suspect?" And once again this fell on deaf ears. The male officer reached into the glove box and pulled out a snippet of dress material, which had been used as a sample for dress's that was to be used in the pantomime.

"Where is the rest of the dress?" inquired the officer. He dangled the piece of material close to my eyes. I explained why it had come into my possession, but I don't believe that he believed a word I said. He then found a jar of Vaseline in the glove box and took it out, opened the lid and asked me if I usually carried it and what it was for.

Rapidly thinking of some explanation that he might understand, I replied - "I only wear leather shoes occasionally. If the shoes are synthetic, my feet perspire and cause an itch between my toes requiring the use of the Vaseline."

"Very strange," he muttered. Then, after replacing the lid he said, sarcastically - "You'll have to buy leather in future, but I have a strong suspicion that you have another use for this stuff."

My only thought at this time was - is this for real? I went from cold to hot and God only knows what scale my blood pressure had reached, or dropped down to. My mind was playing tricks and I was beginning to wonder, if, in fact, a crime had been committed with me as perpetrator. My mouth became dry. I felt nauseous, but deep inside was fear.

The encircling shadows became denser, as the interrogation proceeded. Then, in the back of the glove box the policeman found a magazine which had been bought from a stall in Flinders Street, purchased solely for the

Chapter 13 - Australian Transformation

advertised interview, inside, with Oliver Reed. He had been a friend of mine and I had been interested to see what Ollie's latest pranks might have been, but I had hardly done more than glance briefly, at the magazine through lack of time. And I had certainly not been interested in what may have been shown in the centre. But that was precisely what the police were enthusiastically interested in, and might send me to be entertained at Her Majesty's pleasure. As you have undoubtedly guessed, the centrefold showed the photo of a fully nude lady, complete with an enticing look on her face, well captured by the photographer. She certainly did not help my case at that moment, with a budding Sherlock Holmes hot on my tail.

"Are you a collector of this sort of art?" he asked. I instantly knew that my life was about to plunge for the worst, deep into the mire. I attempted to explain my reasons why I had bought the wretched book. He turned to the other officer and both regarded me with deep suspicion. Then, in a voice totally devoid of emotion he dropped his bombshell. "I'm not satisfied with your answers," he said, standing close to me. "A trip to the station may get at the truth, so, into the van you get - not your car! -He opened the door of the van and beckoned me to get in, which I did. Once I was inside he banged the door shut and locked it.

I sat and looked around this mini prison and wondered how many innocent souls had been incarcerated here, in this metal jail. I sat on that seat with my heart pounding, feeling completely drained. I pinched my side, hoping that the pain inflicted would awaken me from this dream, to no avail. The engine spluttered and jerked, stopping sharply and causing me to lose my balance and my ending up on the floor. After another few tries of the engine we were on our way. The van stopped finally, the door was opened and my captors ushered me into the station's interview area. The place seemed to be manned by police, who looked to me like the Gestapo.

I was left alone in a room whose display on the walls advertised current wanted criminals. On the opposite wall hung a further exhibition of past and present murderers and burglars. Would I ever escape this dreaded art gallery and end up in Melbourne's main prison, where all hardened criminals are incarcerated to serve sentences befitting their crimes?

Enter the first interrogator. He was shorter in length than the average policeman, but his expression was equally cold and menacing. Beating a school ruler on his arm this man obviously meant business. His voice broke the silence, as he continued to wave the ruler around in the fashion that Mr. Fulford used, when he was about to deliver corporal punishment. In school language it used to be called The Cuts. And so, with a swish of his measuring piece, he continued with his threat.

"If you persist in not giving me the right answers... do you imagine that I am an easy person to deal with?" Swish, swish. His words made it quite obvious to me what the ruler was for, in the hands of this sadistic keeper of the law. "I will return in a few minutes, expecting your co-operation. Think about it," he concluded and left the room.

I was speechless; then, no sooner had he left than 'Mr.Charmer' appeared. He was all smiles and insisted on shaking my hand. Would this man get me out of the mess, I wondered? Still smiling he said - "My colleague does not come across as friendly, does he? But he needs your co-operation Bernard. I will help you if you tell me the facts - where you have hidden the body."

Hidden the body?! At those words my mind worked overtime to prove my innocence. "I do not know anything about hiding a body," I stammered. "I have not killed anyone. My life as a nurse is to save life, not take it. However did you conclude that I could have committed such a crime?"

Mr. Nice continued, in measured tones - "We received information that you stopped your car, grabbed a child on the highway going to Frankston. Were my ears playing tricks? As panic began to overtake me,I prayed to God to save me from this nightmare.

"Let me face the person who made this accusation," I pleaded.

"We were informed by phone," he told me. "Till we can prove that your answers are true, you will remain under suspicion. Your son in law will be here shortly and we trust that he will be able to clear your name. He is coming in place of your wife because she was not at home when we called."

Val duly arrived and seemed not at all to be anxious about my predicament. In fact, he treated the whole thing as a joke. When he was shown the

Chapter 13 - Australian Transformation

contents of the glove box ,he said calmly - "Mr. Blestel is a bit of a hoarder. He never throws anything away."

"Please tell them why I've saved them," I said to him. "This is serious."

Val looked at the offending materials and said - "I can only guess that the material is for costumes for the panto." He ignored the article about Oliver Reed and looked at the centre fold picture of the nude girl for a moment. "Hm, very nice. I admire your choice," he remarked, smiling. The jar of Vaseline received no comment (thank God). Aware that I was not getting any help from Val, I turned to the Gestapo chief again to plead my innocence.

When he returned to the chamber of horrors, because that is where I imagined this charade was being conducted, he spoke to one of my captors - "He is free to go," he said. "Get him to sign the book confirming that he was not abused in any way during the interview." Then, with his eyes cast down he marched out of the room as if I had never existed. There was never a word of apology. I learnt, from the 'kindly' policeman that the phone call had been a hoax! After signing the book, which, I did much against my will, my mind slowly returned to normal. If there is any such thing as normal.

Chapter 14

Lending a Sympathetic Ear

Due to the change of politics after Matron Henderson retired, I endeavoured to find another hospital that would employ me. Glancing again through the Yellow Pages, my eye was caught by the name Mayflower, a medical complex in Brighton.

Supervised by another capable Director, June Mackenzie, I applied for and was accepted to a position which lasted for ten years, before an injured back forced me to find a job with less lifting.

During my nursing career, I cared for patients with many and varied illnesses and disabilities, all requiring special needs in their treatment. In some cases the prognosis was not good though we continued to give the best care possible.

Mrs. Poynton was one lady in my care. She was as bright as a button at 106 years! At bedtime she would kneel to say her prayers, while few would have followed her example; choosing instead to pray in the comfort of their beds. But not this lady. She said that Jesus had said 'kneel and pray' and so she carried out His instructions. "Till these poor old bones say enough is enough," she insisted quietly. She was a dear Christian lady with a great sense of humour.

Talking about humour - one night, shortly before dawn, the fire alarm went off. The system was undergoing repairs, and because of this, we were inclined to call the fire brigade out on a false errand. Of course, this happened on a night when I was on duty. So, I waited at the entrance to let the brigade know that everything was okay when, strolling along the footpath, came a young policeman. On spying me standing there in my dressing gown, he crossed the road towards me, saying - "It's a cold night, sir, and it's gone three o'clock."

"Good morning, constable," I responded. "I'm waiting, for the fire brigade - though there is no fire."

"I think you'd better go back to bed, sir," he said solicitously. "No use catching pneumonia. Back you go before you get into trouble with the Matron," he advised.

"No, officer," I said. "I'm in charge here. The system is faulty and is being overhauled."

The kindly constable looked me up and down, as if he was suspicious of my explanation then turned to go. "Well, if you say so. I'll be on my way then, but you'd better wait for them in your bed, because, you never know - they might never turn up." Unfortunately the concerned PC had already disappeared when the clanging vehicle arrived poste haste to quell the non-existent flames.

When all the excitement had finally died down and things were normal again, I found my way back to my room. I surveyed myself in the mirror to satisfy myself that the policeman had made a mistake. Surely I did not look that old? Like one of my patients? Anyway, that's my story and I'm sticking to it. On the other hand, perhaps he needed to have his eyes tested?

There was the day, when Lily, a lady, more English than the English, rang for me in the early hours of the morning to tell me that 'those buggers' had crept under her door. I never found out who the 'buggers' were. She informed me that they had taken her false teeth out of her mouth as she

Chapter 14 - Lending a Sympathetic Ear

slept and that she could not sleep without them. The search for the missing teeth began in the dark of the early morning. Bed covers were removed and the mattress were upturned to no avail. Wardrobes and clothes were inspected, and, down on hands and knees, we groped under bed. While this operation was taking place, Lily sat quietly muttering - "You won't find them. Those buggers have taken them." In desperation I realised that there was only one other place to look - the commode. I lifted the lid and there, neatly laid out, and seeming to smile, were the offending teeth. "You found me," they seemed to be saying.

Lily responded with a toothless smile of her own. "You found them," she said. "But you never know where these buggers will put them!" After a good scrub the Happy Wanderers were put back where they belonged, and dear contented Lily settled down for the rest of the night. Lily loved to sing, so, when she was down in the dumps, we would render Lily of Laguna, her favourite sang. This always brought a smile, especially when we came to the line - 'I know she loves me, because she said so.' At the end of the song she would give me a kiss on the cheek, God bless her.

On the other side of the coin were patients who needed another kind of support. Maybe they had family problems, or suffered the death of a friend, or were afraid of dying themselves, not knowing what the future might hold for them. When we are young, we have all the time in the world, but in the autumn of our lives the leaves fall swiftly and to many the future is bleak. I try to brush away the shadows by reminding those, who are fearful, that birth is a coming out into the unknown, but usually brings good and comforting circumstances. And death, which is also like stepping into the unknown could well have similarly good and comforting consequences.

Jean, who came from a farm, near Castlemaine, was very close to her sister Mary. Both were pianists. Jean taught music on the farm and fell in love. Her father did not approve of her choice and poor Jean had to obey him, so the lovers parted. Such was the way of life in those days. There is very little chance of a father ruling his daughter's life these days. Jean always regretted the loss and spoke with sadness when she recollected her past. Mary married twice, having lost her first husband in the war. Jean loved poetry. She loved tape recordings of poems and bible readings interspersed with music, which I recorded for her. Jean spent hours many listening, as her sight was failing. This was my way of supporting her, and every night she offered up a prayer on my behalf regarding my work. Such a dear Christian lady.

There were times when members of staff would approach me with some of their personal problems, in the hope that I could save them. This was not always easy.

I remember one young male, nurse who had been living in the shadows in secret, for some time. He believed that people would show no understanding of his predicament. One day he arrived at work with a swollen lip and a black eye. Apparently, while returning home, with his partner John they came face to face with a gang of louts, who referred to themselves as 'poofter bashers'.

Eric was a good-looking lad with a gentle and caring nature who had decided, from an early age, to train as a nurse. He joined the staff at Mayflower on his twenty-fifth birthday and was loved by his patients, because nothing was too much trouble for him, whenever he was asked to carry out a request of any kind. He wept, as I compassionately took him into my arms, and poured out his whole story. He and John had attended school together and developed a close friendship, and this grew stronger in their teenage years. They decided to live together as a gay couple and this was kept secret from their parents. Both fathers would have been appalled, if they had found out what was going on, and would undoubtedly have turned their backs on them. Between sobs he intimated that I too would probably be disgusted by his behaviour. I assured him that nothing was further from my mind and invited him, when his shift was over, to talk his problem through with me. He was more composed when we met later, and he told me that he had explained to the patients that he had met with a slight accident, which they accepted. He was ready to confide in me.

It seemed that in many ways he felt guilty, and obviously the first step would be to get rid of that guilt. Over a cup of tea, I asked him whom he thought might be the most important person in his life. I suggested that he, himself

Chapter 14 - Lending a Sympathetic Ear

was without doubt that person. "If you are not right with yourself then you are no use to anyone," I told him.

"Where do I begin?" he asked me.

I told him that he should begin with himself. "Let's start with the guilt," I continued. "You did not ask to be gay. Like millions the world over, it developed in your sexuality. Whatever the cause maybe, a quirk of nature or a part of nature's pattern, remember that there are over 1500 different species of animal that are bi-sexual. Did they have a choice? You are what you are. Guilt smothers us even when we are not responsible for the position we might have taken, even when this is often against the mores of society or our family." He listened carefully as I went on. "You are living in the shadows, and it is time that you recognised that you are not alone in this situation. Let God be your judge, not others who are bigoted against your lifestyle. God's concern is about how we exit this world. He is not looking for flaws we might gather along the way. Our sexuality is not a problem in God's eyes. He is concerned with how we handle our situation during our journey in this ever-changing world."

"Frequently, our behaviour towards each other becomes lax and standards are lowered. There is drug abuse with drugs being pushed in schools and work places, and there is terrorism and fraud, racial hatred and murder, etc, etc. These are just a few of the things that sadden God's heart. Many years ago, Kirk Douglas acquired a Cameroonian carving, about two feet tall, of a nude figure. One side had a female organ and the other was male. It was not an idol but the representation of the human psyche or of our individuality or persona. It is remarkable that those African natives knew long ago that every human being has a feminine and masculine side. The people, who made that statue understood the complexity of the human psyche. It's all about balance, isn't it? The feminine side is a symbol of creativity, while the masculine, gives us the perseverance and strength."

I saw that he was smiling and smiled with him. "Why don't you ring Gayline for further help? And turn towards the light, which, in your case, is understanding what it is that is causing unrest in your life."

Thankfully, he did seek the help of a counsellor, and slowly came to terms with his dilemma. Both lads faced their parents who mercifully did not take any drastic action. They began to understand that they were not separated from their families or friends, as had been the case before their choice had become common knowledge. The shadows have dispersed and they are beginning to feel the warmth of love radiating from the sunshine of friends and families.

Mildred always worried that some catastrophe would come to me, as I returned home from work. (Mind you, things did seem to happen to me and no one else ...) She always begged me to phone her on the way, and, while the road is paved with good intentions, mostly I did phone at some stage.

On this particular night the sudden inspiration to be a dutiful husband entered my mind and urged me to find a phone. Phones seemed to be nonexistent at first, but then I saw one on a side road, adjacent to a park.

Standing outside the phone box was a young man, in his early twenties, leaning against the boundary pole. I got out of the car and asked him if he was making a call.

"No, mate, go ahead," he said.

My long-suffering wife has had the patience of Job over the years regarding my time keeping. This time I felt that I had done the right thing and told her that I was on my way and would be home in half an hour. Truly, as God is my witness. The road to hell is paved with good intentions, and fate thought otherwise. The young man bid me goodnight, and, as he spoke, I detected that something was wrong. Oh boy, was I right!

"Are you alright?" I asked him.

"No, mate I'm not. You can't help me," he replied, not looking at me.

"Try me," I said, without knowing the problem. The light from the phone booth gave enough illumination for me to see the person, who was about to reveal the distress which presently engulfed his young life. He was dressed in the typical fashion of the seventies.---- a cap with the peak turned

Chapter 14 - Lending a Sympathetic Ear

backwards, almost entirely covering his blonde hair. His eyes showed a trace of melancholia and his voice was clearly Australian accented.

He told me that his father had emigrated from the war-ravaged city of Cologne, in Germany, in 1947 and married a country girl from Gippsland. His mother was one of three children, two girls and a brother, who had been born blind. He stopped talking and introduced himself as Ben, shook my hand and asked my name.

"Bernard, but most people call me Bernie," I told him. Finally, we got down to why he was waiting by the phone booth. It seemed that his mother had accused him of taking a hundred dollars from her housekeeping, which he denied. She did not believe him and this led to an unholy row, which terminated with her throwing him out of the house. 'She said that; if a son steals from his mother, then he's not worth being called a son."

"Forgive me for asking," I ventured. "But you never touched the money, did you?"

"Of course I fucken didn't," he retorted hotly. "She should know me better than that! I wouldn't rob her, even if I were on drugs! Which I am not I never touched a cent of hers, believe me Bernie. I was tempted, I was no angel, but I never stole to buy the stuff. I had other means, which I suppose was as bad as stealing..."

He went onto explain how he had fed his habit. Apparently ,some ladies of the blue rinse set whose rich husbands denied them sex, asked Ben to be their stud, which usually started as a drinking session and subsequently led to bed for which he duly received a fee.

"But Bernie," he said, not looking at me. "I was dishonest in the fact that I tried my best to get them so pissed that they wouldn't know if they'd been fucked or not. Still, they always seemed happy when I left, and asked me to return. In those days I served some thirty odd ladies, so l had to cut down my input which is why I had to get them pissed. Eventually, some woman who never drank got me into rehab. She said she loved me, but I suspect it was my cock she loved. He stopped for a moment and grinned. "Not a pretty history, Bernie. But now that's-all behind me and I've been off the drugs for three years. Now, to crown it all, I've lost my job through inflation. The boss said he was sorry to lose such a good worker, but he couldn't afford my wages. What's the use of being a good worker, when nobody employs you? So, Bernie - what am I to do?"

As he spoke, I felt his sensitivity. The poor lad was close to tears once again. I sensed that he was telling the truth, not covering his faults, which I suspected in the past had caused much heartache for his mother.

At this precise moment in time he needed direction, with a capital D. I gave myself a few seconds, as I considered what advice I could offer him ,and finally suggested that he should go back to his mother and apologise for upsetting her. "Tell her that, whatever she may think, you did not steal her money and, that, as soon as you get another job you will replace the hundred dollars, which someone else must have stolen or which she might have lost. Remember, she is still your mother and lam sure she still loves you and will forgive you, as she has done in the past."

"Do you think it will work, Bernie? My mother can be a bugger at times."

"So can we all, Ben," I said. "You can but try," I went on. When you apply for a job take anything on offer and use it as a stepping stone for a better position."

By the look on his face I could see that he was uncertain that his conversation with his mother would succeed or be futile. I am sure that he thought I had more faith in his making peace with his mother than he did. I must admit that a few silent prayers were needed in this situation.

I glanced at my watch and realised that the half hour I had promised Mildred had well and truly passed. Ben thanked me and we exchanged phone numbers, so that I could be informed about his future progress, and we parted company---- I on my merry way to the Home Front, and, Ben, going back, not knowing what sort of reaction he would receive. We were both apprehensive.

Poor suffering Mildred was not amused, to say the least. My usual explanation, when I arrived home late was –"you'll never believe this", to which Mildred would reply- "Where have you been? I've been worried

Chapter 14 - Lending a Sympathetic Ear

sick. You said half an hour and you appear three hours later, as if nothing had happened. You're impossible!" I told her about my meeting with Ben and Mildred responded with – "Can't I impress on you, that if you are delayed, you use your bloody phone?" By her inserting that word I knew that she was not impressed. "It's a wonder that you didn't bring Ben home for the night – as you so often do on odd occasions ..." she concluded. Once the storm had subsided she asked me if Ben would be alright. The answer came by phone a few days later. Yes, his mother had welcomed him back home and he had found a job. "Thank you, Bernie," he said. "Do you know why I was standing outside that phone box? Well, I was waiting for the biggest truck to come along so that I could throw myself under it."

How sad. Reaching the stage, when you want to wipe out the very breath given to you at birth. When you descend into a well of loneliness, thinking that no one cares, if you live or die-----unable to see a glimmer of light to guide you from the path of self destruction. Who is to blame for the dramatic increase in suicides affecting all age groups? Have we lost the art of coping?

When deep shadows cross our paths, have our parents failed by providing too much of modern welfare, while the pursuit of money takes-up whatever time is available to them, leaving the family unit in second place or non-existent? All this assisted by unscrupulous dealers who say that trendy drugs will assist by transporting everyone to a world where cares are wiped away, and forgetting to point out that annihilation is on the cards, through the use of cannabis and chroming, amphetamines, ecstasy, cocaine or heroin---- and hallucinogens like LSD, magic mushrooms and not forgetting alcohol. All of them bent on Mind Changing, giving a false impression of life. What is the answer? Do we ignore the situation? Treating the syndrome, not the cause. Is pleasure put before life or is life a humbug to be injured and dispensed at will? The breath given to us is worth saving whatever the odds.

To me it was worth the wrath of Mildred. Once again it was people who counted;. to be of any use, we sometimes have to enter their world of shadows. This means involvement, which can be irritating to your family, often unwittingly neglecting them of your time. I sometimes feel, that, because I live in such a rush, I leave no time to spare----perhaps losing time for spirituality and communion with nature and those around us.

I often felt that, though Mildred supported me, she never fully understood my desire to help people to rid themselves of their shadows. Her love for me required me to be within reach twenty four hours a day, and I certainly considered it a compliment to be wanted. Deeply as I loved her, this was impossible for me. Time was the only thing I denied her, while I loved her in all other respects and it was reciprocated. Fifty-three years together proved the commitment we made all those years ago in the Holy Trinity Church. Love does not ask you to give up your individuality; it does expect you to respect each other as individuals. To merge as one ,though, even in the best of marriages, it is sometimes difficult to find fulfilment in all aspects of life together. It takes a lot of hard work, Plus great understanding, to achieve the way to find all the colours of the rainbow during the journey.

Chapter 15

Hope Abandoned

I would like to deal with the light and the shadows that can be cast.

We all have the ability to radiate light to others in the form of understanding. We have the power to enhance or destroy the lives of others. In other words, our bodies and brains are capable of transmitting good or evil. Very often it is not our choice to cast shadows; we are used as instruments to increase the power of evil. Or, often, the last glimmer of light fades, leaving us in complete oblivion, a suffocating darkness. Our only hope then is to focus on the light however faint it might be.

Shadows are only cast by light. When the light is diminished, we are in BIG trouble. As I have said before, light is life, generated by each one of us. Our lives should be committed to each other, to disperse the shadows.

Where do we get our particular light or strength from? For each one of us the source is different. Some receive it through moral teaching, by goals you set yourself to achieve. For others, it is the adoption of the Christian faith. In many cases one may look for religious teachings from around the world, like Buddhism, Muslim teachings, Judaism and so on.

Whatever dynamo charges, the light is unimportant, as long as the wattage or amperage behind the source is love. Love knows no colour nor creed, embracing all. Love is patient and kind---it does not envy, it does not boast, it is not proud and it is not rude. It is not self-seeking and it is not easily angered. It keeps no record of wrongs and does not delight in evil, but rejoices in the truth. Love never ends. So, faith, hope and love abide - of these three the greatest love. If I have not got love, then I have nothing.

How many can say that they have embraced all three? This should be our aim - shouldn't it?

When I started writing this book, I did not intend it to have any religious connotations. The sole purpose was to show what motivated me through my life. At times I did rely on divine power giving me the strength to fight the most intense shadows, and you can believe that I've been through quite a few. My desire is to show how an ordinary person like myself can face the trials and tribulations,when things seem hopeless.

Due to lifting patients over the years, my lower back began to give me a lot of pain. I decided to leave Mayflower which was a great disappointment, as I had enjoyed my stay. The patients presented me with parting gifts and it was with great sadness that my journey there had ended.

My next move was to a different field of work. Bailey Lodge catered for twenty intellectually handicapped people from teenagers to seniors. I enjoyed the job, and, thankfully, it did not include much heavy lifting.

The place was not run as an institution but rather as a home, where we treated everyone as if they had no handicaps at all. I grew to love them and this was reciprocated, I smile now, when I remember the humorous side of it all at Fewster Road. Olga was one of the seniors at the Lodge. Her mother had worked as an usherette in the local cinema when Gone with the Wind was first shown in the early forties. Dear Olga told me that she had seen it twenty-four times and hated every moment of one of the greatest movie classics. Olga loved to peel carrots and potatoes, though the taste made her sick. Chips and raw carrots were okay. She was a character.

Chapter 15 - Hope Abandoned

I was on a cooking roster four days a week with a cap and apron part of my attire. Those days were not a hardship for me, as I enjoyed cooking. Previously, at Mayflower, if the chef was sick or had days off and a replacement could not be found, I would take over the kitchen, which gave my back a rest from lifting. I stayed at Bailey Lodge till my retirement. I missed our Bailey Lodge family when I left---dear Olga, Marion, Carol, Patrick, Darien, Jillene and Steven etc,

I'll never forget dear Margaret Jones who wanted to buy every item in the supermarket, when we shopped for supplies. It was a battle, returning tins to shelves which she took back as quickly as they were replaced. She had an uncanny way of filling her basket. Once, when dear Margaret put on her usual show at the checkout, another customer surveyed her antics with obvious disdain. I considered it unkind and turned to her. "It's a shame," I said. "Margaret was just like you a month ago." Needless, to say I hope this gave the woman some food for thought.

Kevin and Trudy, both with Downs Syndrome, were always ready to help. They were delightful people. I have mentioned just a few who were handicapped, living in the shadows. Even so, they endeavoured to turn to the light, enjoying life within their limitations. The staff gave loving care and I considered it a privilege to work there, in spite of the fact that the patients could be a little naughty at times. There was not an ounce of evil in their personalities. God bless them.

I have included an appreciation of my care, from the manager of Bailey Lodge, Mr. John McDonald. I do so humbly. Not for any glory but for the way they responded to love. "To whom it may concern. I have known Bernard for a period of six years. During this time Bernard has displayed qualities which are rare. The qualities most admired by his colleagues and myself are his compassion, his capability, conscientiousness and willingness for hard work. Whilst employed with me Bernard was well liked by other staff. But he was particularly loved by the disabled clients in his care. Who, I may add, are excellent judges of human nature."

After I retired, I continued to accept film and TV engagements, arising at 5am, getting to locations at the crack of dawn, having fun meetings with various stars and other performers. Australian films and TV are shown all over the world. Friends from the other side of the ocean, when viewing Aussie productions were excited when they caught a glimpse of me. Such is fame. No shadows here. I count myself very fortunate to be surrounded by love, even though clouds overshadowed the sunshine at various times. One of my concerns is the plight of those who slide down the scales of life, finding comfort in drugs or alcohol. It is almost impossible to put a brake on their dependence, in spite of their loss of home, work, family and dignity.

A friend, Sue Fisher, asked me if I would be willing to assist with breakfast programme which voluntarily assisted people in need. Yes, I told her that I would be interested. This involved going on a roster, arising at the unearthly hour of 5.30am and travelling to St. Paul's Anglican Church on the border of Frankston. Once there, I would cook (again) bacon and eggs, sausages, tomatoes and beans. Sometimes included was savoury mince, which some kind person would donate. While the cooking was being prepared, they enjoyed toast, a bowl of cereal topped up with fruit salad or the like, plus orange or apple juice and tea or coffee. There was no charge. We catered for a mixed bunch of all ages, all affected maybe through drink, drugs, schizophrenia or just plain loneliness, manic depression or losing the will to work. We often fed up to sixty people and sometimes young children, who had been left to their own devices, joined the meal.

Unfortunately, in this materialistic age, many parents have forfeited the true needs of the family in their search for elusive wealth. How sad to lose those precious years, collecting bric-a-brac to enhance our lives. I considered it a privilege to be included in this volunteer service, where the money that was needed was raised by fund raising and donations. Thanks must be given to Janet McCann and Sue Fisher, who spent endless time ensuring that there was food in the kitchen. There are comments sometimes made by people who are not in touch with others in need, like - "It's their own fault, letting drink or drugs reduce them to becoming the fag ends of society." My answer to that sort of comment is to ask them, if they have ever been on the rocky road to their own downfall or do we have the right to criticise other people? At the end of this book I've included a story called 'No

Chapter 15 - Hope Abandoned

Hoper' which I wrote for a competition. Perhaps you will draw your own conclusion as to who the No Hoper is.

Being involved is an important part of this work. Understanding the problems that face these people by always being on hand with a listening ear, even though you may not be able to alleviate the cause of the problem. Just by suggesting some way that they can tackle it, may help. One of the worst features of this work is when you hear Craig will not be coming anymore, because he died of an overdose, or that John hanged himself in the station toilet or that Shaun who was deeply depressed, threw himself off a cliff top and that his body was found smashed and broken. And then there was Mary. Such a kind caring mother who had reached the end of her tether as the shadows closed in and, was unable to face her future as a single Mum, after breaking up with her partner and threw herself off a convenient bridge. She was clutching her baby in her arms at the time.

Ray and his partner Wayne contracted AIDS. As the disease progressed with no cure in sight, this period required a great deal of thought and mind searching. Both decided that, if the pain and suffering became too much, became unbearable, then either one would assist the other to exit from this earth. A year or so later, Ray lost the will to carry on. Both the mental and physical pain became too much for him. It was time for him to go. The thought of leaving Wayne was unthinkable, but if he stayed, he would lose his dignity as well as all other functions. The nausea, the pain, weight loss and diabetes sent him drifting into a never never land, where there was no more waiting for the ticking of the clock. He fought to avoid being reduced to a vegetable state, and knew it could be years before a cure could put a stop to his nightmare.

Ray knew that both his mother and his father had accepted his partnership with Wayne, because they could see and understand the fact that they loved one another. But the time had come for Ray, and so he asked Wayne to help him end it. Wayne was not yet at the advanced stage of the illness and finally agreed to administer an overdose of morphine. Ray insisted on a farewell glass of champagne, while Wayne left the fatal dose within easy reach of his beloved friend. Ray thanked Wayne for their sharing their lives together so happily for twelve years, and then, after a final embrace, he turned away and swallowed the fatal dose.

One can only imagine how Wayne found the strength to survive the ordeal. The thought of what he had done filled him with guilt. Yes, he had carried out Ray's wish, Ray had chosen to die, Ray had thanked him and that was what they had planned together. But his conscience plagued him as he worried over the other side of the story. You had no right in law ...it's like committing a murder ...a miracle cure may have been found at some time. And so on. His mind was in a state of torment. And then, Wayne decided to spend a pleasant evening with his friends, after which he waved a cheery goodbye and drove his car to the tallest bridge in town, parked close to the edge, clambered over the fence and plunged to his death far below. Did both find peace?

Chapter 16

Magnificent Venice and the Japanese Annihilation

The wonderful thing about the mind is that it allows us to travel backwards and forward. For the time being, I am leaving the shadows behind me and emerging into the sunshine. This period became an exciting part of my life and I will share it with you. Are you ready to step onto my magic carpet to feast your eyes on lands that are far away from Australia?

The journeys were only made possible through the generosity of my dear friend William L. Lowe. [Billie] I met him soon after I arrived in this land which I now call home. We met while I was still nursing at Hedley Sutton, where Billie was visiting another patient. Bill orBillie , as he is known, is a very caring person, a very talented piano teacher who first studied under Ada Corder OBE, one of Australia's most renowned teachers, this lady taught him for fourteen years. He furthered his studies in London under Louis Kentner, a world famous pianist who also taught in the Grand Tradition. After which Billie returned to Australia and continued his studies under Ada Corder .I might add that Billie is a Specialist in his field.

Some years later, Billie had the pleasure of renewing his acquaintance with Kentner at a Violini a Venezia Concerti performance in the Teatro Goldini in Venice. At the same time and at the same Concert I had the opportunity to meet Yehudi Menuhin whose relative by marriage I had nursed during my time at Mayflower. We chatted in the Green Room after the concert. It was Billie, who is usually shy about such encounters, suggested that we should go back stage this time. It proved to be a very great pleasure to both of us. At the Concert the audience were dressed to the nines, and both Mrs. Kentner and Mrs. Menuhin wore diamond-encrusted tiaras which caught the light like sparkling stars. The stage was bedecked with the most gorgeous floral arrangements and the music was superlative.

Menuhin on the violin and Kentner on the piano played the Brahms Sonata in A Major No.2, followed by the Beethoven Sonata in A Major, known as the Kreutzer Sonata, and finally they played the Cesar Frank Sonata in A Major. These three Grand, remarkable works were played with profound depth, and insight, not to mention that the whole performance was play from memory. Due to their advanced years this was a marvellous feat. Unforgettable.!

I remember Venice as a wonderful city of antiquity, a city of canals with gondolas steered by handsome gondoliers who burst into romantic song whenever the occasion arose. There were villas reached by aged stone steps that led to enchanted gardens, and those ancient stone steps seemed to set Venice apart from the rest of the world. I remember numerous narrow streets or pathways taking us to abundant places of interest, over bridges, and canals built long ago by the founders of this great city. Venice is a mixture of past and present with buildings which seem to rise up out of the sea.------ St. Mark's Basilica, the Byzantine religious centre seated in the square, where people participate wholly in the life of the Republic.

After it attended to the promulgation of laws and sentences, this place became an ancient atrium for festivals and ceremonies. The square also houses the Doge's Palace, while screeching gulls and pigeons circle the church dome in perpetual motion, ever watchful of passers by dropping tit - bits, leaving the flying circus as vagrants to fight and gather the spoils dropped by the maddening crowds. And sparrows, cheekily alight

Chapter 16 - Magnificent Venice and the Japanese Annihilation

on tables, steal a crumb or two from the undisturbed visitors and locals enjoying the warm sunshine, as they sip their wine, oblivious of time.

There were couples, hand in hand, their eyes speaking of love, stopping to look or buy from the plentiful novelty shops, Or to acquire a work of art, or, if they were lucky, an icon. The icons were supposedly blessed by a Saint who had suffered martyrdom. Romantic Venice, a city set deep in the pages of history. Upon its stage a mixture of intrigue, drama of all sorts and love. Gathered together to become the city we see today, a city which seduces the traveller to return. You are intoxicated by the beauty that radiates from a culture whose heritage is impregnated within its walls and waterways. Perhaps the stones have a patron Saint? St. James' anniversary is on the 25th July.

Consider how much there is to see and enjoy! Rio delle Torres Elle, Rio di San Vio, the Academia Bridge, which spans the Grand Canal, the Church of San Vidal, Rio di San Toma, the Rialto Bridge, the Bridge of Sighs and the museums, the art galleries and the sculptures. A plaque, on the wall of the Casino di Venezia states that Richard Wagner had lived there. And the Island of Murano, so famous for its glass.

We dined in a restaurant overlooking the Grand Canal, eating Leisurely and watching gondolas plying to and fro. Oh, what sights to behold! My friend Billie summed up our stay -"Words pale into insignificance alongside this wondrous city, so steeped in history and time. With the waters of the Adriatic, St. Marks Square and St. Marks Basilica, the buildings that fired the imagination of Tintoretto, Guardi and countless others. And the warm, caring Italians, Causing the tears to well up in one's very eyes."

True to form, getting there was an adventure, which seems to happen to us on our travels. We arrived in Paris and made our way to the station to catch the connection to Venice. After being directed to a train whose carriages seemed to stretch for a mile, with the place a hive of activity and porters barely being able to understand our French, we finally made our way to the first class carriages. Yes Messieurs, it goes to Venice, our porter told us. Billie tipped him and he eyed the francs in surprise after which he loaded our luggage onto the train, touched his cap and said 'au revoir'.

Billie turned to me as we sank thankfully into our reserved seats. "Do you think I gave him enough?" he asked.

"Well," I replied. "With the look on his face it was either too much or you paid him slave labour."

On through the night sped the train, as people of all nationalities came and went, while both of us slept in fits and starts. Then it happened. The train slowed down, then came to a final halt. It remained stationary for an indeterminate period. Half asleep I asked Billie what was going on? I had no sooner uttered the words, when the carriage was invaded by three male cleaners armed with mops, brushes, buckets and all the other paraphernalia required to thoroughly cleanse our environment. The look on their and our faces was indescribable. It appears that we were the only passengers left. All the others left while we were sleeping. The cleaner's spokesman who managed to communicate with us in broken English asked us why we were there.

"We are on our way to Venice," replied. Billie with confidence. After a few seconds we were shattered, when the spokesman threw up his hands in despair.

"No, no, go to Venezia! Go to Milano! No Venezia, Milano! We go to Milano!" he yelled. Billie looked out of the window, and, to our amazement, we saw that the whole carriage had been slipped, awaiting another engine to hook up to and then on its merry way to Milano. Our invaders thought that our situation was a huge joke, bursting into sporadic laughter which we felt we should join, though this was no laughing matter for us.

Thankfully, the head cleaner seemed to understand our predicament and beckoned us to follow him out of the carriage with our luggage, then tripping over the railway lines in fear that some express would mow us down before we could see the wonders of Venice, and, still laughing, he bade us goodbye after putting us on a shunting train that took us to the right platform, where we would finally board the Venice bound train. Out of breath, but feeling better, Billie handed our saviour some money. This time, unlike the earlier porter in Paris, he looked thankful, so Billie must have got it right.

Chapter 16 - Magnificent Venice and the Japanese Annihilation

We eventually arrived in Venice at 4am. I left Billie sitting with all our cases around him, in an empty room of the station, assuring him that I would be back as soon as possible after I had found a hotel. It would have been no use both of us trudging around with the luggage without knowing where to go. So off I went, without the slightest idea of where we would find the abode we wanted. My last view of Billie was of him sitting comfortably on the cases looking somewhat gnome-like and wondering what our future might hold.

Trekking through unknown territory I eventually found the Hotel which we had booked. But I was quickly informed that the booking had been for two months earlier! Someone - and I mean someone had booked by mistake and it had not been us. My blood ran from hot to cold at this latest adventure (disaster?). The proprietor shook his head, and waved his arms around, much like a Maestro conducting a symphony and uttering as fast as the Concorde in full flight. "No room, you made mistake, no room!" Thankfully, those very words started a cat and mouse game and - the mice won! We got the room.

I returned to Billie, and, behold, - he was now sitting in a room full of vagrants. Apparently all the down and outs gathered there to sleep. It had become a doss house for the night, and I have to say it did not smell of ashes of roses. Needless to say, Billie was not amused at my choice of waiting rooms.

After leaving beautiful Venice we made our way to Amsterdam via Rome. We stayed in Rome for a few days and visited the Coliseum, picturing this showplace in ancient times as an arena of death where lions and gladiators fought to kill. What barbaric times they were. Yet, have we altered our ways of killing? Perhaps we just choose more devious ways and now we kill in thousands, or should I say millions. In wars, acts of terrorism and so on.

The Coliseum is now a place where you can enjoy festivals, plays, music, the blood that flowed freely long ago, now redeemed by songs and laughter, together with audience appreciation in this open-air art centre. The shadows have lifted from this place of slaughter and sorrow. May the light shine, as long as the Coliseum stands.

Crossing the Roman roads was a feat of endurance with the traffic zigzagging at breakneck speed. No wonder the Pope lives here. You have not visited Rome if climbing the Spanish Steps is not on your agenda. When you reach the top of the steps you enter the Borghese Gardens and gaze upon the busts of past Emperors looking down on the city below, as they have done over the ages. Rome, the Eternal city, is built on seven hills. As you walk along its streets, your eyes catch the wonder of a past Empire. Little did the architects know that when they built this breathtaking seat of Imperial Rome that it would survive for so many eternities. Nor did they know that the Vatican would rise with all its pomp and ceremony to become the focal point for all the myriad followers of Roman Catholicism.

It is August 6th and a glorious sunny day in Rome. Happy days. The birds are singing in the leafy trees bordering the park. Sparrows are pecking over a carpet of green grass, hoping to find insects or worms to satisfy their needs. For all creatures, human or otherwise must eat - or die. Children play hide and seek behind a fountain whose cool water splashes into a lily pond, where goldfish scurry for shelter under broad leaves of pink and white lilies. The sweet fragrance of the flowers tantalises our nostrils. The hustle and bustle of people and traffic make us feel alive. A vendor is sitting on a stool, selling today's newspapers. Though the papers had been Italian, I glance at the date. It is August 6th.

The mirror of Rome fades and becomes silent, as I remember another time. I remember August 6th, 1945, and coldness invades my body. VE Day brought us victory in Europe and everyone thought that the Japanese would soon surrender. The Italians had capitulated, leaving Germany and Japan to fight on. Germany surrendered on May 9th, 1945. The Japanese did not follow suit until one of the greatest crimes ever committed against humanity was dropped upon them from the skies. The Japanese decided to call it quits on August 16th.

The war in Europe had ceased three months earlier and with it came the liberation of our dear Channel Isles. As stated by Winston Churchill during his speech to the nation, - the refugees from the Channel Isles were eagerly anticipating the OK to return home after their five years of exile.

Chapter 16 - Magnificent Venice and the Japanese Annihilation

The sun shone at its brightest on that hot summer's day. Far away, in Hiroshima, on a day that none will ever forget, the terrible atomic cloud encircled the many thousands of inhabitants as they went about their everyday business. The Americans who flew in that aircraft had never visited their destination or knew those who dwelt there. All they had to know was that the people far below were Japanese and enemies of the free world. The plane was on a mission and in its gates sat a bomb like no other before it, designed, nurtured and brought to life by top scientists. Their job, to create a juggernaut, so powerful that it held, in its 28 by 120 inches, a weapon that could change or destroy this planet. The monster's brainchild was neatly attached to a parachute which enabled it to float calmly from a high altitude to a position where it will explode to rain death in a form never before seen. One might inquire as to what was so special about that insignificant looking object? The answer came when it hit the ground and an explosion occurred that let loose the fires of hell in its mushroom cloud. The atom split and this so-called insignificant object now possessed the power to hold the world to ransom. Evil reigned.

The powers, who instigated that murderous attack, sent yet another on a mission at 11.02 on August 9th. Nagasaki was the target, and, as a result, 39,000 people were killed and 25,000 or more were injured for life as were so many thousands in Hiroshima. Did the shadows from those who organised the Manhattan project ever lift? I was thankful that I was not old enough for military service, old enough to kill or inflict suffering on a fellow human. Deo Gratias. War is not the answer to any nation's problems. Politicians on every side goad each other to commit acts of opportunism, regardless of the aftermath, which will come to the people they are supposed to represent. Those bombs, Agent Orange and so much else, should never have been used to destroy.

I might have included all that earlier in my journey, because, at the time it seemed justifiable ---- to hasten the peace. But maturity has brought understanding to me and I know now that aggression is totally unforgivable.

Chapter 17

Shadows Tinged with Hope

Up and away to our journey from Rome to London, where we visited all the tourist spots. And then, a brief stay in Guernsey. Here we were in the land of my birth, staying in a guest house in George Road near the top of the Valle de Terres.

Trudging up that hill was taxing. It was built by the unemployed in the 1930's and once again I spied the granite marking stone which informed us that the Prince of Wales, later to briefly become Edward Eighth, had opened this road.

Did my eyes play tricks or did my memory come rushing back? Here I was as a small boy watching the ceremony on my father's shoulders. The sun was blazing down on uncovered heads. No one had heard of skin cancer. The meadows bordering the road were a maze of yellow and white---- Buttercups and daisies caught waving in the warm breeze as if joining the spectators. Flags were waved in welcome of our Prince with schoolchildren lined along both sides of the road and cheering, as they had been given a holiday for the occasion. The Prince was escorted by the Governor - I remember a festive day.

Suddenly the picture changes, because the taxi has parked in front of St. Georges Villa, our home for a few days. Thank God for good memories.

Portsmouth came after Guernsey, for the sole reason that I needed to find out (if possible) what had happened to our furnishings. The fat gross English agent hardly gave us the time of day. In fact, when I intimated that there could be a court action, his reply was that as far as he was concerned our conversation had never taken place! It was quite obvious that both he and his firm were crooked. Subsequently, through a taxi driver, I heard that many pantechnicons had been stolen at that time. I assumed that ours was included. The insurance company never paid us a penny, saying that we had no proof that it was lost or stolen. And so another shadow was dealt with as we turned towards the light, and got on with our lives. We were thankful that no lives were lost and that our loss

was only about things. People are more important.

We continued on to Stockholm and then to New York and San Francisco, finally returning to Melbourne and home. It had been a wonderful trip; thanks to Billie. There is so much I could tell you about our travels, but it would take another book. Who knows, I may write a sequel?

I am going back a bit here to the time just before our great trip. The trip was on offer and I wanted it - at any price. Perhaps this was selfish or due .to some kind of male menopause, but my determination did bring some shadows with it. I had not told Billie that I had not confided it to my family. I knew that Mildred had always wanted me nearby and would have not agreed to let me go, perhaps even fearing that I might not return, which of course was never in my mind. I thought that I richly deserved this holiday, and, unknown, to Billie, I paid a taxi driver to put an explanatory letter in our letter box for Mildred. I enclosed an opal ring with the letter to soften the blow. What a coward, I should have faced the problem. This was a case of not leaving the shadows.

Oh, the plans of mice and men. The letter was found sooner than I had expected, at Sydney Airport. Kay phoned and was not amused. She virtually ordered me to return. But we were already in the plane and it was ready for take-off, so there was no possibility of a return. My discomfort

Chapter 17 - Shadows Tinged with Hope

continued throughout the plane trip and when we reached London, I immediately phoned home, and made my peace with the promise that I would phone Mildred every day. It took some time for the shadow to disappear. I shudder now when I recall that telephone bill. It was enough to break the Bank of Monte Carlo. But all through this period my love for Mildred never faltered, or hers for me. One does stupid things and there was a lesson to be learnt. I hope I learnt it.

Time flies as you get older on life's journey. All sorts of wonderful things filled our lives Mildred, Delma and I became founder members of the Peninsula Singers in 1987, and continued to warble at annual concerts which I produced. As this was a community choir, we sang at various venues like nursing homes and hospitals under the baton of our very capable musical director Joy Hilleir.

You can well imagine that nursing, filming and never-ending social work kept me on my toes. Yet, the journey was tinged with sadness, My father-in-law died 18 months after we arrived in Australia, and my mother-in-law, dear Linda, passed a way few years later, to join her husband Cecil. Delma's health had always been very good, but it became a worry ending with a spell in hospital, where she needed an operation for a gall bladder. Then on top of it all, our darling daughter Kay, who has been such a blessing in our lives, a loving caring person, went through a period of one failed, one unhappy marriage and then a broken relationship. As you can imagine, this caused great distress to Mildred and to me. Also during this restless period Kay required a overay to be removed. Thank God not Cancerous

Our grandsons and family supported her during this difficult time. Finally, Cupid shot his arrow once again, and this time at dear Russell with whom she found love. After all that adversity she found the man of her life. The union brought us a granddaughter Emma by Russell's first marriage.

One day we returned from a piano recital given by extremely gifted Tatiana Kolesova. She came second in the Sydney International Piano Competition of Australia. Her playing was sheer magic and we were sure that this young lady had her life before her to bring music to international audiences. Billie and I congratulated her after the performance. It was a wonderful evening.

When we returned home, my eye was caught by the headlines in the Herald Sun. Bold letters announced 'Mark's Demons' to the world. A photo of a young Mark Priestley, TV star, was displayed. He had jumped from his 23rd floor window to his death below. Thus ended the life of a young man who had everything going for him - apparently. Friends and relatives had forecast a great future for him.

So why suicide? It appears that, somewhere along the way, he had turned from the light into the shadows. The bright illumination of light was replaced by depression, the shadows bringing total hell and darkness, where demons torment ones's very being. Taken away were his love for himself and those around him. Problems arose in his life. There were broken relationships and a feeling of despair reaching into the very depths of his soul. He believed that everything he had achieved was worthless and that he sought peace, but never found it. Those tormenting demons were always there to make sure that peace was never found.

Demons take on the guises of Jekyll and Hyde. To Mark's friends and relatives he presented a good facade of being normal, as he always had been. Meanwhile, the devious demons were working up to the grand finale in tragic circumstances.

But once the main character in this saga has gone, it is the bereaved who will suffer. They will question why it happened. They had been kept away from the truth, which would only have been revealed to those who had themselves been in that land of darkness.

I never met Mark Priestley, but I place him among the many I have actually met on my journey----. -- --those who were suffering from bipolar or manic depression, which contain the selfdestructing demons that diminish the will to live. And there is one thing that I have learnt, depression attacks all ages, races and colours. Those who are afflicted need love, support and understanding. There is a trek back to the light, if help is at hand. Remember, some day this might be you. Mark may have chosen to die. Did he make the right decision? Did he have the right to bring grief to his loved ones and friends? Are we controlled by destiny? If so, the choice is not ours. Who knows?

Chapter 17 - Shadows Tinged with Hope

This I do know. Life is for living and each moment is precious. Use it as though it is the last, and remember that we don't have another chance ,as we journey and make our way to the exit call. The important thing in life is to care for not only for ourselves and family but to others. A , word, handshake with understanding may save those, who are in the pit of self annihilation

And now I would like to write about another courageous battle from shadow to sunlight. I first met Mary at St. Paul's Church in Frankston.

Frankston was a fast growing city about 35 kilometres from Melbourne. Mary's cheery and smiling disposition proclaimed that she enjoyed life and people's company. She was born into a Christian family and had a happy childhood. As the years passed she became a happy kindergarten teacher, married and raised a family.

Enter the shadows. She had previously been through a few torrid years. Her parents died and then her niece. Then came the breakup of her marriage. In spite of the looming divorce, she managed to adjust and to take stock of the positives that still existed in her life. The shadows dissolved behind her and she got on with living.

Suddenly, she became ill, saying, as so many women do – tomorrow, I will feel better. But no, the tomorrow never dawned and Mary felt even worse. A flickering light was casting an unsteady shadow, as her doctor quietly told her that she was suffering from auto immune disease, primary Schlerosing Cholangitis. Unknown to her she had had an infection for some years or an infection in the bile duct. Her immune system went into action to fight the infection ,but forgot to turn itself off, destroying the bile duct and in turn affecting her liver function.

The prognosis was not good and so the doctor referred her to the Austin Hospital. The outcome of that visit was that Mary required a healthy liver to regain the strength she needed to regain the strength to banish the persistent nausea, which was clouding her life throughout the day.

A liver transplant - it can't be that serious! But how long would Mary have to wait for a transplant? It became a question of time, of waiting for that life threatening operation. If one could not be found, then the inevitable would happen. Hold on a bit. Was she hearing right? Her liver was diseased and she would need to have a transplant? Mary takes up the story –

"After the doctor explained the nature of my illness I did not fully understand the seriousness of my condition, or maybe I closed my mind to the situation I was facing. Deep down, the fear of dying never entered my thoughts. I had no intention of leaving this earth. My family needed me. On the other side of the coin, I needed them, to feel their supportive love. Yes, the operation will be successful.

Suddenly the bitter truth hit me. I will live. The gift of life will be mine at the cost of someone dying. A thousand thoughts crossed my mind - guilt included. Did I have the right to accept that vital part from a body that had been mutilated on my behalf, and others who will use donated organs??"

"Oh, how I fought with the shadows. This became the basis of my prayers. Slowly I turned my negative thoughts to positive as we must do on our journey, or we will forever be destined to remain in the shadows. Lifting my head my eyes caught the light. The shadow took up a rear position. We must always go forward, whatever the odds. The donation of organs is the greatest gift a person can give, so I must accept the donation with grace, in the knowledge that the transplant will enable the recipient to continue their journey with renewed health and quality.

On reflection, I think of the time after the operation. I wrote to the parents of the daughter who gave me a second chance, thanking them in gratitude of the gift they had given. I received a beautiful reply. Both letters on either side were charged with emotion. Their reply giving me the assurance in my sadness, their daughter definitely wished parts of her body be put to alleviate suffering. I think, in a way they drew comfort that she was still living in another form. I praise God for those words of assurance that cast away my guilt. My only regret, that I did not write before the operation. It may have saved me a lot of soul searching."

Chapter 18

The Gift of Life and Its Compensations

"I continued to work for the next fifteen months," Mary continues. Day by day life became a chore as I advanced in my illness. More and more admissions to hospital with serious infections. Suddenly my life took a rapid change; I was no longer the organiser, becoming dependant on others. I loved being in control. In the past I foolishly thought no one could replace my skills of running a house. How wrong can you be? Run, a household? I couldn't even decide if I felt like eating, let alone cooking a meal. Was this me or was this a sort of nightmare? Oh, how I cried when the dishwasher broke. I cried, not because it was out of action. I just did not know how to handle the situation. I became incapable of making decisions. My liver was no longer doing its job, a toxic build-up affecting my brain. The independence raped from me by the insidious poisons.

Oh God, what will become of me? Am I to be left in a wilderness? My children have their lives to lead. Please take me out of the shadows. God is no man's debtor. My beloved family became my carers, seeing to my every need. I had no need to feel humiliated through helplessness. I felt great pride in their commitment and love. The shadows lingered deep in my mind. I, Mary, who enjoyed the very essences of life, was now a failure, forced retirement and unable to do the things I enjoyed. This was not living.

Oh God, save my dignity! My love of reading became less and less. Concentration began to wane. At times I was stupid in conversation, on the telephone stopping to think the right words. The seeds of love were within my brothers and sisters and their families, also my friends. It was at my time of helplessness their love blossomed, regularly coming to stay to give my children a well-earned break. Days I would indulge in self pity, crying at the injustice of the situation. Oh, when will that telephone ring? Perhaps it will remain silent, no match being found.

Is my suffering a prelude to death? No, death is not on my agenda. The strange thing, I had no fear of dying, even though I knew that the operation was touch and go. Somewhere inside of me my voice assured me that the transplant would be successful. Oh ye, of little faith!

The phone did ring but not before my health was fast reaching rock bottom. Every six weeks the Austin Hospital became a home from home. Then another shock. My beloved uncle, who had helped in my caring died suddenly. He was not given the chance to see my recovery. More tears. I became despondent, nearly on the verge of depression. Only those who have trodden the same road know how easy it is for you to refuse to continue the journey. Ring, ring, ring. Every time the phone rang I approached it calmly. Was this the summons to change my life, and in some ways my thinking? As much as I wanted the transplant I knew the donor's family would be in grief.

Finally, in December 2004, the phone rang. This was it! I gathered my hospital bag, which had been packed in readiness for my journey into the unknown. Yes, unknown, because I had never passed that way before. Many thoughts were in my head as I looked out of my window, gazing at the calm sea. I had seen the view many times. Today it seemed calmer than ever, instilling a calm within me. One last look at my home, if I was never to see it again. Yet the thought never entered my head. Unlike Mark I was on my way to a new era in my life. God had given me a second chance.

Chapter 18 - The Gift of Life and Its Compensations

The family gathered at the hospital. I felt at peace as we took Communion together. The peace that passed all understanding, I had no negative thoughts of dying, my attitude was positive on that day.

Off to the theatre; this is no three-act play; this was for real, the drama played out by modern surgery. When I awoke the transplant had been carried out. Within me was a new liver and a new life. Tubes were dangling from all parts of my body, the worst one down my throat - which prevented me from talking. The only fear I had - would my body reject my inheritance? The medicine I received prevented this. Oh what joy and jubilation when, 13 hours after surgery my family was united with the new me.

All was not over yet. Healing takes time and the road to recovery is hard and challenging. Slowly but surely I returned to my old self, but not before, two months later, I was confronted with some alien emotions. It was as if I had lost my way completely. On one hand I was so lucky to have had a successful transplant. I was so grateful to my donor and her family for my amazing gift. I had a wonderful family, great friends, my faith and everything to look forward to. But what was everything? Will my life return to carry on to do what I did before my illness? I was at my lowest ebb, feeling so ungrateful when I should have felt on top of the world. I'd finally got the chance of a new life, but what was this life with so many unanswered questions and so many uncertainties? I prayed for this to end but my prayers seemed faraway and I cried for the least thing. I was re-admitted to hospital and my medication was reviewed. I saw a psychiatrist to see me through this difficult time, to be told that it's perfectly normal to feel this way. I'm told that it will get better. Still, I felt desperate and angry. A surprise to me because I rarely got angry. I couldn't even identify what I was angry about. With time, patience, counselling and lots of prayer I came to terms with my feeling. As always, I was fortunate to be surrounded by a supportive and loving family and friends, plus the fact that everyone kept telling me how amazing I was to have remained positive and conquered so much. But I had so many doubts. Just where do I begin to pick up my life?

I wake up every day and give thanks for the day ahead and my renewed health. I still have moments when I hardly believe this has happened to me. This was no dream. Over several months I had spells in hospital because there are always risks with transplants. But I have the strength and courage to confront the issues and work towards overcoming these."

Overcome these Mary did. Today she is back to being a mother, grandmother, teacher and sportswoman. For Mary became interested in the Australian Transplant Games in Geelong, and through this she took part in the 2008 Australian transplant games in Perth. She won silver and three bronze medals for swimming and bowls for Victoria. Not bad for a woman who four years earlier was seriously ill and hardly getting through her day. Mary looked towards the light and then the shadows fell behind. Some say it is not right to have transplants from another human body. I wonder, if we asked Mary for her views on the subject what her answer would be. Would transplant patients forfeit their happiness for the sake of a principle?

I am glad I met Mary on my journey. Seeing her happiness and that of her family has made me decide to give my body parts to be used to overcome debilitating illness.

I will return to the shadows later, but first let me tell you about the wonderful places I visited through the generosity of my friend Biliel. True to form they did not go without incident. The time arrived for us to go on an overseas trip. My passport was renewed, visa included and the cases were packed well in advance. Dollars were exchanged for foreign currency, the travelogue was checked flight tickets okay and everything re-examined to the last detail. Billie remarked how well we had organised our trip, with praise to our two very capable travel agents - Rosamond at Flight Centre and Belinda from Jet Set.

As the day approached the air was filled with excitement. Due to our early departure ,we decided to stay at the airport Travel Lodge. Next morning, ablutions completed we were fortified by a breakfast fit for a king - you do tend to indulge when on holiday. What the hell! Never mind the weight, what's the problem in gaining a few kilos? You'll soon come back to earth when the carnival is over. Final checks. Nothing is left in the unit. Often, when you're on the other side of the world your glasses, or, worse still, your false teeth are sitting comfortably in the lost property office, never to see

Chapter 18 - The Gift of Life and Its Compensations

the light of day again. Imagine spending your travels as a toothless wonder. Travellers beware! The doors were locked as dawn was breaking with a chill in the air - collars up. The warm reception office greeted us as we came to settle our account and returned the plastic key now replacing metal. This is the age of synthetic wonders, unfortunately not given to longevity. We were bidden a bon voyage by the young male receptionist with a cheery disposition who gave us the impression that he might have been on the other side of the fence. "Have fun, darlings," were his final words as we set off on what turned out in many ways to be a memorable holiday.

All is well in the state of Denmark- or are the clouds of trouble lurking to turn sunshine into stormy weather? No fear of that as we had scrutinized all aspects of our departure and were stepping out with confidence. We made our way to the departure gate as the airport was beginning to come to life. Passengers were hurrying to join the unending queue to have their passports or visas stamped. Thank God I've updated mine! Canberra renewed the requirements for my stay in Australia, coining the Oz expression - "No worries, mate."

Quoting Billie - "Until we are seated in the plane, enjoying a brandy and dry with the compliments of the airways - then I feel that we're on our way." Here we come, London, Bath, Switzerland, Germany, Poland and Guernsey, etc, etc. Oh, what a beautiful morning!

It was - until we entered the International Passport check-in. The man at the desk seemed harmless enough as he stamped Billie's passport. Admittedly he seemed to be a man of few words, flicking his head as if to say move on. His outstretched hand snatched my passport, as he glanced at me with an intense look which to my mind spelt disaster.

"Is this your photo?" he asked. Apparently satisfied by a nod of my head he continued, as if I were in prison - "Line up, spell your name." Please and thank you did not exist in his vocabulary.

"B.L.E.S.T.E.L.," I responded.

He leaned towards me with a look that could only be interpreted as trouble and spoke in a third degree voice. To me, the days of the inquisition had arrived. "Then, why is it spelt BLETEL on your visa?"

"I've no idea," I replied. "An oversight on Canberra's part since my passport was renewed recently?"

"Are you suggesting that Canberra is at fault?"

By this time I was beginning to feel a little prickly, and my intuition knew that Billie was on the same wavelength. Commonsense prevailed and I held my temper. "I am not suggesting anything - at my age I do know how to spell my name," I said quietly.

Without removing his eyes from the offending document he muttered "Canberra rarely makes mistakes. This I do know. If your name is not rectified you will not be given the right or allowed to re-enter Australia. Understand?"

I was dismissed with another flick of the head, accompanied by an outstretched finger, not crooked, indicating that we must obey, pronto. This vital part of his anatomy pointed to an offside room into which we were ushered by another servant of the Government. This lady proved to be a little more co-operative.

Billie gave me a knowing look as much as if to say - "Here goes the brandy and dry." The plans of mice and men go astray and this one was certainly on its way.

"You may sit if you wish," she suggested. "If your name is not spelt correctly, or you did not bother to have it changed, quite likely it may take some time, weeks or a year, which may cause you difficulties regarding your re-entry," she said.

She spoke as if we had all the time in the world. After hearing her pronouncement it was not only goodbye to the brandy and dry, but also to all the wonderful places on our travels, the joy of visiting the lands on our itinerary. Suddenly they seemed to be wiped out by the descending shadows of beaurocracy.

Chapter 18 - The Gift of Life and Its Compensations

Billie, who has acute hearing, did not miss a syllable and released his tongue with the word - well! "What are we going to do with all our fares paid? We are due on the Continent in a week's time. Mr. Blestel relied on his passport being returned correctly. A Government blunder. Surely Canberra should have noted the spelling did not correspond."

"Canberra handles many renewasl. An oversight on their part is unfortunate for you, but it's happened," She said with a shrug of her shoulders. Whether it was compassion or guilt I never knew, but a glint of light shone through the shadows. "All I can suggest is that you go to your Embassy when you arrive in London. They may be able to help though forms will have to be filled in," she said.

Throughout this drama I had decided to withhold my feelings for fear of losing my temper. And now it was over to me. "We are only passing through London then straight on to Bath," I ventured. "Can't you phone Canberra to explain the predicament? It's their mistake." I went on.

Her attitude warmed slightly, as she said - "I'm afraid that will not help. It's their policy to view the passport before changing any written matter. Sorry, but you will have to phone when you arrive in Bath, trusting they will be of assistance. Best of luck." She offered her hand and ushered us to the door.

Billie, by this time, was foreseeing gloom and doom in the not too distant future. "Disgraceful behaviour on their part," he said angrily. "We will certainly write to complain. No wonder the country is in strife. How many poor souls are subject to what we are enduring? Disgraceful! Imagine some elderly person travelling on their own and being told they might not get back!" Billie always spared a thought for the elderly. I can picture my mother in the same situation. Disgraceful. Poor Mother wouldn't know what to do.

As we boarded the plane, Billie remarked - "What else can go wrong?"

"Treat it as an adventure. Have faith, Billie ," I replied. As it turned out our faith was sorely tested. We were finally seated in our window seats with belts fastened. Both female and male stewards looked after us with impeccable charm as the plane soared upwards, carrying a full complement of passengers. One cannot cease to wonder how this mechanical bird ever gets off the ground into a world of fluffy white clouds. Beneath us, the purity of the golden sun, truly a world akin to fairyland. It was all the more enchanting as we sipped our complimentary brandy and dry. God is yet good.

Sitting next to me were newly-weds from India who had saved to have their honeymoon in Australia. They were sort of surveying the land as they would have liked to immigrate. The hardest part would be if they had to leave their close-knit family. Billie, meanwhile conversed with a delightful ballet teacher who was recuperating from a nasty bout of flu. We enjoyed hearing about the countries she had visited in the course of her work. It was all very interesting, but I think it proved to be our undoing, because, in a few days, we both a terrible flu. I never laid down in bed for three days. Cough, cough, and sounding like Puffing Billy. I've never felt so terrible. Bill's flu developed a few days later. At one stage the doctor said, that, if there were no improvement by the following day, hospital would become his holiday home. Luckily it did not come to that, if any reader has been taken ill on holiday then you know the Drama.

We continued on our not so merry way. On our arrival in Bath we were greeted by our friend John James. 'John of Bath' was a fun name given to him by Billie, saying his name went well with the aged city, while John's feline friend, Petra, was also named after an ancient city. There will be a great sadness in him when his beloved companion goes to the place in the sky - or wherever our pets find peace and tranquillity. His charming house at Entry Hill overlooks green fields interspersed with cottages built in a bygone era. On the horizon, one catches a glimpse of the city, like Rome, built on seven hills. It is a city of culture with many places for the visitor to enjoy. There are the Roman Baths, almost untouched, since Caesar's legions marched through the city's cobbled streets to conquer as yet untouched lands, for, like Hitler, Caesar hoped to rule the world by creating the Great Roman Empire.

Bath is a city whose walls are steeped in history. Close your eyes. It takes very little to imagine you are back in yesteryear feeling the presence of Jane Austin who sometimes dwelt and wrote in this beautiful city, though she

Chapter 18 - The Gift of Life and Its Compensations

was not impressed on her first visit, when the town was bathed in rain. Yet, she declared later that it was more beautiful in the rain. Those who enjoy architecture in all shapes and forms then Bath is for Australians, a place on which to feast their eyes.

The Royal Crescent is to be seen to be believed. Famous actors have trodden the boards in Bath's renowned theatre. In the Street of Strangers antiques are to be found in quaint shops. Bath Abbey offers organ recitals together with Oratorios by choirs which perform throughout the year. museums, art galleries and parks abound in the city. There are canals with barges which carried freight in the past and were now given over to trippers to enjoy the lovely scenery. Along the banks are primroses, bluebells, hollyhocks and foxgloves amidst other wild flora, mingled with private cottage residences. A serene picture for the eyes as we travel.

Lunch or afternoon tea is served as the barge meanders along the quiet waters. We pass through lochs, past meadows where sheep safely graze, sharing their pasture with cows chewing the cud. Oh, what tranquillity! How can this be spoiled and taken away due to a phone call to the Embassy in London regarding my ..... yes, you've guessed it - my visa.

The day after our arrival I lost no time in making the call. The conversation remains in my mind. Dialling the number, waiting for an eternity. This is how it went - Australian Embassy: (A,E) "Good morning. This is the Australian Embassy."

Bernard: "I need to renew my passport and visa."

A,E: "What is your full name?"

B: "Bernard Anthony" (in my best B.B.C.voice)

A.E: "Full name. Please. Christian and surname and date of birth."

B: "Bernard Anthony Blestel. 30.12.29."

A.E: "How can I help?"

B: "My passport was renewed and somewhere along the line the spelling of my surname on the visa did not correspond with the passport. An 'S' was left out. By leaving out that S it has caused me and my travelling companion no end of worry, due to immigration informing me that I will not be allowed to re-enter if this is not rectified. We are leaving next week for the Continent."

The inquisition continued.

A.E: "When was the mistake noticed?"

B: "Not until the officer pointed it out, asking why there were two different spellings. I did glance at it when it arrived, but failed to notice the missing 'S'. One does not expect errors from the Government on such an important document."

A.E: "One must be more vigilant in the future. Canberra has a heavy workload. It is unusual for a Government department not to see the error before mailing it back."

Plus not liking her attitude, I had a gut feeling that the blame was due to Canberra for their inefficiency. "How long before I receive my passport back?" I asked, fearing a negative answer.

"Normally, four to six weeks," she answered in a voice that did nothing to boost my morale.

In desperation I reiterated that we were leaving next week.

The next question floored me. "Have you got a computer, with you?" she asked.

"No, we are on holiday," I replied.

A.E: "Then you will require forms to be filled in. I will post the documents to you on Monday. When you return them include a return envelope with a cheque for post and packing--- 120 pounds which includes the fee for alteration."

I thought my ears had received the wrong message. One hundred and twenty pounds for some balls-up in Canberra?! Excuse the French.

"Would it be any quicker, if I motored up to London to deliver my passport to the Embassy?" I asked.

Chapter 18 - The Gift of Life and Its Compensations

A.E"If there were any other way for you to receive the forms earlier, I would have suggested it," was the response. "The office is only open for two hours, with no set hours, plus it is not our procedure to receive documents over the counter. But there may be another option. If a friend has a computer, he or she can email the documents to me today," she suggested.

After she gave me the necessary, dot.comm. etc., I said I would endeavour to get the visa processed as soon as possible.

A.E"Thank you for your enquiry," she said and with that the line went dead.

By luck, John of Bath his dear neighbour Christine kindly used her office computer to acquire eleven nightmare pages of forms. By this time I was in such a state that Billie offered to complete the questions, with my gratitude. We did this in the nearest building to the Post Office, Bath's Public Library, so that we could get the wretched stuff sent back post haste,. Thank you Billie.

The following days were spent worrying. Our friend at the Embassy has, in fact sorted out and sent the passport which arrived at Beckley. Our friend and host Jo gave us the happy news. God was yet good. The week we stayed with Jo and Kevin went like wildfire. We continued our journey battling colds.. The worst we ever had.

Drama number one was over. I would be able to return. Drama number two was coming up. I have to have a Warfarin test every so often due to a heart condition. Pathology took the test, and then promptly lost my blood, which meant travelling many kilometres to have another sample taken. Then, because he was at a loss to know the right dosage, the doctor overcame this by guesswork which must have been right because I am still breathing.

Drama number three. The landlady at Inverness in Scotland forgot to book our room, even though we had made the booking in Australia. When we reached Inverness, a kindly petrol station attendant directed me to Telford Street, telling me that we would definitely be accommodated in one of the many B and B's there. I left Billy in the car as he was still in no fit state to go searching for a place to lay two sick heads. The attendant was right when he said that there were many guest houses in Telford Street. What he didn't tell me was that nearly all had 'No Vacancy' signs boldly displayed in their windows or on their front gates. I thought we might have had to sleep in the car for the night, but, as I was about to return to Billie, I noticed a little cottage which offered bed and breakfast. Is my luck turning? I knocked on the door, in the high hope that the sweet grey-head lady who answered it would take pity on two poor weary Aussies.

"Good evening," I said. "Do you have a room for tonight? We had booked our accommodation in Australia, but the guest house misplaced our booking. Can you help??" I said with a look of desperation.

"Yes," she answered. "I may be able to help. I've one room left with a double bed. A pretty room, painted in blush pink. Will that suit your requirements?" She spoke those words in a strong Scots accent and it was nectar to my ears.

"Thank you, we will take the room and I'm sure it's a nice pleasant room," I replied with a sigh of relief.

"And where is the wee wife?" she asked.

"I'm afraid my wife died " I replied.

"And who, may I ask, will be sleeping with you?" she continued, looking around.

"My friend of many years. Even though we are not related we are brothers in every sense," I informed her.

The 'sweet little old lady' suddenly found that the blush pink room was no longer available. She endeavoured to shut the door, making sure that we did not darken her doorstep.

"I don't take men," she said; with finality.

End of story. It's funny how often people jump to the wrong conclusions.

Two doors away I was confronted by the same reaction. Perhaps, if I dressed in drag we might have found a comfortable bed for the night? Poor Billie, who was waiting for my overdue return bearing good news, began to panic

Chapter 18 - The Gift of Life and Its Compensations

in small stages, thinking I was in the hands of thugs, attacked and robbed, leaving me to join the angels or their counterparts.

On I trod, in the vain hope that I would find a room, or even a shed. If Joseph was content with a stable, then who am I to complain? As yet, no shed or stable had been offered to me. I turned away from disappointing Telford Street and came across an artistically painted notice board advertising B and B. There was also a sign which said No Vacancies. But, by this time I was truly desperate and knocked on the door to ask if the occupants knew of a room.

Isobel, the owner, answered and smilingly asked my reason for calling. I repeated my well-worn request and told her the sad story of the ridiculous mistake with our booking. Mercifully she was a kind soul who took pity on two larrikins from 'down under'. The shadow lifted, when, out of her mouth, shone a ray of hope.

"I have a room vacant tonight ,as I have people staying tomorrow. So, seeing your predicament you may stay for one night," she said.

I returned to Bill post-- haste with the good news. After we motored down from the wind-swept Orkneys we stayed with Isobel for the night. Then on to Inverness Airport to leave the car as previously arranged, before flying on to London. Having left the car at the airport, another drama occurred, but I will refer to that later.

On reaching London we caught the train to Waterloo ,where we boarded the EuroStar which would take us under the Channel to Brussels. Then on to Basle in Switzerland to embark on the Viking King. The boat would travel up the Rhine to Cologne. Our two young friends lived in that city . Lucas and his German wife Suzanne, just had their first new born baby. Arriving at their home we had our first glimpse of their child. Lucas is a gifted violinist, living in one of the many cities that were razed to the ground during World War II. He plays with the Cologne Orchestra which we had the privilege of hearing. Lucas left Australia at the age of sixteen, and, having won a scholarship to study music in Germany, he stayed to further his studies.

Cologne Cathedral survived the war. Hundreds of pilgrims pay homage in this building, which has stood the test of time. Each day the crowds move slowly through the Cathedral and it is almost claustrophobic, but, in spite of this ,we were glad that we had visited this monument to the Lord.

Our cruise on the Rhine was all that we had expected. The weather was as beautiful as were the wondrous sights we passed. Billie and I have visited some wonderful countries. Denmark, Norway which was the birthplace of Billie's grandfather, Sweden and the city of Stockholm ,where our Australian friend, Kevin, teaches English. Apart from those already mentioned, were France, Italy. Poland, Holland and England, Scotland and America. We visited the Orkneys, and, of course, the Isles of Scilly. Guernsey and Sark are among the many lands we have implanted in our memories.---

--'Where sheep may safely graze.' ' Buttercups and daisies are nodding as if they are greeting the passerby, for this is the Isle of peace. Far removed from the time when jackboots trod the very same paths. Brown and white Guernsey cows, famous for their rich milk, lie lazily in the shade, while heifers prance about in the luscious grass, oblivious of their future.

In Sark, Granite built Stocks Hotel comes into sight, reminiscent of Mrs. de Winter catching a glimpse of Manderley. But this is no Manderley and houses no sinister Mrs. Danvers. You may relax within its walls, enjoying the comforts it has to offer. Stocks has been a landmark for generations both for the Sarkees and visitors. In post war years it was run by the FaIle family who have long since relinquished the lease, then refurbished by Phillip and family, tastefully. On arrival you will always receive a warm welcome with a touch of humour from his mother, a delightful lady. In keeping with the character of the island the guests at Stocks will experience old world charm, retiring to your bedroom after a nightcap in the cosy bar. The bedside lamp gives a cosy glow and the bed covers are already turned back giving a feeling of care. Meals to whet the appetite in the Dining Room restaurant are a compliment to the chef and staff.

The Channel Isles, which were once part of the Duchy of Normandy, received a charter from William the Conqueror declaring the islands independent, self governing. Yet, owing allegiance to the English crown.

Chapter 18 - The Gift of Life and Its Compensations

Today, Sark is under the guidance of the Seigneur Michael Beaumont. His grandmother was Sybil Hathaway, known as the Dame of Sark. A remarkable lady, who, during the German occupation kept the Germans on their toes and received very little trouble from the occupying forces. In fact, one of the previous owners, Sheila Falle fell in love with one of the German soldiers - love knows no bounds - and married him after the war. One of the conditions to the marriage was that he change his name to Falle to continue the male line.

La Coupee is the rocky, precipitous isthmus or narrow stretch of land connecting Sark and Little Sark. Before the occupation you took your life in your hands, crossing the rugged path. There was no railing to protect you from a sheer drop of hundreds of feet on either side. It was certainly impossible to make the other side in windy weather. If it were attempted, there could be fatal consequences, with high winds sending one over the edge - which happened. The Germans constructed a railed concrete causeway. Thanks to them the passage is safe. The mode of travel on Sark is by horse and carriage with cycles for the fit and healthy.

Billie and I, during a previous visit, cycled around the island. Returning years later time had caught up with us and Shanks's pony was the order of the day. Motorcars are not allowed on the island, so that tractors convey freight wherever it is needed, as well as transporting visitors to their hotels or guesthouses. The magic of its folk lore still lives on.

In previous centuries knitters would gather in the island's cottages, catching up on the day's gossip as the needles clicked away. Knitting was also traditional in Guernsey where the beautiful jumpers were made, mainly for seafarers from oiled wool, which protected the wearer from rain or sea spray in rough weather. The fisher folk have always been a tough breed, defying the elements to land their catch. The women of yesteryear heard numerous stories of smugglers, pirates, ghosts and witchcraft, and retold those stories. Writers Edith Carey and Sybil Hathaway wrote so that the legends lived on.

Sark is truly a unique part-of the world, with its sandy bays and coves and strange rock formations and arches----. all carved out by the forces of nature, while the song of the sea creates a concerto in union with the ever changing wind. The cry of the gulls, tinkling bicycle bells, the clip of horse's hooves hitting the unpaved lanes as they trot carefree towards La Sablonnerie, bird songs, fluttering wings and the happy laughter of people as they sip and dine, relaxing together in peace. All these ingredients together form a Sark Sonata. Let the orchestra play! Let the shadows of the egotistical developers be obliterated by the applause of heritage!

Sark belongs to the Sarkees. Their forefathers moulded the land, not the Moguls who come in the disguise of benefactors enriching their already bursting wallets. Let sunshine, not shadow, reign in this fairisle of tranquillity.

Of the various countries we have visited, each holds fond memories. Norway, with its magnificent falls and fjords – breathtaking and have to, be seen to be believed. If fish is on your menu, then the quay market in Bergen is a must. Sitting by the water's edge one can indulge ones self in eating fish sandwiches with either crab or lobster served in a shell - a gourmet paradise! In the foreground fishing boats are moored, while many others return with their holds filled to capacity. The catch will be sold to agents after which it will move on to the purveyors to end up gracing your table.

As we sat, we caught sight of the Kong Harald the boat we joined at the top of Norway after we had flown from Oslo. We spent nine wonderful days on this working ship akin to a cruise boat calling at picturesque towns, villages and fjords during which time we met fellow travellers from all over the world. They showed interest in purchasing this story when it is published and assured me that they would look for it on the bookshelves.

If only life continued in a state of joy without pain or sadness, though, we, as humans, seem always to find something to grumble about. Shadows loomed. Shadows that would alter both mine and my family's life. Though it was a time, when I had learnt to accept the trials and to adopt a positive attitude, and to realise that we cannot always achieve what we want on our perilous journey.

In hindsight the conclusion became clear. Are we in the hands of destiny or of God? Yet how, we tackle the problem is the problem. I placed myself in

Chapter 18 - The Gift of Life and Its Compensations

God's hands, realising that He also controls the hands of destiny. Without His help the rocky paths I was soon to encounter would have left my feet sore, wounded.

In the meantime, the storm clouds had not blotted out the sunshine that we were enjoying. After I retired, the family consisted of Mildred, Delma, Kay and her then partner Charles and Matthew and Ben. We all packed our bags and travelled overseas, visiting London and parts of England and then America. The itinerary included a day at Disneyland which was much enjoyed by my two grandsons and Delma, who braved the rigors of fast-moving rides, which, watched by Mill and I, made us feel sick. Good on you Delma. She came away unscathed, or should I say no worse for wear. Mildred and I remained on terra firma. My excuse was my heart condition, which, made it unwise to tempt fate. "That's my story and I'm sticking to it."

One of the major highlights of the trip for me was touring Universal Studios. Unfortunately, it rained on the day that we had chosen, so we had to purchase rain mack's and umbrellas. Still, the day did not dampen our spirits and the boys had a great time. Then on to San Francisco where Kay and the boys visited the infamous Alcatraz, while Mildred and I toured Fishermen's Walk and did some shopping. Billie and I had visited there some years earlier and he had bought me my first Greek fisherman's cap, a style of hat that has since become synonymous with my identity in that it never left my head since that first day. Or the replica I now buy from Aussie Disposals, the original hat having long since gone to dust.

We bid farewell to America and returned to London, where we caught up with Charles who had remained in England with his deceased mother's ashes. His mother had wished that her ashes should be scattered in the place of her birth. So, with the roar of the metropolitan traffic and the bemusement of passers-by and armed with a trowel, we proceeded to grant Charles' mother her last wish. Bizarre as it now seems, she lies half in Hyde Park and the other portion is near Marble Arch. Far from the shores of Australia. My only hope is, that, on the day of resurrection, the two halves will be united - you've got to have a sense of humour, haven't you?

The last lap of the journey was spent in Guernsey where we caught up with relatives and friends. The telephonists with whom Delma had worked at

STD laid on a surprise reunion at St. Martins Hotel. This proved to be not the only surprise of the day. A few people thought I had gone to God! I had to assure them that I was no ghost.

Finally, we travelled down to Cape Town where our bridesmaid and her husband, my pal Courtney, who was also my workmate at the SED lived. What a reunion after so many years! We also met Scottie, who had married Susan, whose mother Molly is our bridesmaid's daughter. We thoroughly enjoyed going back to the days of our youth and reliving past memories. All things must come to an end and so we bade "au revoir, or, as we say in Guernsey," a la prochaine" (till the next time). There were tears amongst the laughter as you can imagine.

A few years later Billie and I stayed in Cape Town, and I was able to introduce him to my friends, plus their son Steven, whom I had missed seeing on the previous occasion. The overseas trip was the last one that we, as a family, spent all together. The shadowy clouds were fast approaching and, as a result, life would take on a very different aspect. While we were away I kept in touch with Billie, whose weather reports stated that temperatures were so high that it was almost unbearable.

Poor Mildred who, like so many others, detests the high temperatures, was thankful that we were in the cool English climate at the time. Luckily, when we returned the weather was more moderate. Even so, a few days, proved almost too much for Mildred. I, myself enjoy the hot weather, swimming in the warm Australian sea. As much as I enjoy returning to Guernsey, Australia is my adopted home. In a sense I have come to terms by belonging to both. At this point in time I do not wish to live anywhere other than Australia.

Life is full of surprises. Well! If you had told me that this vast continent would become my home I would not have believed it. But God had other plans. My working life found fulfilment in nursing patients with all manner of illnesses. This did not trouble me, because I became a link between those I nursed and their loved ones. The question which at times invaded my mind was how would I cope, if I had a mentally retarded child or one given to epilepsy or autism. Or if I saw my wife or loved ones dying of cancer or

Chapter 18 - The Gift of Life and Its Compensations

some other life-threatening disease? How would I feel facing a lifetime in a wheelchair through paralysis?

Until we are faced with the situation with dark flickering shadows cast in our mind, we stay in the cloak of shadow. It is our safety zone. We have no desire to turn to the light for fear of a negative answer. Anyway - it happens to others. We are immune to those situations, or so we think. A false euphoria.

The time came when I was put to the test. Meanwhile, life continued on smoothly. Delma and I enjoyed our retirement and helping out doing voluntary work. Delma was approached by the Rev. Bill Peacock who asked if she could help in St. Paul's Church office two days a week. It would have to be a labour of love. She accepted the office and became secretary for the choir which kept her busy.

Mildred had given up work in a Melbourne takeaway due to arthritis, but her condition did not interfere as a member of the choir. Our daughter Kay was now happily married to Russ. His daughter Emma, from a previous marriage meant that I had now acquired another grandchild. Kay's son Matthew worked at his mother's optical business in Mornington, another lovely seaside resort approximately 40 kilometres from Melbourne. His brother Ben became a masseur.

Yours truly was acting on TV and in films at the time when my agent of many years (Jill's Casting) had found a suitable role for me. I also cooked for various functions, paid or unpaid, banishing the hours to minutes. Time no longer marches on. It flies by Super Jet.

It was decided, as the two boys were living with us permanently, to purchase a larger house with two extra bedrooms, which we did, with the help of Billie. However, this became a financial downfall through circumstances which I will relate later. On the face of it, all was well in the State of Denmark, but unforseen were the deep dark shadows encircling and threatening our lives. Shortly the light will cease to illuminate the darkness. Tears will flow before the light is rekindled. The only saving grace was our faith which was sorely tested.

We must not forget in life's turbulence that our faith can be undermined by the Devil, using his co-partner seeds of evil which grow and flourish in all walks of life. There are times when one is blinded by the fact that this force exists. I've learnt on my journey that positive thoughts are from God and the negative are from Satan. Each one of us has a path to tread and, in doing so we can tune in to either the positive or the negative, good or evil. Our minds act as receivers, a sort of radio or TV set. Both forces are in conflict with each other, the positive the builder, the negative the destroyer. It seems as if the world has embraced the negative wave. It is important that we do not get distortion, making sure that the waveband is tuned correctly and receives the messages loud and clear.

We must not forget in life's turbulence that our faith can be undermined by the Devil, using his co-partner, seeds of evil, which grow and flourish in all walks of life. There are times when one is blinded by the fact that this force exists. I've learnt on my journey that positive thoughts are from God and the negative from Satan. Each one of us has a path to tread, and, in doing so, we can tune in to either the positive or the negative, good or evil. Our mind act as receivers, a sort of radio or T.V. set both forces are in conflict with each other, the positive the builder, the negative the destroyer. It seems as if the world has embraced the negative way. It is important that we do not get distortion, making sure the waveband get tuned correctly and receives the messages loud and clear.

Chapter 19

Caring for Loved Ones

Mildred received a message in 1997. There was no mistake in her reception. She had been feeling listless, with a bloated tummy, as if she had been over eating. She brushed both these symptoms away saying that she must lose weight and go on a diet. Mildred was always a law unto herself inasmuch as going to see our family GP, Dr. David Thompson, saying - it will pass. When I and the family prompted her, she saw our concern and decided to see him. Luckily a periodic appointment had been made in regard to her arthritis, plus a blood pressure check, so there was no way she could not confide her condition to David.

At the time we did not feel unduly worried as she remained bright and cheerful, going about the usual household chores and seeing to the needs of the six of us as best she could, under the circumstances. Mildred managed to laugh which she always did when humorous' situations arose. .Even though she was coping with arthritis ,but this meant Delma , I and the boys leant a hand.

Previously, on our overseas trips, there were no signs of what was in store. The only thing hampering her was the arthritis which necessitated a wheelchair, taking the strain off her legs. It proved to be a boon in getting her through officialdom so that there was no waiting in endless queues.

David our GP arranged for Catscan's and blood tests. Kay, I and the rest of the family waited not too patiently for the results. Mildred was diagnosed with having Microcytic Anaemia, which could be treated. The real cause of the problem lay hidden. She soldiered on with medication -for twelve months, during which time we were both anxious and concerned over her loss of weight. She lost over two stones without dieting. Sunshine cast real shadows over both our lives.

David suggested further Catscans and X-rays as a result of which he suggested that Mildred should see a gynaecologist in Carlton, in outer Melbourne. Dr. Maxwell Cole and Professor Michael Quinn were truly dedicated to their work in alleviating pain and instilling hope to .those whose lives are plagued at times with incurable diseases. Mildred had every confidence in the treatment suggested by them and we considered them as friends, singing their praises to others who may have needed treatment.

To me this was a time when I suddenly realised that this was not some person I nursed, returning home after my duty was finished, leaving the grieving to their family whatever the outcome. This was my loved one with whom I had grown up from the age of sixteen, married, fathered a child. This was a person who had shared my joys, my disappointments, our arguments, sorrows, the bereavement of family and friends and one who had trusted my decisions - which at times had been unwise. She had stood up for me when others were critical, and laughed and supported me when the chips were down. She had loved me in spite of my misgivings. This was my wife, with whom I had hoped to celebrate our golden wedding. It is now my turn to know the anguish of a husband whose wife may be terminally ill.

Mildred first presented herself to Dr. Cole on the twenty-third of October 1998 for a routine gynaecological check-up. Examination at that stage confirmed a worrying distension of her abdomen, with a hard mass that appeared to be palpable in her left abdominal area. The uterus appeared fixed and there was evidence of pelvis induration ,although her ovaries

Chapter 19 - Caring for Loved Ones

could not be identified at that stage. A previous ultrasound had suggested the presence of cholinethisis together with an amount of ascites.

I am ever grateful to the family, Billie and friends for giving us love and support, but things were not looking good at that stage.

A follow-up CT scan of her abdomen confirmed the presence of a large omental cake with a considerable amount of peritoneal opacity. This was thought to be suggestive of primary ovarian carcinoma with widespread peritoneal metastatic disease ,although no gross uterine lesion was identified at that stage. A Ca 125 -was markedly elevated at 26,950.

Poor Mildred endured these examinations with fortitude, still managing to smile through the shadows. What was particularly nasty was the fact that her small veins made it difficult to insert the needles when collecting blood or injecting medication. The patient nurses had to try three or four times, which was very distressing both for Mildred and for the nurses.

I remember saying to Mildred"Do you ever think why me?"-and her reply would be - "I've got it. Let's get on with it." A brave lady. What she had to get on with was no easy road.

Dr. Cole recommended Professor Quinn at the Royal Women's Hospital to carry out further investigations. This tall Scot won Mildred's heart with his charm and complete understanding. Kay and I knew, that, between Dr. Cole and Michael Quinn, Mildred would receive the best possible treatment and they would keep us posted with either good or bad news.

Arrangements were made that on the 9th of November 1998 at 7am along with Dr. Cole, Professor Quinn would perform a laparotomy. They found a massive intra abdominal tumour. A biopsy was performed and no further treatment was undertaken. The abdomen was closed.

Kay and I waited patiently in the ward for the results. Just after 8am Michael Quinn entered the room. His face did not show the concern that was in his heart. He told us later that he was worried about what the biopsy would reveal. But what he said on that cold morning did not fill us with hope.

"I am afraid the news is not good;" he said. "I've never seen such a large ovarian cancer. Removing it at this stage may cause a secondary in some other part of her body."

That was the bad news. He followed-this up with what he considered to be the best line of attack, which gave us hope. "I will give Mildred six months of strong chemotherapy together with blood transfusions," he told us.

The shadows were not good. It took a couple of minutes for the full impact of the news to sink in. I've heard the same news in the course of my nursing career, then expressing condolences. But this time it was different. It was Mildred who had enjoyed a healthy life except for the usual childish ailments and colds. No, it can't be that serious! My eyes turned to Kay to see how she was coping with the news. She gave me a knowing look and clasped my hand, denoting the depth of her love and the warmth.

This very gesture brought the tears to my eyes. It is not till such times that you realise how blessed you are to have a caring family. Over the years, my darling daughter has been a source of comfort in many ways. And Matt, Ben and Delma were always there to lend a hand, which made life easier. The selfish part of me did not want to heed the advice I had given to others. I wanted to stay in the safety of the shadows. Turning to the light might have meant challenges which I had no desire to tackle. During the time of those dark threatening shadows I indulged in self pity, and would return to the light when it became safe to do so. So I dwelt. It is a facet of humans to take the safe path.

Dawn had not yet broken when the awful truth dawned. What possible use am I to Mildred and to others in a zone I deemed safe? This was a way of thinking that was entirely new to me. Throughout my life I had faced up to problems, battling against whatever the odds may have been, but this case was entirely out of my control. Mildred's future lay in the hands of the surgeons I will support her in prayer. Readers may say that prayers are useless, not answering their devotions. But prayers never go unanswered. It is not until we look back in hindsight that we see the way prayer has been fulfilled.

Chapter 19 - Caring for Loved Ones

I will see that all Mildred's needs are cared for. I will try to grant any wish she may have, but I will not emerge from the false euphoria of the shadows to see her in pain. The doctors and nurses will attend to whatever discomfort she may have, just as I did for my patients, where at times I walked that extra mile feeling privileged that I was able to.

This was a time of soul searching, digging deep as to why I felt the way I did. The truth of the matter was that I felt afraid, that, if Mildred died, I was to blame. I had nursed many patients whose conditions were much worse who, through, my good efforts, had returned to health. I had been praised by relatives for the time I had spent; caring for them. So, perhaps my thinking was up the creek. I've a saying – today's problems can be tomorrow's joys. How often have we worried about certain things which then turned out well? I don't say that it was a joy nursing Mildred, but it was a privilege, which drew us closer together.

I came out of the shadows, buried my fears and turned to the light, receiving a warmth within me and a strength that will assuredly be given to me to carry me along this unhappy journey.

Fortunately, Mildred made an excellent recovery postoperatively, though the shadows were still with us. The biopsy confirmed the presence of a primary carcinoma of the ovary and she remained in Professor Quinn's care.

There was a remarkable response to her chemotherapy with excellent resolution to her tumour and she gained a remission of four years. Prior to this, Michael had performed a full hysterectomy.

During the interim periods Mildred and I visited the Royal Women's Hospital once a month, enabling her to have chemotherapy. Professor Quinn would assess her condition. According to him, Mildred was an amazing lady having survived the cancer which had been diagnosed in such an advanced stage. He often remarked that 'someone upstairs must be giving her a helping hand'.

And we would reply - "Yes but not without your help." We were extremely lucky that both doctors were top drawer.

As time progressed we encountered a few nasties. I was keeping an eye on things, and her bowel movements were showing blood, which needed attention in hospital, so back we went. The staff would welcome us as long lost friends, assuring us that all would be well. Wonderful people. On numerous occasions her low blood count required another transfusion, which was always difficult for the nurses, but Mildred never complained. She felt more sorry for the nurses than for herself. This was typical of how she faced her illness very often with a smile. A positive lady with a determined spirit fighting the wretched cancer.

Since I did not want to leave the hospital, they supplied a foldable bed, allowing me to stay overnight. The bed was placed next to Mildred's so that I was able to see to her needs such as toileting, showering and massaging her back and feet. If the patient is in bed for any length of time she has to be turned every so often, which I did. Lying in one position for too long can cause bed sores and luckily I was able to prevent this from happening.

My retirement had not lasted long. I was back doing unpaid nursing. Not true. The salary I received was Mildred's love which cannot be bought with dollars.

The hospital became a second home. One of the doctors asked if she would take part in a special research investigation, entailing taking blood every couple of days. They explained that this would not be of benefit to Mildred, but in participating she might be able to help in narrowing the cause of this insidious cancer. The request certainly meant that she would suffer discomfort due to the smallness of her veins, and so she asked me what I thought! But, of course, she had already made up her mind. If it could be beneficial to others, then that was the least she could do.

One of the saddest memories we have of the chemo ward was seeing young mothers undergoing the treatment----- Knowing that in many cases the prognosis was not good, involving the death of the patient. Mildred unselfishly took part, bless her. Little did we know at the time that a young mother, a friend of Mildred's, who often visited her, would be facing the same situation.

Chapter 19 - Caring for Loved Ones

Because of so many incisions, Mildred's veins became very bruised. This caused concern and it was decided to install a click up her arm. This was a tricky operation which had to be carried out several times before the blood flowed freely. Poor Mildred. What she went through! Yet she never complained and was even able to smile. A brave lady indeed.

During her remission we celebrated our golden wedding. This was a promise that Michael Quinn had hoped to fulfil. The celebration was held at St.Paul's Church Hall and arranged by Kay and Delma. It was a wonderful evening ,where we enjoyed the company of our family and friends, leaving our worries behind.

You may ask how Mildred tackled the cancer. Firstly, she adopted a positive attitude which took her away from the negative side of the illness. Then, once more in the light, her Christian faith upheld her. So many people offered prayers, which, she said, lifted the weight of her suffering. Plus, my support and that of the family. Kay never came without bringing a gift for her comfort and enjoyment, even as far as purchasing a TV and audio player for our 'bedroom'. A very caring and thoughtful daughter.

Due to the chemotherapy Mildred found that all her food had a metallic taste. I spent some time searching the shelves of the Supermarket trying to find a gem that might entice her taste buds. It was a great worry. Even home cooking did not induce her to eat a decent meal. I hit on the idea that iced coffee might tempt her, which it did. So, when food was out of favour, iced coffee became the mainstay of her diet, particularly during the later stages of her illness. Other food or drink was a no, no. The iced coffee was the only thing she enjoyed. At least the milk was food. The four year reprieve enabled Mildred to lead a fairly normal life.

Billie's aged mother entailed both of us giving her support at her home. His father had died some years earlier. Due to her advancing age problems arose. As she became incontinent, the washing machine never rested. And there was the showering and the ever-changing of sheets due to her condition. We cared for her in her house for some ten years in Mount Albert.

One weekend, Billie and I went down with a bug and she fell, though no damage was done. Then we had to make the sad decision of trying to find full time care for her, which was no easy task. Through people are living longer, it created a shortage of beds. Eventually we found the Bryson Hospital which was located not too far from Blenheim Avenue, Billiey's home. This was a godsend as Billie was still teaching piano. We did not know how the dear soul would accept the move, but, luckily she settled in, accepting that this was for her benefit. Her stay at the Bryson was for only a month; the search was still on for a permanent home.

As the time approached for her to leave we were directed, through the grapevine, to Kinross Nursing Home, again not too far from Blenheim Avenue. Truly ,our prayers were answered. We knew very little about the standard of care at Kinross, but over a phone call it seemed to meet our requirements. Yet we wanted to be reassured that we had chosen the right place.

So, with Billie's blessing I checked with a doctor I knew and he okayed it. At 8pm that evening we knew that we had to move quickly, as all vacancies needing to be filled had to be settled within twenty-four hours. Otherwise, the Government reduces the funding.

After meeting the Director of Nursing we decided, as far as we could tell, that Billies's mother would Have a good standard of care. You can imagine what sadness was within our hearts over this decision and that she could no longer stay at home, though she was an independent lady who considered that black was black and white was white, with no shades of grey, When she was asked if she believed in God, she would reply - "I believe in all that is good."

A short lady with high standards. She was brought up in rural Victoria. Her Norwegian father sired a family of ten, and both he and his Australian wife Flora had twice raced to the river for safety from a roaring bush fire. They only managed to save a few of their possessions which included an oil painting, now hanging in Billie's house. Unfortunately, none of these escapades' s had been documented.

Their daughter Sylvia,with her husband William Lowe, had weathered the storm of social depression of the late twenties and early thirties. Sylvia was a person who in times of trouble would stretch out a hand to help those

Chapter 19 - Caring for Loved Ones

in need, and, as a mother, she would encourage her son in music. She also saw to it that he was taught by one of the best teachers in Australia , Ada Corder.O.B.E. of whom I have written about earlier Now, in the autumn of her life she deserved the best care.

I am glad that she did receive it, due to a wonderful son and with my support .Sylvia, bless her, was moved from Kinross to the new home Bellvue, which the owners of Kinross had built this was situated in Oakleigh were the extra beds and facilities were up to modern standards.During the time that she was in the nursing home we both kept a watchful eye to make sure that she was happy and in the best environment possible.

 Sylvia was in their care for seven, years until she passed away at the great age of ninety-sevenand a half.

Billie , a very caring son, visited his mother every day unless his teaching prevented it. I would also visit and we often went for walks together. When she died, Bill sat on one side of the bed, holding her hand and I sat on the other side, clasping her left hand. Praise God she passed away peacefully .after a life well spent.

Chapter 20

Faith Rewarded

Much was taking place during that time. During the last two years of Mildred's life the shadows deepened. Professor Quinn told us that the cancer was prevalent and that further chemotherapy was needed. On top of this, Mildred developed gout which is extremely painful. This became a chronic condition, which necessitated her taking strong tablets to cleanse the system. It was not pleasant.

One bright morning in April 2000 the phone rang. "Hello Dad," said a bright and cheery voice on the other end.

I recognised the voice as Kay's immediately. "Hello, darling. What can I do for you?" I asked. Little did I know what would follow her simple request, which was to deliver an exercise bike to her home. This entailed carrying the bike up a few steps. Some things linger in ones memory .I shall never forget that Wednesday. As I carried the bike up the steps on that sunny day, the bike felt a little heavy. But things do seem to be heavier as one goes through the passage of time. I had everything to feel thankful for. My health was good, apart from my heart condition, which never seemed to bother me provided I took my Warfarin and other medication. Apart from the regular blood tests, Mildred, in remission was coping well, while a lovely family gave Mildred and me support. On that Wednesday afternoon the shadows drew closer.

My arms suddenly felt lethargic, as if I had been scrubbing floors and on the following day my calves hurt as if flu was on its way. Val asked me to move my car in the driveway. The ignition key required me to use both hands in order to turn the engine on. On Friday, my condition grew worse and a visit to the doctor became necessary. He concluded that the condition was due to flu or a virus.

On Saturday morning, Mildred asked me if I was staying in bed, then, as I tried to move my arms and legs, the bitter truth hit me. I was paralysed from the neck down. Neither speech nor mind were affected, but all my limbs were out of action. I knew this was not a stroke, I would probably have been dead if it had been so. Can you imagine my anguish? I was angry with God and asked - why me? The me who had always tried to serve Him. Is this my reward? I, who had been so active - useless.

Hold on. Did I not preach to others, particularly to my patients that nothing is useless, unless you make it so? Take stock, Bernard. Turn the 'why me' into the 'why not me'. Thousands, no millions are worse off than I am. Why do I think I'm so special? Turn the why's into 'use me' for the benefit of others, which did happen while I was in hospital.

Poor Mildred now had two things on her plate. The cancer though still in remission and a husband who may never use his limbs again. The shadows were bleak. Very bleak indeed. Kay, who was naturally distressed at the news, arrived post haste. Dr. Thompson came, but was unsure about my condition, and an ambulance was called to take me to the Peninsula Hospital Where Dr. Scott took over my case.

CAT scan, MIR, and so on were undertaken to find out what malady dwelt within. Dr. Scott, after perusing my X-rays, stated that my neck was the cause of the trouble. Expert treatment was needed and this could only be carried out by Dr. So at the Alfred Hospital in Melbourne.

Chapter 20 - Faith Rewarded

This threw my whole family into turmoil. The ambulance was booked for 9.30am. I had an appointment with Dr. So at 10.30 which was all very well in theory, but the wretched thing did not turn up until an hour later, which meant that I missed the appointment. Unfortunately, the doctor was unavailable till later, since he was operating all day. Those words of cheer were spoken by the charge sister. She also said that they did not have a bed available in the meantime.

"Don't worry, you will be transferred to Casualty, then to a ward after doctor has made his diagnosis."

So, down to the Casualty Department. Once there it became an experience I will never forget. Those poor nurses - what they had to cope with. As I lay in my bed, I surveyed the comings and goings of people seeking help. All races and creeds. One coloured gentleman was continually pacing up and down, uttering abuse at the staff. Another person insisted that he was well. The nurse gently informed him that as he had lost the use of his legs it would be impossible for him to live alone. He then shouted at her to bugger off in a voice large enough for all to hear. The poor nurse patted his hand. "The doctor has said that you must stay till you are walking without help."

"You can tell the doctor that he is an arsehole. Fuck off!" was the response.

Among this mixture of humanity an elderly woman was crying in pain, informing the staff that she wanted to die as she had nowhere to live. Her son had refused to have her in the house. Then a fight broke out between two druggies, who were warned that if there were any more trouble, they would not receive treatment. But they continued snarling at each other.

Lying there in my bed, unable to move and with tubes attached to my arms, plus not knowing what was wrong, I was a little frightened by the carrying on around me. Kay and Mildred came and went, returning later. Bless them. Dinner arrived at 6pm with still no sign of Dr. So. The time lying there seemed endless. Then at 8.30 Dr. So's assistant arrived, shook my hand and apologised for the doctor's absence. He was still operating. He then went on to give me a case history of what was in store, which sounded horrendous.

After Dr. So had examined the X-rays he decided that an operation was the way to go. It would have to be carried out that night. He intended to move the throat artery, presently attached to the neck to one side so that it performed properly, taking bone from the left leg and grafting it, so that the nerves are no longer trapped. He told me that this was a serious operation, but with every chance of success in the right hands. It would take several hours. Meanwhile, I would be fitted with a cervical collar which would keep my neck stationary. I was certainly not impressed with what I had heard. In fact, to put it mildly, I was bloody scared. Oh those shadows! When I asked for the name of my condition he muttered something inaudible, then went on to say that he had arranged with Physio to bring my collar, after which he disappeared. A short time later the wretched collar arrived and was fitted. I now felt completely trapped. Moving my head from side to side had been my only movement, but now I was no longer in control. My thoughts went back to one of my ex-patients who had become a paraplegic. At the time I was full of sympathy and caring, but not feeling or understanding the anguish he was experiencing. On top of that, his wife had found the pressure too much and divorced him. So sad. He also told me that be was taunted, because his sex drive was as strong as ever, which caused him problems. He could do nothing at all to relieve his tensions, because his hands were totally paralysed.

What could I say? What hope could I give him? I could only resort to prayer. He was in his early thirties. While nursing him I made sure that every possible care was given to him, he nevertheless rested in the enforced shadows. Now it was I who lay there in the same circumstances. It was I and no one else doubting whether I would ever recover. Perhaps I would die? The thought frightened me. I had no wish to leave this earth. Hold on. What is so special about me, I thought. Millions of people die every day. I wanted to return to the light. At that moment I did not know what I was fighting. Claustrophobia, that horrible breathless feeling overtook my very being, but I must not panic. Please God help me.

The curtains are drawn. What is happening now? A short dark-skinned man appeared as if from nowhere. He introduced himself as having come

Chapter 20 - Faith Rewarded

from Sri Lanka. I did not catch his name, probably because I was too concerned with my own feelings, but I did hear what he said next.

"I am a neurologist," he told me. "I would like to see what is causing all your symptoms."

This piece of news gave me hope. Perhaps they will not have to cut my throat. After much pulling of my limbs and asking numerous questions and testing my reflexes he came up with a response that seemed to me to be on the right track.

"You have a virus which only one in three hundred thousand contract," he said, looking over his spectacles with a little smile. "You will not have to have an operation. You have been struck down with Guillain-Barre Syndrome. The cause of the disorder is yet to be discovered. Anyone at any age can come down with the inflammatory neuropathy, which destroys the sheathing around the nerves. Muscle weakness tingling and general weakness are all symptoms of the disease, which can be overcome in some cases with treatment. This entails physio, exercises and swimming. With perseverance you will win the battle. Occasionally patients are left with a weakness in their limbs. As for the collar, you may dispense with it. It is not needed."

This news certainly answered a prayer from Heaven. In my mind doubts lingered, but I was filled with hope. As my saviour left he said - "I will be interested to hear of your progress." He then opened the curtains and left. I did not know his name, but I was grateful for his news.

Kay and Mildred came, and, after hearing the good news, they left for a cuppa. One of the staff came to see if I wanted a drink. I asked her to take the collar off but she shook her head.

"I'm afraid only the doctor can order its removal. Sorry dear," she said, gave me a sweet smile and left before I could continue.

Not satisfied with her response I called out to be released from my prison. This time the charge sister received my wrath.

"Will you please remove this strangulating instrument of torture from my neck," I said angrily. By this time the best of my nature was not to the fore.

"As much as I would like to grant your request, only the doc ..."

She did not finish the word. "Doctor or no doctor," I raged. "I want it off! Please." I had a feeling that my efforts were in vain. But the poor soul could see that she was on the losing side and went off for reinforcements. Kay returned to quell the storm.

"Now, Dad. You know that nurses have to obey the rules. You know that as a nurse yourself," she said gently.

"I know that rules can be broken, especially if the patient is distressed, and believe me I am distressed! Anyway, the neurologist said it could come off!" I stated. Kay reminded me that he was not the one who had ordered it to be fitted in the first place. Now I was about to use my very nasty and last trump card.

"Kay," I said seriously. "If they won't remove it I'll worry about bringing on a heart attack. Then it will be on the conscience of those who refused."

Kay looked at me. "Tut, tut," she said and summoned the nurse who unclipped the band and placed it in a cupboard, much to my relief. I don't usually resort to such methods but the Sri Lankan had said to get rid of it. I was only obeying doctor's orders.

Once the diagnosis had been confirmed I was transferred to a ward, where peace reigned. I was thankful to be out of the chamber of horrors. My only hope was that conditions had improved for the poor nurses in casualty.

The staff on the ward positioned me, where they could observe if there was any change in my condition. They were excellent in serving my needs. I was completely immobile, having to be fed, toileted and bed bathed. Showering was out of the question. They changed my pyjamas for me, saw to it that I drank enough liquids and checked my breathing with a sort of pressure tube into which I had to blow with the best force I could muster. Between the measuring of my heart beats and blood pressure an endless trail of doctors and students arrived to view this unusual case. They would poke and jab my limbs. They asked questions regarding my general health and specifically the Guillain-Barre Syndrome. Regular visits from the physio therapists gave me passive exercises.

Chapter 20 - Faith Rewarded

Even though everything was being done to return me to optimum health, I still felt angry with God and was unsure whether I would ever fully recover. I was still dwelling in the shadows.

Mildred, Delma and the rest of the family paid me regular visits as well as Billie, who picked Mildred up for the long drive to the Alfred Hospital. I value his friendship.; he has supported and helped me in many ways over the years and is still doing so.

Mildred asked me if I wanted anything brought from home. You may remember Mary Evans and her sister in a previous chapter of this book. In appreciation of my kindness to their mother they gave me the book Daily Light as a daily reading to help me on my journey. My wife brought the book in, knowing that I was still despondent regarding my condition and in need of reassurance so that I might make a full recovery.

After Mildred left I tried my best to flick through the pages. To this day I do not know how I managed because the strength had completely gone from my fingers, but, there in front of me, was written, in bold letters -

RECOVERY FROM SICKNESS

The Lord that healeth thee.
I shall not die, but live and declare the works of the Lord.
The Lord hath chastened me sore;
But hath not given me over to death.

As I read those words, I knew that the passage was there to give me hope and the courage to continue on. I realised again that I must leave the shadows behind me, while asking the Lord to use me, which he did. That book had been given to me twenty years earlier. I believe that its sole purpose was to give me strength in my sickness.

Little did Mary and Lorna know, when they gave me the Daily Light just how much comfort I would later derive from their gift!

As I already stated, many student nurses gathered around my bed, interested in my condition. Some of them told me that they had heard that I had been a nurse and asked what made a good nurse. For what it was worth I told them that the main ingredient would be TLC or tender loving care. I also told them that the commodity they would be dealing with is very weak and they were very strong, meaning that they could either make or break the patient, depending on how they were treated. Treat them as you would wish to be treated yourself if you were in the same position, I advised them.

I repeated this over and over again, and, as they stood at my bedside, they told me that it would give a new slant to their thinking and that they would remember my words while they were training.

The Lord is no man's debtor. Serve Him, trust Him. Never doubt His power and He will lead you out of the shadows. Believe it. I've proved it.

While the staff did all they could for my comfort they also had to turn me-constantly, thus avoiding bed sores from my lying in the same position for too long, I was finally given a waterbed which was heaven after the hard mattress.

Each week brought a little progress and gradually my limbs were encouraged to move. The physio and the doctors were pleased with the way things were going. On the humorous side, I said to a little Asian doctor who told me that there was definite progress without complications - "Yes, thanks to the staff," and at the same time I pointed up to the ceiling. "With a little help from up there," I told him.

"Yes," he replied. "We have a good physio department."

I think he got the wrong message. After I responded well to exercises in the ward ,I was moved to the physiotherapy room where various aides were used to induce my limbs to get back into action, with the encouragement of the staff and twelve bottles of antibodies which hastened the improvement.

As the weeks went by, the next step was rehabilitation. Mount Eliza Rehab was chosen. It was set in beautiful surroundings on the outskirts of Frankston, overlooking the sea. An ideal setting to get on the road to recovery. So I bid farewell to the staff at the Alfred Hospital and was transported by ambulance to my new home where I would stay until I was fit and fairly independent.

I received a warm welcome with assurances that my stay would be enjoyable at the Rehabilitation Centre. Later, through the grapevine I learnt that the

Chapter 20 – Faith Rewarded

Alfred Hospital had informed them that I was an agreeable patient, thus assuring the staff that we would get on well. I must say that I was touched by their remarks, but I responded laughingly – "Just wait. I'm a grumpy old so and so when you get to know me."

The lovely receptionist replied in a jovial manner - "We have a place for anyone with the grumps." Just where this could be I was not game to ask. I was never grumpy so I never experienced the threatened abode. I felt that I would be happy during my stay. How could I be otherwise when they treated me as someone 'special', for some reason.

A big shock came when I was taken to the ward. There, in front of me was, dare I say it, a collection of old grey-headed male and female patients, complete with walking sticks and wheelchairs and some with evidence of facial disfigurement due to strokes, or permanently paralysed limbs. Some people projected a look of despair and I had every sympathy for them.

Faint shadows were appearing and I must quickly about face. I had been the instrument in the past of comforting and helping those in similar circumstances. Now on the road to recovery, the situation was entirely different. I was no longer the nurse. I would have to obey the rules. I was no longer in control. No matter how I felt, the boot was now on the other foot. This was a hard pill to swallow. I had no wish to join this group in God's waiting room.

Hold on. As I surveyed the scene before me, I realised that some people were my age. No, this cannot be a reflection of me, I thought. I still had my wits, my sense of humour. I could still hold a sensible conversation, and, above all, my faith in the knowledge that I will be healed.

I was determined that the shadows would not be cast over my faith on this rather hard road to recovery. Think positive thoughts and half the battle will be won.

During my stay I was able to help many patients in a small way, injecting into their lives a sense of purpose, even though they were confined to a wheelchair or a bed. The wisdom they had thus hopefully gathered, plus their own experience, could be passed on to staff and visitors, especially the young. By coming to terms with their handicaps many learnt to feel that they were helping to banish the idea of 'uselessness'.

To aid my recovery, physiotherapy and exercises in the hydro pool and cookery were chosen as part of the daily agenda. This suited me. I enjoyed making scones or biscuits which were shared with the other patients during morning tea. But I received a nasty shock when I was told that my driving licence would be suspended, until my doctor stated that I would be safe behind the wheel. This meant, of course, that I had to pass another road test. Fortunately, due to my response in gaining the use of my limbs it was not required. The test, which is required by law in the cases where a person had suffered a stroke or any disability of limbs or brain was wavered in my case, because I made a full recovery. During that time I had the use of a wheelchair which brightened my day, because I was not confined to the ward.

The shadows were behind me after several weeks and the time came for my departure. I went home with the aid of a walking stick which gave me confidence when I felt a bit unsteady. Trips to the hydro pool continued to strengthen my muscles and Mildred also attended the pool, because Dr. Thompson suggested that it might improve her arthritis.

Thankfully, Mildred stayed in remission while my drama was centre stage. The worst as far as she was concerned was yet to come. But luckily, not before I was able to regain my strength, mobility and independence. This enabled me to nurse her again. Though it became a full-time job at times ,I felt that it was a privilege.

I spent the time doing very little while I was at home. I read or watched TV with Mildred who unselfishly enjoyed my company at home, not at work.

One highlight during this convalescence was a visit to Ben's school to see a student performance of Oedipus. The stage had been built by Ben who is very clever with his hands. Both of my grandsons are very precious to me. Sometimes we do have the odd disagreement, mostly because Grandpa did not accept the views of the young. The generation gap is close-knit in our family and we say what we think, at times upsetting each other. But it is done in love and once done it is finished. Then we get on with our love

Chapter 20 - Faith Rewarded

for one another. I'm very blessed to have the family and my dear friend Billie, who is always there. A great comfort in my life is my wonderful daughter Kay and her husband Russ,. both unselfishly caring and stretching out their hands to those who have fallen on hard times, easing their burdens or lending an ear to their problems.

Mildred remained in remission, while my recovery and progress led to a fairly normal life. Between check-ups at the Royal Women's Hospital Mildred put on a brave face after chemo, which can be extremely unpleasant. She told me how she felt during this period, "I am in the world, yet out of it," she said. She needed my help to walk or shower, but she remained steadfast in her faith during this unsettling time, and her thoughts remained positive. She trusted Professor Michael Quinn and other doctors with whom she came in contact. Mr. Max Cole also held a special place in her heart. He now keeps an eye on Kay for any signs of cancer. You may remember I stated earlier a few years earlier she had a benign tumour removed from the ovaries. Mildred could not speak highly enough of the wonderful staff at the Royal Women's Hospital----a place were joy and sorrow go hand in hand .It is also a place of hope.

As we journey through life, we meet special people. Marian Louise South (nee Stanley) was one such person. She was born to Christian parents Mary and Ian on the 7th of April, 1974, and her life subsequently centred around her Church at St. Paul's in Frankston. The Church introduced us to this rather shy and retiring girl, though from an early age she had projected a determination and strong will. She soon let you know, in the course of a conversation, whether she agreed or disagreed with the topic by the expression on her face. She had an infectious smile when she greeted you, betraying a quick wit and a sense of humour. Marian was a fun-loving person in spite of her shyness and became involved with Scottish Country Dancing, enjoying the lessons with her father as teacher and her mother as his trusted assistant.

Marian grew up with her brothers Keith and Christopher in a stable family background. Her grandparents on each side were involved in church work. in fact, her grandfather became a vicar after he married. Her father-in-law was also a minister, so it was no surprise, that, after she left, school, then on to Melbourne University she became interested in autism. Her interest grew enough for her to focus on this subject for her assignments.

At the time she did not fully understand why she was led to study this particular subject. Deep in the back of her mind she felt that the reason would be revealed later. Acquiring this knowledge became a bonus later in her life. It is a true saying that in this world nothing is wasted. It is how you use it that matters.

Ridley College brought Marian a step further in her life study of theology. She knew that somewhere along the line God had special work for her, though she was certain that it was not that she would be ordained as a Minister of the Church. Her calling would be revealed in His own time. Marian left a channel open for guidance.

She was a young lady of many parts and used her gifts to the full. Music was always important to her. She studied piano and organ and taught herself to play the flute. Since she also had a lovely singing voice, she used her gifts in her worship at St. Paul's and played a large part in forming Refresh which was an evening service for people who did not attend the traditional services.

Marian loved the Church where she was baptised in the baptismal robe, which was a family heirloom dating back to her great grandmother in Tasmania from the 1880's. On her first Christmas a cuddly bear entered her life and it stayed with her through thick and thin for the rest of her days.

When she attended a week-end training course at Merricks, which was a part of the Ridley curriculum, Cupid shot his bow as she met a young man from Traralgon. Love blossomed. He was on her wave-length as regard working for the Lord and they married in due course. Two adorable boys, Stephen and Isaac, arrived and Marian's and her husband Matthew's happiness was complete. But shadows lurked and the boys were diagnosed as autistic. Through her assignments at Ridley Marian knew how to cope with it, turning to the light which gave her the strength to deal with her family. Unfortunately, there were more shadows on the horizon.

Chapter 20 - Faith Rewarded

I've included Marian's story, because somehow, with her incredible faith, she found the time to visit Mildred with the two boys. Mildred enjoyed those times together which brought them close and for that I am eternally grateful. Marian was always thinking of and caring for others, loving people and children, and so she became a registered carer for children with special needs, particularly when she accompanied a child to a to a weekend camp.

Later, when the shadows cast their silhouette on her, she was overwhelmed by the love and gifts she received as well as donations for her treatment, much of it from complete strangers. She began a scrap book project on her web site, thus remaining in contact with others who wanted to share their special moments with her. She had many strings to her bow which created music for all those with whom she came in contact.

Life was good for Marian, with a loving husband, two adorable children and a stable family background with two brothers whom, I suspect spoilt her as brothers do to an only sister. Yes, life was good. Tyabb proved to be a great place and friendships blossomed from a remarkable bunch of mothers from the kindergarten and then from Tyabb Primary School. Marian loved a joke, which sometimes led to mischief. The school, in the midst of fund-raising ,displayed a large jar containing multi-coloured jelly beans. The idea was to guess how many beans were in the jar. Marian and her friends decided that there were too many and laughingly relieved the jar of a handful. No harm was done, but doing it transported them back to the happy days of childhood when one purloined some fruit from mother, as she was mixing her cake. It was fun.

Here is a note Marian wrote on the 25th April, 2007 - 'I am 33 year's old. Two days before my 33rd birthday I was told my cancer was terminal. I've been given two to five years at best. With a wonderful husband and two adorable children I have much to live for, so the fight for life is on. Although I'm fighting with every fibre in my being, death is a real possibility.'

She also wrote -

'I am a child of God!

I am a reader. I love children's books, mysteries and fantasy.

I am an artist. I love to create, to paint, to draw, to ,create.

I love to scrap - to write down the memory of the moment a photo was taken.'

Marian was not so heavenly minded that she was of no earthly use. She had a human side to her, which, through her spiritual side, allowed both sides of her personality to emerge.

Once Marian sensed where her cancer was leading her, though weary in struggling with chronic fatigue syndrome, a crummy kidney condition plus the advancement of cancer throughout her body, she decided to be the architect of her own Memorial Service. Each part was planned to the last detail. The service was meant to be a gift to each one of us. The songs, the Bible readings and all those taking part were hand-picked.

She wanted the Service to be bright' and colourful. Party balloons hung from pillars. She did not want her boys to think that this was a dreary occasion. Each member of the congregation received a small box containing coloured jelly beans and a caption -

> 'A bag of jelly beans
> Colourful and sweet
> Is a prayer
> Is a promise
> Is a special treat.
> May the joy of Christ's resurrection
> Fill your heart
> And bless your life.
> Red is for the blood He gave
> Green is for the grass He made
> Yellow is for the sun so bright
> Orange is for the edge of night
> Black is for the sin we made
> White is for the grace He gave
> Purple is for the hour of sorrow
> Blue is for our new tomorrow.'

Chapter 20 - Faith Rewarded

The precious gift that was packaged during the service was the gift of eternal life, offered by Marian loving God through her belief in the death and resurrection of Jesus Christ.

Wow. What faith. Here was a young woman who turned her back on the shadows, unblinded by the radiant light that gave her warmth in her coldest hours, who lit the pathway to her eternal life. Here was a person who had everything to live for with a happy marriage and two young children, who, at their age, needed the care and love of a mother. Although the cancer robbed her of all that was most precious to her, she felt no bitterness. Her one aim was to see that she left her house in order. Leaving her loved ones and friends with the knowledge that they had nothing to fear. She was stepping into the future, to be there for all of us to be reunited in the presence of One who had become her trusted companion on her journey.

Marian passed away peacefully in the presence of her family in March 2008. As Marian drew her final breath, Mary, her mother, had what she described as an ethereal experience. Three of her late grandparents and Mildred, who had also passed away, stood together and seemed to be welcoming her on the final part of her journey here on earth.

Mary swore that this was no dream, it was real. Marian's story has been told to give hope and strength to those who live in the shadows. God bless you Marian.

The shadows loomed again for us in the year 2003. Mildred's cancer was once more raising its nasty head, necessitating further chemo and blood transfusions and short stays in hospital. Michael Quinn and the nursing staff were amazed at how well she had tackled her illness. Because her veins made injections difficult, a permanent site was suggested. The procedure is known as a PICC Line. Needless to say, this was a tricky procedure in Mildred's case. There were four trips to the theatre before it was successful, though, as usual, she took it in her stride and even saw humour in the situation. Truly an amazing lady, fighting it all with fortitude and courage. The fact that I could stay at the hospital overnight, and, was, therefore, able to help. This was her support.

Kay saw to her every need----buying her new nightwear if needed and often bringing in a book, cuddly bear or embroidered cushion, with loving woven words or sometimes, a printed humorous picture or helpful verse. Delma supplied clean laundry and the rest of the family helped and supported in every way as did Billie, knowing what a trying time this was for all of us. Mildred continued giving small amounts of blood after her chemo, as the hospital researched ways that might ultimately be of help to patients.

During the last twelve months of her life, Mildred and I had to decide whether to continue chemotherapy - or not. We both knew, as did the rest of the family, what the final outcome might be if it were, stopped and so we left this final decision to her. Loving her and wanting her to live was not enough to justify the pain and the indignities she was suffering.

There is a time to be born and a time to die. Had the time for Mildred to complete her journey here on earth finished? The actual time for our final breath is not governed by us. What we can do is hasten the step by refusing to take medication. This is what Mildred chose to do.

In her case she knew that the odds of recovery were not on the books. Day by day she knew that it was useless to fight her body which was not responding to treatment. When she was asked why she was refusing to go on with chemotherapy, her answer was - 'What is the use if you have no quality of life? I am thankful that I had a few years of remission, while there are some patients who are not so blessed. We managed to celebrate our Golden Wedding, plus a three-year bonus.'

As she spoke, I remembered the young people undergoing chemo. Some lives were cut off before they had the chance to live. Life seems to be unfair. We all entered this world nursed in our mother's womb, yet, on entering, each one of us is on a different path. Each one of us must strive to do our best. The shadows must be obliterated. The choice is ours, to dwell in the shadows or to find the light. Have no regrets for the past and cherish each hour of today, tomorrow's dawn may not be for you. It's later than you think.

During the next few months, if I found that there was any turn for the worst in Mildred's condition, I would phone the hospital who would refer

Chapter 20 - Faith Rewarded

me to Michael Quinn, who, thankfully, never minded how often I rang. Mildred had put her trust in my nursing, asking me to nurse her to the end. She had no wish to die in hospital. This was a great responsibility for me, even though I had nursed to the best of my ability before retirement, this time the patient was my loving wife who I loved. This was the person who had shared the ups and downs for more than 50 years.

When, during the latter part of her illness I suggested that perhaps she should go back to the hospital, Mildred would not have a bar of it, saying that she had every confidence in my nursing.

As the weeks and months went by her legs swelled up with oedema and water blisters occurred due to the tightness of her skin. There was a constant battle against ulcers and making sure that dehydration did not set in, also seeing fluid intake was appropriate. On top of all this Mildred developed a fear of inconstancy. There were many sleepless nights, where, every ten minutes ,she would have to go to the commode. Getting her to eat was another problem. It was a losing battle. It was amazing to see that she continued to live on iced coffee.

On the last visit to Professor Quinn, as we sat waiting, he came over to us, took hold of her hand and kissed her face saying as he did so - 'I do not usually kiss my patients, but this is an amazing lady.'

Yes, she was certainly that. Always being positive in her attitude during her illness. Letting the trust in her faith support her and thankful that she had a loving family, which sad sadly she did not want to leave. Realizing that the clock of her life was slowly unwinding, she accepted this with grace and dignity.

For my birthday on the 30th of December, Mildred gave me two cards. One was humorous and the other contained loving words. She signed it with - 'Thank you for all you have done for me, especially the last two years. With all my love.'

Those cards are very precious. They were the last she wrote.

On the 12th January Mildred wished us all goodnight. Matthew helped me to turn her on her side. She I kissed him and told him to go to bed and get some sleep. Ben went out to see a friend. I said I would sit up in the chair. It was no use going to bed as she needed the toilet every ten minutes. Kay offered to stay, but Mildred insisted that she should go home, assuring her that I would phone if she were needed. Against her better judgement Kay left. Mildred told me very firmly to lie in bed and get some well earned rest which I reluctantly did. I fell asleep almost immediately.

At about 1.30am on the morning of the 13th Ben returned with cries of 'Gran, Gran!' arousing me from my sleep. He had felt for her in her bed, but she was not there. She was lying on the floor. I quickly searched for her pulse, but I knew that her earthly journey was over.

Oh, how angry I was with God that he had robbed me of those final moments! Guilt set in. If only, if only I had stayed up she might still be alive. The thought that she had died because of the fall haunted me. Perhaps she had lain on the floor in pain while I had been oblivious to her calling? Oh God, why did you forsake us?

Such were my selfish thoughts. I cried for my loss. I cried in anger.

My darling daughter arrived with Russ to comfort me in my loss.

"Mum's suffering is over. No more pain," she assured me.

"Yes, my love," I agreed. "But, If only I'd stayed awake'. The words hammered through my brain. If only, if only. Even today those words haunt me. I gained little comfort when the doctor assured me that she would have been dead before she reached the floor.

The law states that when any person is found to be dead, the police must be informed in case there are suspicious circumstances. The rest of that early morning was spent with the comings and goings of the doctor, the police and our friend and minister the Reverend Bill Peacock, offering prayers and reassurance that we will be reunited with Mildred in Heaven when our journey here is complete.

Beautiful words, but in those shadows the cancerous thoughts come to the fore. Is this true, or false? Are we deluded into believing that the journey on earth is over? No eternal life, no Jesus, He is a myth. Do our bodies, which we have nourished and cared for, end up in the cold ground to rot, or

Chapter 20 - Faith Rewarded

are we just burnt in a fiery furnace? If this is so, then life has no meaning for me. It is up to us on our journey to search for the truth, deciding whether or not our souls will dwell in the house of the Lord.

I am sitting here on this beautiful Easter Monday, writing. The sun is shining in a clear blue sky. I am seeing the last autumn flowers, and trees, which are dressed for the finality of the season in rich warm colours. They are dying, but they will be resurrected in spring with gowns of green. This is nature's way. And we too go through the span of our lives. We are born, grow, blossom and die, to be reborn with new bodies. I have proved the Easter message to be true. And so did Marian and Mildred.

On our journey let us search for truth, and may we find the answer to give us the peace that passes all understanding. The days following Mildred's passing remain blurred.

Finally, the mist began to lift, leaving me in a sort of limbo while there were so many things that needed immediate attention. One was, of course, the funeral. Kay and Russ dealt with this very personal occasion as well as helping to ease the grief which we all have to pass through when we lose a dear one. The Rev. Helen Chick, who was a special friend of my daughter, accompanied us to the funeral parlour.

The parlour staff greeted us offering their condolences and led us to the room where Mildred lay. The moment of truth hit me in this room of reverence. There was soft music as we entered, conjoined with the aroma of blue and white hyacinths. They were Mildred's favourite flowers and for a moment my mind returned to the day of our engagement when I first gave her a white hyacinth.

My eyes took courage to look from the flowers to the polished burial chest. It was not a coffin. Coffin is a word that announces the finality of earthly life, whereas a chest holds a treasure! It was the last gift my family and I could give to Mildred.

Here, amongst the flowers and the music lay Mildred, partly covered by a lace shroud, her features untouched by time. Here lay the girl I fell in love with six decades ago and on her face was a smile. Or, was that only in my imagination? Had she not said just two weeks ago that I could still make her laugh? The way through sunshine and shadow together was over. Cancer has robbed us of any remaining years and only in memory will I hear her song, see her laughing at a joke or at the funny side of a humorous situation.

No more goodnight kisses

No more loving words

No making up after an argument

Time has run out for what I should have said and for what I didn't

No time now to repair a hurt spoken in haste

No time to say I love you

No more excuses covering up a selfish act

I touch the chest and know that Mildred's journey here is over. She will continue on without me. 53 plua years have gone by in the twinkling of an eye. If we banished clocks as Joan Lindsey did at Mulberry Hill, would our life be extended, without the seconds, the minutes, hours and days? Vital measurements that govern night and day. Are we programmed to the ticking clock, with no reprieve to enjoy the nectar of companionship or love? Do we clutch at straws or figments when shadows fall?

This much I did know. I wanted to stay in the shadows. I cannot face the light. It is too strong. There has been too much hurt. Yes, I'll stay to grieve with self pity. These are now my friends and safety valves. I'll live on my memories, staying as if in a cocoon. Encased, protected till it's safe to emerge.

One last hold of Mildred's left hand. There was no ring on her third finger, where it had remained since our wedding day. It was a seal of the vows we had made before God. It had remained on her finger for better or worse, in sickness and in health and for richer or poorer. That ring was removed to be cherished by Kay. Other rings were put on a tray to be sorted at will.

Chapter 20 - Faith Rewarded

There was no look of fear or anguish on her face. She was in repose as if she were sleeping. There were no more shadows, because she had faced her final journey without fear.

Hold on a second. This book, and its very essence are about sunshine and shadows and how we must find a way to turn to the light. There I was, shirking my own advice.

Finally, I turned towards the door with one last glance at the precious wife I had first kissed so many decades ago. I left Mildred. There was nothing more that I could do. The final curtain had come down, but not in darkness. I left her in the light which was the reward for a life well spent.

This was the way I must travel, leaving the valley of the shadow of death. I will fear no evil. A new life is before me. I will plant the seed to bear fruit, Rain will fall in the shape of teardrops. But sunshine will dry the tears in the joys that I will hopefully encounter along the way. And in due season I would have the courage to begin a new life, embracing the old yet stretching out to new horizons.

God gave us memories so that we could have roses in winter----not to dwell on them, but to occasionally take them out from our hearts to once again delight in the sweet fragrances of yesteryear Blossom.

Chapter 21

Marysville Then, Marysville 2009 The Return

Marysville - then

As I write, my mind travels to a little town, or what the English would call a village. It is a place within easy reach of Melbourne, Victoria. Just 90 kilometers away. We drive past tall trees and catch sight of vineyards producing wines for both the rich and poor man's tables. The journey holds our interest, and Billie and I often visit to get away from the crowds during the hurdy gurdy of life; it is here in Marysville that we recharge our batteries, Marysville, where the pace simmers down to the point of total relaxation.

We can recapture the spirit of the past and almost feel and see the miners of 1857 as they search for gold at Enoch's Point. They were probably too busy to enjoy the beauty around them. But we can see the Mystic Mountains, and, across from them, the Acheron Valley with spectacular views of Lake Mountain and the Cathedral mountains. The search for gold continued in the district, when, in 1861, discoveries were made at Woods Point and Jamieson.

We were most fortunate to have friends in that part of the country. Pam and Greg were the superb hosts of the Crossways Historic Country Inn that has stood the test of time since 1920.

As soon as one entered Crossways, one could feel the elegance that pervaded it in an atmosphere of nostalgia. Within its walls were the collectibles of many years gone by and this is where we dined, lit by candlelight and warmed by an open fire. The sumptuous meals were prepared by Pam in Ellie's Licensed Restaurant, which was named after Pam's late mother. Or we might have a tipple in Greg's beautiful red gum bar under his charming but watchful eye, always giving us the assurance that we were welcome. Then, finally, 'when the Sandman called' which was an expression used by my mother when I was young - it was time for bed.

We retired to a delightful cedar wood cottage, six of which are situated in a lush parkland environment. The soothing lullaby which comes from the nearby Steavenson River encouraged us to drift off into the sleep of the gods, to be woken in the morning by the songs of the birds. Sometimes one could hear the rare sound of the lyre bird as it imitated the call of other birds. They can even imitate the sounds of an axe or a chainsaw.

After a hearty breakfast we would set off to explore what Marysville had to offer in this wonderland of nature. Steavenson Falls is one of the tallest in Victoria with five cascades and a total descent of 122 meters, the last having a drop of more than 21 meters. Nights are beautifully floodlit, as Billie and I enjoy one of the many bush walks.

We are so grateful to our friends for their hospitality, truly an oasis in this troubled world. We have visited in all seasons, but autumn is our favourite as the trees are in all their glory. Their leaves radiate gold with tinges of yellow and rustic red, intermingling with the green foliage still waiting to conclude their life span, after which they are adorned in a brownish gown. All the colours boast of lives well spent, as they patiently wait for the time when they will be separated from the boughs which gave them birth.

Chapter 21 - Marysville Then, Marysville 2009 The Return

The leaves will fall gently as they are banished by the wind and scattered, nourishing the earth and encouraging nature to continue its cycle.

In the April of 2008 Billie and I stood by the war memorial, Paying our homage to the sons of Marysville who had paid the supreme sacrifice in the service of their country. As I glanced at those around me, a thought came to mind. In the ongoing uncertainty of life, will we stand here again on Anzac Day in 2009?

Pam and Greg had decided to semi-retire, putting their beloved Inn up for sale. If Crossways were to be sold, would it become a motel? Or maybe a developer would raze it to the ground and put up a building which would have no real connection with the town's past? Will this little haven be obliterated by those who are totally insensitive to its heritage just for the sake of the almighty dollar?

We stood, as tributes for the fallen were spoken in the gently falling rain, as if tears were falling for those who were mourning.

And then we had to bid farewell to Pam, Greg and their friend Daryl, and, as the car drove away, we looked back fondly at Crossways set in its magnificent surroundings. I turned to Billie - "So many people have had great times here. If the Inn could speak it would have some tales to tell. Let's hope it never changes."

As we drove away down the main street of Marysville, we glanced around us at the buildings which had been constructed in another era. They are simple in design, but still serve their purpose in this modern age. We see a ski shop and a lolly store; there is the Cumberland Hotel which some say is out of character with its neighbours, yet it has moulded in with the rest of the town. We see a Meccano shop complete with models which bring joy to children everywhere. There are craft shops with gifts to be bought and a newsagent combined with a supermarket. In a quaint alleyway is Mrs. Mop's Op Shop, selling goods for a good cause. Visitors stroll leisurely by, taking in the beauty of the street which is the hub of commerce for residents and visitors. The War Memorial is on the left of the Bendigo Bank, attached to the Information Centre.

Beyond is a man-made lake where ducks find refuge, and there are trout swimming just below the surface. The lake is situated in a grass and tree-lined park with an oval, where, on weekends and holidays, cricket teams bat out each other. There stands an old water wheel, a feature displayed from yesteryear.

Nearby the ripple of the Steavenson River with its precious cool waters gathers momentum to flow into the dam. And then, advancing down the street one comes across a little cafe called the Corner Cupboard, run by Pam and Greg, the owners of Crossways.

Marysville - 2009 The Return

The heat is oppressive, well over 45°Celsius.

The date is Saturday February 7th 2009.

It is a day to remember in the history of Marysville.

Some six weeks after that dreadful February 7th, we returned. As we drove towards Marysville, we saw the blackened trunks of trees on either side of the road, heralds of what will be seen, as you advance into what was once the town of Marysville. The fires, the destroyer played its trump card then finally was beaten by those who held four aces, the gallant fire fighters. But, as we approached, the smell of smoke still lingered in the air as the essence of death.

We came closer to the town and saw that a church, called Our Lady of the Snow, and which had acted as a signpost, was gone. This quaint, little church had pointed out the way down to the town, but now it was left as a smouldering symbol only, its Christianity destroyed by the hot friends of Hades. The little white church did not suffer alone. Houses, shops, flora and fauna and perhaps most importantly, people of all ages had been reduced to ashes.

Chapter 21 - Marysville Then, Marysville 2009 The Return

Still resting on its makeshift foundations is a quickly built metal shed ,housing those who had survived and who chose without other support to shelter inside. This metal shell is the temporary church wherein the cup of salvation is passed from one to the other, the sacrament giving strength and courage to the believers. Those survivors gave thanks that they were saved from a disaster, which was unequalled in any state of Australia.

Homes that had once bonded family and friends had become nothing more than twisted rubble, some becoming incinerators for those trapped inside. Others had died in their cars or as they fled from a force that showed man it was a power to be reckoned with.

Our reason for returning to Marysville was two-fold. We wanted to visit our dear friends at Crossways, which was only one of the two buildings still standing, though their house in Falls Road had been destroyed. The other survivor was the bakery.

And secondly, we needed to lay to rest in our own minds the horror that had daily been pictured on TV. We wandered around through this ghost town, gazing at the flattened blocks of land and looking in vain for familiar landmarks like the Lolly Shop or Mrs. Mop's Op Shop or the newsagent cum-- supermarket, Pam and Greg's Corner Cupboard, the Meccano shop and the ,Cumberland Hotel opposite the Ski Shop.

As we crossed the bridge on our way to the Inn we saw that the once crystal clear water of the Steavenson River was now a clouded brown, as if in mourning for the charred blackened garments of nature, now dormant along its banks.

As we walked, a silence dwelt here, amidst the sound of a few passing cars and would-be visitors. Yes, the silence was uncanny, as if Marysville was saying - the storm has passed, we are resting to awaken again, when we can turn from the shadows to forge ahead.

May it not be old for new, but old lamps. Repolished to cast light for the future. It should be remembered that the old lamps once shone brightly in the past. Let us hope, that for Marysville, the old and the new will shine together on the pathway leading to the restoration of this historic town.

As we stood at the top of the hill, surveying the view as we so often had in the past, we knew that the buildings were gone. The Anglican Church in the far distance had been violated, only the white Cross stood where worshipers once gave thanks to God. Shops were no longer there or not open - just empty space. The garage and petrol pumps had suffered defeat, and trees and shrubs had been eaten by fire.

There were a few people wandering idly on the streets, perhaps in reverence, for this place had become a cemetery. A wreath had been placed on the Anzac Memorial and its words stood out, "Lest We Forget". There will be no forgetting. While Marysville had become a graveyard in its desolation and silence, one can still hear the solemn music of the mind.

Tears trickled from our eyes, releasing the depths of our emotion, as we returned to the safety and comfort of our friends at Crossways.

What did we learn from our return to Marysville? It is a hard question. I think that it brings to mind that our lives are in orbit, and, that, at any time, they may be diverted to another dimension. Sudden death, illness, financial loss, a road accident, divorce, hatred towards another or pyromania and so on can overcome us. Each one can contribute to a change of course on our journey, the lesson to be learnt.

Cherish each hour of the day, for tomorrow the river of life may change its direction, leaving a drought in your existence, uncertain whether or not the cool waters will flow again to quench the sorrows of your life.

Yes, we are glad that we revisited Crossways in the knowledge that its legend survives to host those who seek refreshment, a meal and love within its walls. Yes, the trees will grow leaves again, the grass will grow, the flowers will bloom and the people will return. Buildings will be restored and the river will run crystal clear once more. The pioneers of 1863 will cast a blessing on the pioneers of today once they exit from the shadows to focus on the light.

Eleanor Roosevelt once wrote this line -

'The future belongs to those who believe in the beauty of their own dreams.'.

Amen.

Chapter 21 - Marysville Then, Marysville 2009 The Return

We have returned many times since. Marysville has turned from the shadows. There is growth in the light, people returning, houses and shops rebuilt and trees and nature regaining their colours. People now have a smile on their faces, faces who have brushed away the ashes. When you visit, don't expect a replica of the old Marysville. Gone is the touch of early pioneer's scenario. Only their spirit lives to encourage the pioneers of today. Marysville died, but now lives in memories and the resurrection of today.

Epilogue

As I sit before my computer, gazing out of the window, my mind turns to the question that has been bothering me for the last few days. How shall I end this journey of mine, on paper. What shall I write?

The weather is not the best. I see dark stormy clouds and hear the pitter patter of raindrops beginning to hit the window, forecasting the coming of a storm. There are people passing by, their heads bowed as they search out the ground before them for puddles and against the wind. Scarves and upturned coat collars hug the meagre warmth of their bodies as protection on this bitterly cold day. (Yes, it does get cold in Australia's winter!) Umbrellas will be useless against the inclement weather, whose rigors seem to have been invading Frankston over the last few weeks. But, thankfully, I am inside, sitting in this warm lounge. I am comfortable even though my mind is temporarily locked in a 'writer's block'.

A schoolboy stops outside my window for a moment. I guess that he is probably about ten years old, dressed in a blue uniform complete with cap and badge. He slides his backpack onto the ground and crouches down to re-tie a shoelace. The task done he settles his heavy backpack over his shoulders again and wipes his wet nose on his wet sleeve before taking off once more. He has been quite oblivious of my observation. The youngster has somehow managed to clear away my negative thoughts and now the block is lifted from my brain and I am attuned to my writing once more. For a second, the kaleidoscope of my life came back before my eyes and the freshness of his youth and mine were intertwined. I remembered my own youth, with small brown case, not backpack.

But the memory left me again, to be replaced by the fear of living. The Alpha and Omega were before me.

What will be accomplished on this transitional journey? Will everything be left to God- or to Destiny? The sword of Damocles is pivoted above me.

I have lived a fulfilled life in two very different islands. In sunshine and in shadow. It could not have been otherwise, reflecting as it did the joys and the pain; the use of whatever gifts I have had. The appreciation of nature, of music and beauty, and theatre and opera. And the giving and receiving of love. A great thankfulness for family and friends and most hopefully - the gaining of wisdom.

If a return journey is granted to anyone of us, may the mistakes I have made towards others to be rectified.

Appendix

"Time approaches for my final exit into a shadow; the time clock is ticking away faster than I can keep up! Did I say shadows? Wait on, Focus to the light, time enough for shadows when they arrive. I am sending the final pages to Nina, my very able and capable editor, for without her valuable help this book may not have seen the light of day, perhaps left on the publisher's desk leaving my voice and thoughts amongst the would be-- authors

Not forgetting Sylvie Blair my publisher, whose friendship I treasure, must be included in my thanks also Katrina Shead. {copy typist.] and William . L .Lowe. a very able Proof Reader.

Time for me to take stock of my life;

Gone is the red shawl babe of long ago, whose life in limbo between adoptive parents, who chose to give him love as their own son, or the alternative solution, placed in a Roman Catholic orphanage, which trained boys for the Priest hood. Thankfully, from his adoptive parents receiving love which formed a bases on which to grow,

For without Love nothing will succeed.

Sophia Loren, grandmothers cooking recipe. Ten per cent ingredients and ninety per cent love. If you don't love what you are doing or for whom you are cooking, then your efforts will be a failure,

This is so right this recipe applies not only to cooking.

  Gone is the schoolboy clutching a suit case and gasmask setting out on an unchartered journey which will change the course of his life?
  Gone is the boy whose childhood was raped by war
  Gone is the Question To whom do I belong.
  Gone is the young adult who desired the glitter of the stage
  Gone is the teenager who fell in love,
  but still held on to the call of the footboards
  Gone is the joy of seeing your new born daughter
  in the arms of her mother
  Gone is 53 years of marriage Through Sunshine and Shadow
  Gone is the witnessing of the pain, suffering and loss of love ones
  A cycle ,only to be renewed as time goes by
  Gone - - Gone – Gone - Gone are so many things
  you wished to keep or lose
  Gone are negative thoughts you no longer wish to reflect upon
  Gone are desires planted in the Secret Garden
  of your heart nurtured but never bearing fruit
  Gone is the hurt healed through forgiveness
  that you once refused to forget.

Now over eighty I am ever grateful, that I received my measure of love throughout my journey

I trust it has been beneficial, as you read through the pages from childhood to manhood then onto what some may tabulate as the most uninteresting phase of our sojourn on this planet, our active transition from the workforce to a state, where mobility may take's second place and memory has a momentary respite,

What the hell Look! at it this way A car breaks down requiring maintenance

Or, worse still, the scrape heap, I've no desire for the heap.

Appendix

So where am I, at this point of time, creating new interest, having written and produced

Tea with Jane Austen, a play with songs and music based on the novelist life, very well received by the audience. Top marks to the cast. I am trying to lead a full interesting life

Enjoying the love of my family, receiving special blessings from Kay, and Russ, who are always supportive with love and understanding, also to Matt, Ben, and Emma, my grandchildren, who bridge the age gap stopping me from becoming a grumpy old man, to Delma, my sister in—law, who became a sister, and to Billie whose generosity and love during the years, earned him a place as a natural brother, a true friend, and soul mate

To all my friends and acquaintances around the world thank you. Also to you the reader and would be readers, who hopefully will await in anticipation the next: two books ".Eighty and still a Virgin" and 'Forbidden Love" (working titles). Yet to be completed

Gone is the search for "To whom do I belong "which had haunted me throughout my childhood years. The answer is simply we belong to each other and the omnipotent, who created the world. Our very being goes back in time to those who first walked this earth, each one of us part of a DNA linking us what we are today.

In many ways, each one of us is akin to an Island surrounded by the sea of humanity whose waves brush our shores bringing Flotsam and Jetsam, salvaged or rejected.

Let us be ever vigilant, that, as an Island, we do not become insular; we are part of an a enigma, which only self can solve or surmise the answer to life's puzzle.

The survival of Islands can only function, unless adjacent to a mainland; thus, like an Island, our survival depends on inter relationship towards each other, regardless of race or creed

Talking of Islands, time to travel. Billie and I planning to have a trip maybe somewhere close. New Zealand sounds and looks inviting Yes, New Zealand !We will give it a try .

Bernard Blestel

Hold on The Plans of Mice And Men are about to go astray.
Cancer loomed again in our life
Yes another shadow cast before us
Billie diagnosed with prostate Cancer
Time for my nurses uniform
Looking to the light the shadows fell behind
Our prayers have been answered
New Zealand became a reality
May I end with a poem by Helen Steiner Rice
Be Glad
Be glad your life has been full and complete,
Be glad that you've tasted the bitter and the sweet.
Be glad that you have walked in sunshine and rain,
Be glad you have felt both pleasure and pain.
Be glad that you've had such a full, happy life,
Be glad for your joy as well as strife.
Be glad that you walked with courage each day, Be glad you've had strength for each step of the way, Be glad for the comfort that you found in prayer.
Be glad for God's blessings, His love, and His care.

www.ingramcontent.com/pod-product-compliance
Lightning Source LLC
Chambersburg PA
CBHW070933230426
43666CB00011B/2426